Praise for *God and Wonder*

"*God and Wonder* will surely capture your imagination. Rarely do articles from a theology conference sparkle like these chapters. Written almost entirely by or about artists, they remind us that artistry reflecting God's own creativity has always been the most effective expression of the Gospel."
—William Dyrness, Fuller Theological Seminary

"A multifaceted investigation of the disposition of wonder that not only constitutes a proper beginning, and end, for the study of theology, but also rightly orients us to all of created reality, this book is fantastic, and I say that very rarely about multiauthor books. What a gift to both scholars and students, and to pastors and artists as well."
—W. David O. Taylor, Fuller Theological Seminary

"This rich collection of essays draws upon the abundance of the arts and the imagination to recover a sense of wonder in the world, the church, and before God. The variety of the contributions from scholars, artists, writers, and teachers produce a book that from Coleridge to Spike Lee explores the challenge of wonder and excites the reader with the riches of the imagination, from the visions of children to the wisdom of Scripture and theology."
—David Jasper, University of Glasgow

"This volume calls all of us to become 'wonderstruck theologians'—a timely call indeed! But how might we learn again to be filled with awe? Here we find mundane answers that give marvelous witness to the glory of God: worship, children, homemaking, art, poetry, iconography, even lament rooted in longing. The essays in this book should reawaken the church to the nature of theological labor."
—Matthew Levering, Mundelein Seminary

"A diverse and rich collection of essays that hone facets of a Christian theology and practice of creative and artistic communication. An important contribution to evangelical theology that often privileges the epistemic element of Christian spirituality and neglects its affective and poetic dimensions. This book shows that wonder begins with an ineffable encounter with God that compels expression. Each chapter explores concrete modes and forms of that theological expression from church to cinema."

—STEVEN M. STUDEBAKER, MCMASTER DIVINITY COLLEGE

God and Wonder

God and Wonder

Theology, Imagination, and the Arts

Edited by
JEFFREY W. BARBEAU and
EMILY HUNTER McGOWIN

CASCADE *Books* • Eugene, Oregon

GOD AND WONDER
Theology, Imagination, and the Arts

Copyright © 2022 Wipf and Stock Publishers. All rights reserved. Except for brief quotations in critical publications or reviews, no part of this book may be reproduced in any manner without prior written permission from the publisher. Write: Permissions, Wipf and Stock Publishers, 199 W. 8th Ave., Suite 3, Eugene, OR 97401.

Cascade Books
An Imprint of Wipf and Stock Publishers
199 W. 8th Ave., Suite 3
Eugene, OR 97401

www.wipfandstock.com

PAPERBACK ISBN: 978-1-6667-0967-4
HARDCOVER ISBN: 978-1-6667-0968-1
EBOOK ISBN: 978-1-6667-0969-8

Cataloguing-in-Publication data:

Names: Barbeau, Jeffrey W., editor. | McGowin, Emily Hunter, editor.

Title: God and wonder : theology, imagination, and the arts / Edited by Jeffrey W. Barbeau and Emily Hunter McGowin.

Description: Eugene, OR: Cascade Books, 2022. | Includes bibliographical references and index.

Identifiers: ISBN 978-1-6667-0967-4 (paperback) | ISBN 978-1-6667-0968-1 (hardcover) | ISBN 978-1-6667-0969-8 (ebook)

Subjects: LCSH: Aesthetics—Religious aspects—Christianity. | Theology—Anthropology. | Christian life.

Classification: BR115.A8 G50 2022 (paperback) | BR115 (ebook)

10/13/22

In honor of
Dennis L. Okholm and
Timothy R. Phillips (1950–2000)

Contents

Acknowledgments | xi
Illustrations | xiii
Contributors | xv

Prelude

1 Wonder and Theology | 3
   Emily Hunter McGowin

Part I | Wonder and Method

The glory of God's beautiful design, Psalm 40:5
Karen An-hwei Lee

2 A Theology of Imagination | 13
   Jeffrey W. Barbeau

3 Children, Wonder, and the Work of Theology | 30
   Emily Hunter McGowin

4 Imagination, Knowing, and Supposing | 44
   Scott Cairns

Part II | Wonder and Creation

The illumination of beloved statutes, Psalm 119:129–130
Karen An-hwei Lee

5 Making as an Act of Longing and Lament | 59
   Tish Harrison Warren

x CONTENTS

6   The Artistry of Place | 70
    Andrew Peterson

7   Placed Wonder through the Arts | 85
    Jennifer Allen Craft

Part III | Wonder and Wisdom

The field of radiant awe, Acts 4:30
Karen An-hwei Lee

8   Encountering the Uncontainable in the Arts | 103
    Jeremy Begbie

9   The Doxological Apostle | 119
    Nijay K. Gupta

10 The Wonder of Cinema in Dorothy L. Sayers and Spike Lee | 133
    Crystal L. Downing

Part IV | Wonder and the Church

Eternity under the olives, Hebrews 2:4
Karen An-hwei Lee

11 Disciplining Wonder in the Orthodox Christian Tradition | 151
    Marcus Plested

12 Songs and Symbols for an Overcoming Church | 167
    Cheryl J. Sanders

13 Evangelical Theology and the Christian Church | 181
    David Lauber

Postlude

14 Waiting on Wonder | 197
    Jeffrey W. Barbeau

On Wonder. . . . (musical score) | 203
Misook Kim

Bibliography | 221

Index | 235

Acknowledgments

This volume originated with papers presented at the thirtieth annual meeting of the Wheaton College Theology Conference. Due to the onset of a global pandemic, speakers presented their work remotely as participants from around the world engaged the topic online. Subsequent discussion and reflection led to the collection of these fuller, revised essays. While this volume has been edited by two of the conference organizers—Jeffrey Barbeau and Emily McGowin—a tremendous debt is due to Dean David Lauber and Krista Sanchez, formerly administrative assistant to the graduate program of the School of Biblical and Theological Studies—who each helped organize the conference and worked tirelessly to make it a resounding success. Thanks are also due to members of Wipf and Stock for their kind support, including Michael Thomson, Rodney Clapp, George Callihan, Kara Barlow, and Savanah N. Landerholm. Several administrators at Wheaton College deserve special notice for their support, including President Philip Ryken, Provost Karen An-hwei Lee, former provost Margaret Diddams, and Dean Michael Wilder of the Conservatory of Music and Division of Arts and Communication. Other help was provided by Jeremy Root, Linda Bretz, Greg Waybright, Donté Ford, Marilyn Brenner, Tiffany Eberle Kriner, Mary Leiser, Zoe's Feet Dance Ministry, and Brian Miller. Sam Ashton assisted with various editorial duties commendably. The editors thank Plough Publishing House for their permission to feature the entirety of Jane Tyson Clements' poem, "Child, Though I Take Your Hand." We also gratefully acknowledge the support of our families, who cheerfully encouraged us as we planned, organized, rearranged, and adapted to make the conference and this volume possible. Finally, we have dedicated this collection to the visionary leadership of Dennis L. Okholm and the late Timothy R. Phillips. Their work inspired three decades of groundbreaking evangelical scholarship at Wheaton College and far beyond.

Illustrations

Figure 1. *Christ in Limbo*. Fra Angelico, Museum of San Marco, Cell 31, Florence, Italy. Wikimedia Commons.

Figure 2. Statue of Julian of Norwich. Norwich Cathedral, Norwich, England (2000). David Holgate, FSDC. Wikimedia Commons.

Figure 3. *Christ Blessing the Children*. Oil on panel, Wawel Castle, Kraków, Poland (1537). Lucas Cranach the Elder. Wikimedia Commons.

Figure 4. Draft of Coleridge's poem *Kubla Khan*. Samuel Taylor Coleridge (between 1797 and 1816). Wikimedia Commons.

Figure 5. *March 20 / Grapefruit with Dish* (from *40 Days of Trees & Ordinary Things*). © Kari Dunham. Gouache on paper, 6"x9", 2020.

Figure 6. *#1 (burn) Okaloosa County, Florida 2012* (from *The Pines*). Chuck Hemard. Original in color. © Chuck Hemard.

Figure 7. *La Conversión de San Pablo* (c. 1675–82). Bartolomé Esteban Murillo (c. 1675–1682), Museo del Prado, Madrid, Spain. Wikimedia Commons.

Figure 8. *Christ Pantocrator*. Encaustic icon on panel (sixth century). Saint Catherine's Monastery, Mount Sinai, Egypt. Wikimedia Commons.

Figure 9. *The Revelation of St John: 2. St John's Vision of Christ and the Seven Candlesticks* (1497–98). Albrecht Dürer, Woodcut, Cleveland Museum of Art, Cleveland, OH. Wikimedia Commons.

Figure 10. *Jonah Cast on the Shore by the Fish*, engraving and print (c. 1585). Antonius Wierix II. The Elisha Whittelsey Collection, The Elisha Whittelsey Fund, 1951, Metropolitan Museum of Art. Wikimedia Commons.

Contributors

JEFFREY W. BARBEAU is Professor of Theology at Wheaton College. He is the author or editor of several books, including *The Cambridge Companion to British Romanticism and Religion* (2021), *The Spirit of Methodism: From the Wesleys to a Global Communion* (2019), and *Religion in Romantic England: An Anthology of Primary Sources* (2018).

JEREMY BEGBIE is Thomas A. Langford Distinguished Research Professor of Theology at Duke Divinity School and the McDonald Agape Director of Duke Initiatives in Theology and the Arts. He is also a Senior Member at Wolfson College, Cambridge, and an Affiliated Lecturer in the Faculty of Music at the University of Cambridge. Among his many publications are *Resounding Truth: Christian Wisdom in the World of Music* (2007), *Music, Modernity, and God* (2013), and *A Peculiar Orthodoxy: Reflections on Theology and the Arts* (2018).

SCOTT CAIRNS, recipient of a Guggenheim Fellowship and the Denise Levertov Award, directs the low-residency MFA Program at Seattle Pacific University. His works have appeared in *Poetry, Paris Review, The Atlantic Monthly, The New Republic*, and have been anthologized in multiple editions of *Best American Spiritual Writing*. Recent books include *Slow Pilgrim: The Collected Poems* (2015) and *Anaphora* (2019).

JENNIFER ALLEN CRAFT is Associate Professor of Theology and Humanities at Point University in West Point, Georgia. She is author of the book *Placemaking and the Arts: Cultivating the Christian Life* (2018) and is on the board of Christians in the Visual Arts (CIVA).

CRYSTAL L. DOWNING is co-director of the Marion E. Wade Center at Wheaton College. She has published two award-winning books on Dorothy L. Sayers, *Writing Performances* (2004) and *Subversive: Christ, Culture, and the Shocking Dorothy L. Sayers* (2020), as well as three books about the intersection between Christianity and cultural studies: *How Postmodernism Serves (My) Faith* (2006); *Changing Signs of Truth* (2012); and *Salvation from Cinema* (2016).

NIJAY K. GUPTA is Professor of New Testament at Northern Seminary. He is co-editor of *The State of New Testament Studies* (2019) and author of *Paul and the Language of Faith* (2020) and *A Beginner's Guide to New Testament Studies* (2020).

MISOOK KIM is a composer and pianist on the faculty at the Conservatory of Music at Wheaton College. She has won the International Alliance for Women in Music (IAWM) Judith Zaimont Award and the Long Island Arts Council International Composition Competition in 2007. She has also won the 2008 International Sejong Music Composition Competition and The Global Music Award in 2018.

KAREN AN-HWEI LEE is a provost and poet at Wheaton College. Her recent collection is *Rose Is a Verb: Neo-Georgics* (2021).

DAVID LAUBER is Professor of Theology and Dean of the School of Biblical and Theological Studies at Wheaton College. He is the author or co-editor of several books, including *Life Questions Every Student Asks: Faithful Responses to Common Issues* (2020), *The T & T Clark Companion to the Doctrine of Sin* (2016), and *Theology Questions Everyone Asks: Christian Faith in Plain Language* (2014).

EMILY HUNTER MCGOWIN is Assistant Professor of Theology at Wheaton College. She is also a priest and canon theologian in the Anglican Diocese of Churches for the Sake of Others (C4SO). Her most recent book is *Quivering Families: The Quiverfull Movement and Evangelical Theology of the Family* (2018).

ANDREW PETERSON is an award-winning singer-songwriter and the author of *Adorning the Dark* (2019), *The God of the Garden* (2021), and *The Wingfeather Saga*, which is currently in production as an animated series. In 2008, driven by a desire to cultivate a strong Christian arts community, Andrew founded a ministry called The Rabbit Room, which led to a yearly conference, symposiums, and Rabbit Room Press, which has published more than thirty books to date.

MARCUS PLESTED is Professor of Theology at Marquette University. He is the author of three books: *The Macarian Legacy: The Place of Macarius-Symeon in the Eastern Christian Tradition* (2004); *Orthodox Readings of Aquinas* (2012); and *Wisdom in Christian Tradition: The Patristic Roots of Modern Russian Sophiology* (2022). He is also co-editor of *The Oxford Handbook to the Reception of Aquinas* (2021).

CHERYL J. SANDERS is Professor of Christian Ethics at Howard University School of Divinity, Senior Pastor of the Third Street Church of God in Washington, DC, and past president of the American Theological Society. She is the author of several books, including *Ministry at the Margins* (1997), *Saints in Exile* (1996), and *Empowerment Ethics for a Liberated People* (1995).

TISH HARRISON WARREN is a priest in the Anglican Church in North America. She is the author of *Liturgy of the Ordinary: Sacred Practices in Everyday Life* (2016) and *Prayer in the Night: For Those Who Work, or Watch, or Weep* (2021), both of which were recognized as *Christianity Today's* Book of the Year (2018 and 2021). Her articles and essays have appeared in numerous outlets, including a weekly newsletter for *The New York Times*.

Prelude

I

Wonder and Theology

Emily Hunter McGowin

My fascination with theology began with a fresco. More precisely, it was a photo of a fresco by Fra Angelico included in the guidebook to the Museum of San Marco in Florence, Italy. My mother had visited Italy on a two-week trip one summer and returned with countless photographs and souvenirs. But nothing fascinated me like the glossy-paged guidebook. As a newly baptized Christian, I found the painted scenes from the life of Jesus, Mary, and the saints endlessly fascinating. I paged through the book over and over, inserting Post-it Notes throughout the volume with my various comments and questions.

The scene that captured my imagination most intensely is found in the museum's thirty-first cell in the third corridor. Titled "Christ in Limbo" (c. 1442), the fresco shows the resurrected Christ, robed in white, clasping a flag of victory as he stands in the doorway of a cave. He clasps the hand of a bearded man at the front of a crowd, the first among a throng of gold-haloed figures emerging from the depths into the light. The cave's thick wooden door lies fallen beneath Christ's feet, having collapsed, unhinged, on top of a demonic form. Other fiendish figures cower at the opposite edge of the frame.

Figure 1. Fra Angelico, *Christ in Limbo*.

Before observing this image, I had never considered the consequences of Christ's salvific work on behalf of people who had already died. But here was a Renaissance painting of the triumphant Christ emptying limbo and freeing the sainted figures found within. The thought was wondrous to me: unexpected, surprising, and mysterious. What does this mean, I asked? Is this what Christ's death and resurrection did for those long dead? When my pastor's response to my questions did not satisfy, he handed me his theology books. Twenty-something years later, I now teach and write theology for a living. If only I could tell Fra Angelico!

Obviously, not every theologian gets their start with an awe-inspiring Italian fresco. And not all who generate theology make academic theology their profession. Indeed, theology is being done every day in pulpits and conservatories, gardens and dining rooms, workshops and art studios. But I am convinced the origin of all theology, whether by practitioners or professionals, is wonder—specifically, wonder at the triune God revealed in Jesus Christ. Whether acknowledged or not, wonder is the sustaining lifeblood of the theological endeavor.

Theology and Wonder

Plato famously claims that the beginning of philosophy is to feel a sense of wonder. In its classical definition, wonder is "the passion that arises from consciousness of ignorance," which then leads to the pursuit of "knowledge of things in their causes."[1] Wonder is amazement elicited by something unexpected and mysterious. It contains surprise because the cause of wonder is unanticipated. Wonder often leads to ambivalence in the wonderer—being drawn toward what perplexes and being repelled by it at the same time.[2] One who wonders is at once excited by the novelty encountered and fearful of the unknown. In fact, fear of the unknown is why Thomas Aquinas classified wonder as a species of fear.[3] To wonder is to become conscious of one's ignorance. Only those conscious of their ignorance experience the desire for knowledge and become capable of pursuing it.[4]

Theology, like philosophy, has its origins in wonder. Karl Barth says as much in *Evangelical Theology*:

> A quite specific *astonishment* stands at the beginning of every theological perception, inquiry, and thought, in fact at the root of every theological word. This astonishment is indispensable if theology is to exist and be perpetually renewed as a modest, free, critical, and happy science. If such astonishment is lacking, the whole enterprise of even the best theologian would canker at the roots.[5]

---

1. Quinn, *Iris Exiled*, 11.
2. Scorgie, "Wonder and the Revitalization of Evangelical Theology," 19.
3. That is to say, fear of ignorance. Thomas says wonder is the only form of fear that is pleasurable. In Thomas's words, "Wonder gives pleasure, not because it implies ignorance, but in so far as it includes the desire of learning the cause, and in so far as the wonderer learns something new" (*Summa Theologiae*, I-II, q. 32, a. 8).
4. For some, recognition of ignorance can itself usher in the divine presence.
5. Barth, *Evangelical Theology*, 64.

Wonder initiates theology because the subject of theology is, ultimately, God.[6] For Christians, we mean the triune God revealed through Jesus Christ by the power of the Spirit, the fulfillment of Israel's hopes. What could be more unanticipated, surprising, and confusing than the self-revelation of the transcendent, holy God in Jesus of Nazareth? Certainly, this is something that does not coincide with what humankind has experienced before—an entirely unique event in the history of the world. In Barth's words again, "Christ is the infinitely wondrous event which compels a person, so far as he experiences and comprehends this event, to be necessarily, profoundly, wholly, and irrevocably astonished."[7]

In the face of this infinitely wondrous event, ambivalence is a natural response, as is fear.[8] Heather Ohaneson says, "[The works of God] cause us to kneel in awe even as we run toward the glorious source of our confusion."[9] Indeed, the Word made flesh confronts us with how much we don't know. And, faced with this realization, we must choose: Retreat into ignorance or pursue knowledge. To quote Ohaneson again, "The wondrousness of God means paradoxically that we *cannot* think more and that we *must* think more."[10] If the desire for and pursuit of knowledge is allowed to grow, one can move from fear into admiration, curiosity, and contemplation. The theologian's work, then, arises from wonder that leads to the desire for and pursuit of knowledge—knowledge of the God revealed in Jesus Christ.

What, then, does it mean to be a wonderstruck theologian? Among other things, a central characteristic is humility.[11] Because wonder is rooted in the knowledge of one's ignorance, pride is unsustainable.[12] There is something beyond us and our limited perspective, and we will not be able to master it.[13] As we are confronted by "the wondrous reality of the living

---

6. Ohaneson coins the term "omnipelaic" (from the Hebrew *pele*) to refer to God as the all-wondrous one, comparable to the traditional omni- attributes of classical theology (see "Perfection of God," 227).

7. Barth, *Evangelical Theology*, 71.

8. There is a larger conversation about the correlation between biblical fear (i.e., "the fear of the Lord is the beginning of wisdom" [Prov 9:10]) and wonder. Rubenstein posits the similarity between "fear" (Heb., *yirah*) and wonder in *Strange Wonder*, 12.

9. Ohaneson, "Perfection of God," 221.

10. Ohaneson, "Perfection of God," 222 (emphasis mine).

11. For more on the relation between wonder and humility, rooted in the biblical notion of fear (*yirah*), see Ohaneson, "Perfection of God," 222–23.

12. I have suggested elsewhere it might be appropriate to consider wonder a virtue (see McGowin, "Response," in *The Wonders of Creation*). This is something Kristján Kristjánsson argues in "Scientific Practice, Wonder, and Awe."

13. Because, of course, the "it" is God (see Scorgie, "Wonder and the Revitalization of Evangelical Theology," 20).

God," we come to recognize we are entirely dependent upon divine enlightenment.[14] Thus, wonder at God ultimately leads to wonder at one's self. As Barth says, "[N]o one can become and remain a theologian unless he is compelled again and again to be astonished at himself. . . . After all, who am I to be a theologian?"[15] And if one is truly taken up into wonder, then one is inevitably changed.[16]

Unfortunately, there are approaches to theology that work against wonder and the humility it produces. Indeed, some theologies appear to be aimed, perhaps unintentionally, at the dissolution of wonder. Why this is the case is a longer story for another time. But I will note that doing theology under the conditions of modernity led some to approach Christian faith in scientific and mechanistic terms. If theology is a modern scientific discipline, then it becomes primarily concerned with cataloguing, analyzing, and systematizing facts about God.[17] Viewed in this light, wonder is a deadly threat. It advertises our incompetence and undermines control. And in the face of many modern challenges to Christian faith—the historical-critical method, atheistic evolutionary theory, two world wars, and the slow dissolution of white hegemonic patriarchy, to name a few—some concluded such lack of control cannot stand. The answer, then, was to banish wonder through the acquisition of settled, verifiable certainty. But, as poet Patrick Kavanagh writes, "God must be allowed to surprise us."[18] And surprise us God will.

Let's return to my starting premise: Theology begins in a felt sense of wonder, specifically wonder at Christ, "the infinitely wondrous event." But to say wonder begins theology does not mean wonder ceases with the beginning of knowledge. Wonder is the "beginning" in the sense that it persists throughout the theological endeavor, sustaining it over time and increasing as one proceeds.[19] To paraphrase Flannery O'Connor: Wonder isn't something that is gradually evaporating in the theological endeavor;

---

14. Barth, *Evangelical Theology*, 72.

15. Barth, *Evangelical Theology*, 71.

16. Wonder produces, in Howard Wettstein's estimation, "a generosity of spirit, a lack of pettiness, increased ability to forgive, and to contain anger and disappointment" (*Significance of Religious Experience*, 32).

17. Howard Parsons suggests people under modern conditions are less capable or less given to wonder because our sensitivities have become dull, in part due to the rise of the natural sciences (see Parsons, "Philosophy of Wonder").

18. Kavanagh, "Having Confessed," 149.

19. Abraham Heschel, discussing the Hebrew prophets, says wonder "does not come to an end when knowledge is acquired; it is an attitude that never ceases" (*God in Search of Man*, 46).

it grows along with knowledge.[20] If theology is the study of God and God's world, then sustained contemplation and comprehension of God is simply impossible without wonder.

Furthermore, wonder not only begins and sustains theology, but it also constitutes the goal of theology. That is to say, the primary end of theology (not to mention Christian education in general) is the cultivation of wonder.[21] Recently, theologians such as Miroslav Volf have invited Christian theologians to see their work as focused on the cultivation of flourishing—for ourselves, our neighbors, and our world.[22] I have deep sympathies with this approach. Still, it's unnecessary to pit wonder at beholding God against the flourishing of creation. Indeed, I would say the one entails, and is simply impossible without, the other.[23] So, I submit as a starting point that wonder begins, sustains, and ends the theological endeavor, with the happy result that it contributes to the flourishing of the world.

Wonder and Theology in this Book

The essays in this collection, penned by scholars, pastors, artists, and poets from a variety of traditions, demonstrate the inseparability of theology and wonder. Each was written for the thirtieth annual Wheaton Theology Conference, which convened April 4–5, 2021 around the theme "God and Wonder."

In retrospect, it seems like a special kind of madness to convene a conference on theology, imagination, and the arts in the midst of a global pandemic. By the time we gathered, every aspect of the proceedings had to be reimagined for an online format: music and dance performances, poetry readings, paper presentations, interviews, and more. But we pressed on, dedicated to the premise that wonder is a crucial part of our Christian vocation even—maybe even *especially*—in the midst of worldwide upheaval. *God and Wonder: Theology, Imagination, and the Arts* is the fruit of our conversations, both in April and throughout the months that followed.

---

20. O'Connor, *The Habit of Being*.

21. Kallistos Ware sees wonder as the chief end of all Christian education, too (Ware, "Sense of Wonder," 71). He goes on to say, "The university, then, is a structured environment in which we are to develop our sense of wonder before the universe God has made." I couldn't agree more.

22. Volf and Croasmun, *For the Life of the World*.

23. My assertion contradicts Martha Nussbaum's claim that wonder is only minimally related to human flourishing, a case she makes in *Upheavals of Thought*. A full explanation of our differences exceeds the scope of this essay.

The first group of essays considers wonder with reference to what we might call theological method. Jeffrey W. Barbeau's "A Theology of Imagination" recovers the work of poet Samuel Taylor Coleridge on the faculty of imagination to explore the theological genius of medieval mystic Julian of Norwich. My essay, "Children, Wonder, and the Work of Theology," explores wonder as the vocation of children, and asks theologians to consider modifying their theological method to do theology with children in their midst. Finally, poet Scott Cairns's "Imagination, Knowing, and Supposing" draws on Coleridge to consider how imagination helps us span the gap between objective reality and our subjective apprehension of it, weaving together insights from philosophy, rabbinics, Scripture, and the creative process to ponder the never-ending human effort to encounter and communicate the divine.

The second group of essays reflects on wonder's role in creation, especially creating art and cultivating place. In "Making as an Act of Longing and Lament," Tish Harrison Warren reflects on the interplay between wonder and grief in the creative process. Drawing on the insights of numerous writers, as well as her own life, Warren demonstrates the interrelatedness of longing and lament in both artmaking and the Christian life. Then, Andrew Peterson's "The Artistry of Place" offers an artist's reflections on the human work of place-making. Peterson draws on his experience of making a home for his family in Tennessee to reflect theologically on the human calling to make places for living, gathering, and enjoying God's creation. Finally, in "Placed Wonder through the Arts," Jennifer Allen Craft makes a theological case for the centrality of art in place-making, especially in the home. In interaction with place theory and a variety of artists, Craft asks us to consider wonder through art as a central practice of Christian homemaking today.

The third group of essays are united around the theme of wonder and wisdom. In "Encountering the Uncontainable in the Arts," Jeremy Begbie explores the unique capacity of art to cultivate wonder and gesture toward the unbounded God. But he also cautions us to recall that the infinite, uncontainable God is revealed climactically in Jesus Christ, a reality that has implications for artmaking, worship, and theology. Nijay Gupta's "The Doxological Apostle" explores the doxological pericopes in the Pauline Epistles, inviting us to see the apostle Paul in a new light: as an awestruck worshiper of God revealed in Christ. Lastly, Crystal Downing in "The Wonder of Cinema in Dorothy L. Sayers and Spike Lee" draws upon the trinitarian theology of creativity found in Dorothy L. Sayers's writings as a lens through which to understand the cinematic artistry of director Spike Lee.

The fourth group of essays focuses on the relationship of wonder and the church, both what wonder offers to churches and what churches have to offer on the topic of wonder. In "Songs and Symbols for an Overcoming

Church," Cheryl Sanders mines the rich imagery of the book of Revelation to extend both challenge and encouragement for churches grappling with the troubles of the contemporary Western context. Marcus Plested's "Disciplining Wonder in the Orthodox Christian Tradition" reflects on the theme of wonder in the tradition of the Orthodox Church. He explores Orthodox liturgy and worship, saints and icons, as well as teaching on spiritual senses and mystical experience. Orthodoxy's is not wonder without limits, however, as he concludes with an explanation of the ascetic and theological disciplining inherent within the tradition. David Lauber's "Evangelical Theology and the Christian Church" offers reflections on the story of the Wheaton Theology Conference and its lessons for theology today. Though focused on the evangelical context broadly conceived, there is much to be gleaned for Christians of all traditions.

The volume concludes with a homily by my co-editor, Jeffrey Barbeau, "Waiting on Wonder," which was delivered during undergraduate chapel at the conference. In his exhortation, Barbeau draws upon the story of Jonah to highlight the interplay between wonder and grief, praise and lament, in the Christian life. In the end, he invites us to sing to the Lord, even if it is from the belly of a great fish.

Theological essays are not the only works on offer in this volume, though. Each of the groups of essays outlined previously will begin with one of Karen An-hwei Lee's "Four Cantos on Wonder." Inspired by Scripture, these cantos were performed by the New Arts Trio to music composed by Misook Kim for the Wheaton Theology Conference (Kim's musical compositions appear at the close of this collection). In a volume dedicated to wonder, imagination, and the arts, it is fitting that poems of praise would serve as doxological intermissions throughout the book.

To borrow an analogy from musical theory, the contributors to *God and Wonder* present their own compositions each with their own chosen instruments, but all play in the key of wonder. From scholarly analysis of the theme to reflective, homiletic examinations of God's relationship with the world, each of the following essays offers a unique perspective on wonder and Christian faith. We offer the following volume with the hope that it will edify theologians, scholars, pastors, students, and artists of all kinds as they respond in faith to the wonder of God revealed in Jesus Christ by the power of the Holy Spirit.

PART I

Wonder and Method

First canto | Karen An-hwei Lee

The glory of God's beautiful design, Psalm 40:5

O Lord my God, you have performed
many wonders for us. Your plans for us
are too numerous to list.

You have no equal. If I tried to recite
all your wonderful deeds,
I would never come to the end of them.

Your design is a beautiful song
with the brightness of silk
woven on a heavenly loom,

flowing with autumnal fire
and snow outside a chapel,
auburn and silver, our wonder

at the Son of God suffering,
who overcomes the world,
flaming blossom of salvation.

From "Four Cantos on Wonder." Performed by the New Arts Trio to music composed by Misook Kim for the Wheaton Theology Conference (April 2021). Italicized verses: New Living Translation of the Bible (2015) by Tyndale House.

2

A Theology of Imagination

JEFFREY W. BARBEAU

Divine Vision

Christians have long worried over the power of the imagination. The elusive faculty is widely regarded as a fanciful or even a deceptive activity. The imagination, in such a view, depicts that which is decidedly *not real* but rather bizarre, fantastical, or phantasmagorical. Imagination invents, deceives, and leads innocents astray. In the Magnificat, Mary warns against those who are "proud in the imagination of their hearts" (Luke 1:51). Paul similarly cautions that "[i]f anyone imagines that he knows something, he does not yet know as he ought to know" (1 Cor 8:2, ESV) and calls on believers to cast down "imaginations, and every high thing that exalteth itself against the knowledge of God" (2 Cor 10:5, KJV). Such admonitions persist throughout much of Western history.

Some have reasoned that imagination might be dangerous for mind and body alike. Consider one story told by the French philosopher Nicolas Malebranche. A pregnant woman devoted herself just a bit too faithfully to an image of Pope Pius V in times of prayer. When the woman gave birth, the child's face appeared elderly and deformed with eyes cast upwards towards heaven, and carried the resemblance of an inverted miter on the upper torso.[1] The visage of the child, it was claimed, reflected the overactive imagination of its mother—blamed for a steadfast gaze so powerful that the image of the pontiff marked the body of the child.

Others link imagination to feeling and emotion. Inevitably, it seems, women find themselves at the center of attention here, too. This requires greater scrutiny, but suffice it to say for now that eighteenth-century evangelicals were often condemned for the prevalence of women in their meetings. Their prominent roles in the community, testifying to the work of God in the presence of all, seemed only to validate the commonplace assertion that a religion of the heart opposed a religion of the head. Rationality over imprudence hardly seems a choice in matters of faith.

Indeed, stories of imagination run amok are commonplace in the modern world. The rise of natural philosophy seemed to depend on vanquishing the superstitious enthusiasm of an overheated imagination. Enlightened critics cautioned that imagination once indulged could "usurp an entire ascendency over the mind," splashing an array of color where sharp lines of reason ought to predominate: in the words of the English Baptist minister John Foster, "The whole mind may become at length something like a hemisphere of cloud-scenery, filled with an ever-moving train of changing, melting forms, of every color, mingled with rainbows, meteors, and an occasional gleam of pure sunlight."[2]

Yet there are reasons to believe that imagination is essential to life, no less than theology. Imagination allows for beholding, for imagination enables the perception of the world around us. Imagination bridges the chasm between mind and nature, recovering vitality in the face of mechanism and the world reduced to mere machine. Imagination can save us from terrors of our circumstances, building castles that protect us from the real and present dangers. Active imagination leads to reflection on God and the things of God, and, so, imagination leads on to theology.

Indeed, on closer inspection, the biblical narrative depends on acts of wonder, beholding, and imagination. Many commentators believe that the visionary language of the prophets can best be understood with reference to the imagination, and even if one regards Jacob's dream as most certainly a divine revelation, still the recollection and description of the same would undoubtedly require the artistic capacity of the storyteller. Jesus invoked the powers of imagination in his use of metaphors and parables. The call to become "fishers of men," the warning to attend to the plank in your eye,

---

1. Blondel, *Strength of imagination*, 22.
2. Foster, "On the Application of the Epithet Romantic," quoted in Barbeau, "Introduction," xvii.

and the declaration that all must be "born again" each involve figurative, analogical language, and the stories he told of a prodigal son, the laborers in the vineyard, and the sower of seeds invest extraordinary meaning in the most ordinary circumstances.

Still one might ask whether any of this makes any difference to theologians. Theologians trade not in the images of the mind but in the laws of logic. Revelation under the guidance of reason alone is the mode of theology, some might say. But such a move divides, cutting off the artist from any meaningful contribution to the study of faith. At the opening of *Poetic Theology: God and the Poetics of Everyday Life*, William Dyrness dryly laments, "This book seeks to connect poetry and theology. It probably ought to have been written in poetry. But if it were, the poets would not read it because it was theology, and the theologians would not read it because it was poetry."[3]

In this essay, I consider how renewed theological attention to imagination might allow for a more robust conception of its intersection with literature and the arts more generally. I recover the work of two English theologians who help to explain the scope of theological imagination. More specifically, I will take up the most influential modern exposition of the imagination, by the poet and Anglican theologian Samuel Taylor Coleridge, to express how his conception of the faculty of imagination demonstrates the theological genius behind the "showings" of his English predecessor Julian of Norwich. However, while continuing to dialogue with these sources, I press on to what these figures only intimate: namely, the apostatic underside of imagination and need for renewal that more sanguine accounts of imagination inevitably neglect.

Perceptive Imagination

Coleridge's influential definition of the imagination will provide the inspiration for my discussion of the faculty. Coleridge's theory of imagination has shaped the contemporary meaning of the term more than any other in the English language. His contribution to modern theories of the imagination is vast, though he frequently writes on the subject in fragmentary, almost aphoristic, selections. He is capacious in his understanding, too, taking in the vast intellectual traditions that preceded him more than any other, and his reading on the subject shows a close knowledge of criticism from philosophy, psychology, and the arts. Coleridge deserves particular notice in this discussion, since he is the most significant Anglican theologian between

3. Dyrness, *Poetic Theology*, ix.

John Wesley and John Henry Newman, and among the leading theological voices of the nineteenth century.

Coleridge offers his definition in two parts in his monument to literary criticism, the *Biographia Literaria* (1817). He begins by defining what he calls the "primary imagination."

> The primary IMAGINATION I hold to be the living Power and prime Agent of all human Perception, and as a repetition in the finite mind of the eternal act of creation in the infinite I AM.[4]

This sense of the imagination points to the representational capacity of the imagination. Two aspects stand out. First, the primary imagination is the "living Power" and "prime Agent" of human perception. The influence of Immanuel Kant on Coleridge's thought is apparent in this definition. Through the imagination, the individual perceives the world, creating order out of an assemblage of data. The imagination takes sensory images and provides sequence, categories, and organization. And yet there seems to be more. Perception alone could be static and deadening, but Coleridge calls the primary imagination a "living Power" and, more surprisingly, "a repetition in the finite mind of the eternal act of creation." Whatever the primary imagination is—and this is a subject of wide discussion among readers ever since—this living power is active and alive rather than passive and inert.

Relevant to this discussion is a juxtaposition that Coleridge makes between imagination and fancy in the subsequent paragraph. In fancy, the perceptive or representational capacity of imagination is distinguished from memory:

> FANCY, on the contrary, has not other counters to play with, but fixities and definites. The Fancy is indeed no other than a mode of Memory emancipated from the order of time and space; and blended with, and modified by that empirical phenomenon of the will, which we express by the word CHOICE. But equally with the ordinary memory it must receive all its material ready made from the law of association.[5]

This sheds light on the difference between imagination's capacity to organize sensory impressions and actively create through them. While the primary imagination is a living power of perception, the fancy is a mode of memory. Put differently, the imagination involves an act of spontaneous creativity while the latter is only a recollection of experiential, sensory perception. One depends on acts of human will; the other on the mere retention of images.

---

4. Coleridge, *Biographia Literaria*, 1.304.
5. Coleridge, *Biographia Literaria*, 1.305.

Among the most striking features of the primary imagination is Coleridge's *divine inflection*, linking acts of human imagination with the eternal act of creation by God. This means that imagination involves self-consciousness, which he reflects in the willed aspect of the perceptive act. The imagination not only sees images but even recognizes and *knows* them inwardly. The individual recognizes the self as knowing subject and distinguishes perceptions as objects of knowledge. In this, the imagination provides a temporal generation of the eternal act, relating the creative work of the artist to the creativity of God.[6]

Theological Vision

I will return to a second aspect of Coleridge's famous definition of the imagination shortly, but already we can begin to see how his work might begin to illuminate the mystical writings of Julian of Norwich. This investigation might be surprising, perhaps even to Coleridge himself, for he was suspicious of mysticism and warned theological students against falling prey to its allure. In *Aids to Reflection* (1825), his most influential theological publication, Coleridge warned against the mystic tendency to refer to "*inward feelings* and *experiences* . . . as evidences of the truth of any opinion."[7] The mystic depends on sensations and "fancies" to idiosyncratically claim matters of individual temperament as "Permanent Truths, having a subsistence in the Divine Mind, though revealed to himself alone." The mystic, in short, risks descending into fanaticism.

Some have supposed that Julian of Norwich descends into just such a mystic fanaticism. Writing in the fourteenth century, the English anchorite experienced sixteen "showings" in which she came to understand the love of God. The real drama of her story begins in a startling scene of illness and misfortune. In the year 1373, Julian lay near death in a home. The illness sapped her strength and paralyzed her body. Certain the woman would die, members of the household called for a priest to prepare her for death in the last rites of the church. Julian explains that she was already fixed on heaven when the priest directed her to look upon the crucifix: "It seemed to me that I was well as I was."[8] Nevertheless, at his guidance, she "consented."

---

6. On self-consciousness and imagination, see Jessica Oliver, "Self-consciousness and Imagination"; Webster, *Body and Soul*; Reid, "Coleridge and Schelling."

7. Coleridge, *Aids to Reflection*, 389.

8. Julian of Norwich, *Revelations of Divine Love*, 5 (*ST* 2) (all subsequent references to this text will include a page reference followed by a chapter reference for the short or long text as *ST* or *LT*).

Figure 2. Statue of Julian of Norwich.

For three days and nights, the thirty-year-old woman lingered somewhere between heaven and earth. She longed for God and hoped to participate in the sufferings that Christ himself had endured. In this state, her senses were transformed. Her sight failed and the room grew dark—dark as night. Only the cross remained. Her suffering faded but her mind was focused on the passion of Christ alone.

What has this to do with the powers of imagination? I think Julian's sixteen showings are instructive to understanding a theology of imagination. Consider the first showing, where the tone of the whole is set early through a description of the cross of Christ. With her eyes fixed on the crucifix before her, Julian identifies the wounded head of the Savior. Red blood trickled from beneath the crown of thorns. Julian focuses on the bleeding head of Christ: "the roundness of the drops, they were like herring scales as they spread on the forehead."[9] She sees his face and wounded body, but spontaneously expands on the scene. There, as if beside her, is "Lady Saint Mary," a woman of greatness and nobility, looking on Christ as well. Mary provides a visual model for Julian: Mary is small, low, simple, and poor. Most unexpectedly, she introduces the image of a hazelnut: "a little thing" it fit "lying in the palm of my hand" and was "round as any ball."[10]

The vision, which Julian regarded as a gift from Christ himself, was experiential and transformative.[11] Without any diminishment of the marvel she records, Julian's vision came about through an act of imagination. Throughout the first showing, Julian describes the experience as alternately dependent on bodily and spiritual sight. Of course, she never left the room in her home, so we must understand her to mean what she says: the scene before her bodily eyes comes from a combination of identification and representation. Julian's account links the crucifix before her to the meaning of Christ's passion. She identifies with the cross in her persistent "longing" to feel and experience the sufferings of her Savior, beholding the work of God in the image before her. In this, Julian sees a biblical and ecclesial image, identifies herself with the scene, and recognizes the meaning through a series of showings that surpass mere memory of an object or image alone.[12]

Julian's perception of the crucifix provided the material basis of her vision, and yet she has gone far beyond memory alone. Rather than gazing upwards in a reverie, she "consented" to focus on the face of the crucifix. This act of perception, comparable to the function of Coleridge's primary imagination, surpasses fancy. The presentation of the cross initially appears to be a moment of distraction—at first, she is displeased by the priest, for she had already fixed her gaze on Christ internally. But the crucifix unexpectedly proves more crucial than we might suppose. The act of perception required will and understanding as she looked at the crucifix, became aware of her own self (consciousness), and recognized her connection to God in the process. The outcome should not be overlooked: wonder. Fixed on the face of Christ, Julian describes her own surprise: "I was astounded with

---

9. Julian of Norwich, *Revelations of Divine Love*, 51 (LT 7).

10. Julian of Norwich, *Revelations of Divine Love*, 7 (ST, 4; cf. LT 5.47).

11. Julian of Norwich, *Revelations of Divine Love*, 45 (LT 4).

12. For this reason, Julian moves freely between the bleeding head of Christ and the language of the Trinity.

wonder and admiration that he who is so holy and awe-inspiring was willing to be so familiar with a sinful being living in wretched flesh."[13]

Creative Imagination

The role of imagination in Julian of Norwich's *Revelations of Divine Love* might have ended there in that dark room had she not then proceeded to do two things. First, Julian wrote a record of these revelations in the subsequent days. The record is now known as the "short text" of the *Revelations* and provides a basic account of each showing and some initial, fairly spontaneous thoughts on their meaning. Second, she meditated on these ideas for a further twenty years before producing the so-called "long text" that demonstrated her substantially deepened understanding of the original showings, for, as she explains, "when the bodily vision stopped, the spiritual vision remained in my understanding."[14] In committing these revelations to the page, Julian of Norwich moves into another mode of creativity and artistry.

Here, Coleridge again provides helpful guidance for conceptualizing the imaginative act as it relates to aesthetics. Coleridge denominates the creative or poetic aspect of imagination the "secondary imagination."

> The secondary I consider as an echo of the former, co-existing with the conscious will, yet still as identical with the primary in the *kind* of its agency, and differing only in *degree*, and in the *mode* of its operation. It dissolves, diffuses, dissipates, in order to re-create; or where this process is rendered impossible, yet still at all events it struggles to idealize and to unify. It is essentially *vital*, even as all objects (*as* objects) are essentially fixed and dead.[15]

For Coleridge, the secondary imagination is not a different faculty but only a different mode of agency. The perceptive act in relation to the object of the senses remains, but the creative imagination actively connects the same into a unified, coherent whole.

In the *Biographia Literaria*, Coleridge links the secondary imagination to the work of the artist. The creative imagination, echoing the perception of sensory objects in the primary sense of the term, brings the whole into view through the reflective powers of the understanding, balancing

---

13. Julian of Norwich, *Revelations of Divine Love*, 46 (LT 4).
14. Julian of Norwich, *Revelations of Divine Love*, 53 (LT 8).
15. Coleridge, *Biographia Literaria*, 1.304.

and reconciling "opposite or discordant qualities."[16] The poet, according to Coleridge, brings the inward soul into a unified activity as it blends, diffuses, and idealizes in the formation of "all into one graceful and intelligent whole."[17] This remains an act of individual agency but works for a creative and living end. Notably, Coleridge continues to identify the secondary imagination with the divine act of creation. Just as the primary imagination relates the perception of nature to self-consciousness, the secondary imagination leads on to higher knowledge in the creativity of the artist, who reconnects the interior knowledge of the self to the perception of the exterior world but with "a sense of novelty and freshness, with old and familiar objects."[18]

Return now to Julian's *Revelations of Divine Love*. The crucifix before her might have remained but a fanciful image set fixedly in her memory if not for the power of imagination, through which she engaged in an act of spontaneous creativity. She transforms the image of blood on the head of Christ as a participatory symbol of spiritual truth. Julian records not only the image of the cross before her but also, following extended reflection, the theological meaning of the same.[19] In the process, she engages in a poetic act of imagination—an act of theological creativity in which the image is retained even as she relates the meaning of the signs to a wider range of seemingly commonplace sources.

The image of the hazelnut is a case in point. The small nut lying in the palm of her hand serves as an analogy of creation. "'What can this be?' And the answer came to me, 'It is all that is made.'"[20] Julian's text represents a sophisticated act of theological and literary imagination, moving from a description of the crucifix she perceives, to the interior meaning of the image for the soul, and then back to a new analogous image for subsequent reflection. This imaginative oscillation between exterior and interior image and meaning requires readers to engage the mystery of the divine in the work of the cross. In this, she brings "the whole soul" into activity by creating a freshness and novelty in the vision, while suspending theological closure with reminders that "until I become one substance with him, I can never have complete rest or true happiness; that is to say, until I am so bound to him that there is no created thing between my God and me."[21]

---

16. Coleridge, *Biographia Literaria*, 1.304.
17. Coleridge, *Biographia Literaria*, 2.15–18.
18. Coleridge, *Biographia Literaria*, 2.17.
19. In fact, the less she depends on the mere image, moving instead to dissolve in order to unify, the more she engages in an act of "pure" imagination.
20. Julian of Norwich, *Revelations of Divine Love*, 47 (*LT* 5).
21. Julian of Norwich, *Revelations of Divine Love*, 47 (*LT* 5).

The lack of systematization in Julian of Norwich's *Revelations* has long hindered the theological reception of her work. In earlier generations, for instance, no less a figure than the seventeenth-century Anglican Edward Stillingfleet regarded Julian's mysticism primarily as a matter of the heart and "not at all theological."[22] Such an assessment has gradually receded into the background, yet more work remains in order to move from defense to esteem. Janet Soskice, for example, maintains that Julian's *Revelations* is not only within the vein of the dominant Augustinian theology of her day, but "she presses it to a new fruitfulness, especially by her unashamed embrace of the body and temporality."[23] According to Soskice, even if Julian of Norwich never read Augustine's work directly, she would have been well aware of his teachings through the wider ecclesial culture and, as a result, manages to accomplish what few had achieved before her: an innovation on Augustine's teachings on God and the divine image. The images Julian uses are different than those of Augustine—and that's just the point. Whereas Augustine maintained an intellectualist understanding of the Trinity in psychological triads of memory, understanding, and will, Julian of Norwich is able to re-embody the doctrine by drawing on metaphors from family life.

Nowhere is the embodied vision of Christian faith more evident than in Julian's exposition of Jesus as our true mother, which appears as part of an "enlargement" or extended meditation on the idea of union with God in the long text between the fourteenth and fifteenth showings (*LT* ch. 44–63). Julian's expansion should be understood as the product of theological imagination: years after the original, spontaneous act of perceptivity had passed, Julian's sustained reflection on the meaning of the original moment of vision led to a creative "enlargement" on the theme.

In chapter 60, one of the most compelling chapters of her work, Julian links the image of Christ to our own dependence on God in a threefold movement that is simultaneously biblical, liturgical, and eschatological. First, she explains that Christ's motherhood begins in the Virgin's womb. In this, she is extending the earlier meditation on the cross of Christ through a biblical reversal, namely, Christ's sufferings are likened to the embodied sufferings of his own mother in the act of childbirth: "We know that our mothers only bring us into the world to suffer and die, but our true mother, Jesus, he who is all love, bears us into joy and eternal life; blessed may he be!"[24] The sufferings of Jesus are related not as an analogy from a higher truth to a lesser truth but as an extended metaphor that captures the mystery of

22. Soskice, *Kindness of God*, 126.
23. Soskice, *Kindness of God*, 126; cf. Turner, *Julian of Norwich, Theologian*.
24. Julian of Norwich, *Revelations of Divine Love*, 141 (*LT* 60).

divine love in the mystery of the *theotokos*. Even as Mary gave birth to God himself, so Christ gives birth to his children in an act of self-sacrifice. Christ "sustains us" and "labors" until the "sharpest pangs" and "most grievous sufferings" bring him to death.[25] He would do more if he could.

Then, Julian moves to a second aspect of Christ's motherhood: nourishing us with his own self. Here she appeals to the liturgical acts of the church, relying on the biblical image of Christ providing himself as food for his disciples: "Those who eat my flesh and drink my blood have eternal life, and I will raise them up on the last day" (John 6:54 RSV). The bread of heaven that came down as a gift—the flesh and blood of the Son of God—is reimagined in the embodied lives of mothers. In breastfeeding, a mother gives of her very own self in nursing her child: "The mother can give her child her milk to suck, but our dear mother Jesus can feed us with himself, and he does so most generously and most tenderly with the holy sacrament which is the most precious food of life itself."[26] Sacramental grace in the Eucharist, realized through the liturgy of the church, sustains God's children.

Finally, extending the image of Christ our true mother one step further, Julian imagines Christ leading us "into his blessed breast through his sweet open side" in order to raise up the child into full maturity. The image of the wounded side of Christ in the crucifix is reflected on through the philosophical imagination and reimagined in the form of human parentage. Christ's love remains constant in watching tenderly, disciplining, and guiding to full maturity under the care of God, much as the Scriptures teach God's care for his children as well as discipline.[27]

In this way, Julian of Norwich enacts theological imagination to explore spiritual truths that had often been overlooked by the schoolmen. Her prose displays the sort of Coleridgean process of diffusing "in order to re-create" that he labels the "secondary imagination." Her account of Christ our true mother is resonant with biblical language and imagery, refusing to reduce the work of Christ to a legal, intellectual, or disembodied transaction. Her account is eschatological, orienting the child of God to a future made possible by the nurture and care of God. She unifies aspects of faith that are often divided, too, bringing the entire movement of Christian life from new birth to full maturity into view under the lordship of Jesus Christ. In the process, she elevates women's experiences, overturning their

25. The image also recalls, implicitly, the command that all God's children must be born again (John 3).

26. Julian of Norwich, *Revelations of Divine Love*, 141 (LT 60).

27. Notably, Julian distinguishes the use of analogy here, claiming that the birth of a body is "only low, humble and modest compared with the birth of our soul" (*Revelations of Divine Love*, 142 [LT 60]).

subordination in the church and society through an identification between the incarnation and embodied humanity. This places her both within and meaningfully pressing beyond Augustine's theology.[28]

Apostatic Imagination

The sort of theological creativity found in Julian of Norwich has captivated some and troubled others. Right about here we might find ourselves asking whether imagination is always quite as wonderful as this assessment seems to indicate. We are reminded of the warnings about imagination and its liability for abuse. Even in the most common use of the term, we may sense some of the challenge that accompanies its recovery.

Consider the way "imagination" is used in daily speech.[29] On the one hand, when a child cries out in terror for fear of monsters lurking in the closet, the child's parents bring comfort with confident assurances that "it's only your imagination." On the other hand, when we read a moving work of poetry, gaze upon a painted landscape, or listen awestruck to a piece of music, we might honor the artist by proclaiming these works of "unparalleled imagination." The distinction between the two, according to Thomas McFarland, reveals the difference between mere fancy and true imagination: "It is the existence of the unbidden mental phantoms of the first order that sanctions Coleridge's 'fancy', and it is the unified, consciously willed, creative control of the potential ramifications of a situation, signalized by the second use, that sanctions Coleridge's 'imagination.'"[30] The monsters should be rejected as fanciful because they lack the initiating power of will and self-consciousness that are marks of the divine image. But what if some acts of creative imagination are actually more problematic or even marked by evil?

Two commonplace worries about imagination immediately come to the forefront. One of the foremost concerns with imagination has overt theological bearings: idolatry. Coleridge's Anglican predecessor John Wesley warned of just such an error in his sermon on "The Unity of the Divine Being." He claims that many look forward to the delights of heaven but never trouble themselves for a moment with the happiness that God alone can bring in the present. God's rivals are legion. Objects of sense excite a "love of the world" or "desire of the flesh," while "objects of the imagination"

---

28. Cf. Johnson, *She Who Is*, 33–40.

29. I owe the following distinction between the child and the artist to Thomas McFarland's discussion of the topic in *Coleridge and the Pantheist Tradition*, 306–10.

30. McFarland, *Coleridge and the Pantheist Tradition*, 310.

or "things that gratify our fancy, by grandeur, beauty, or novelty" prevent us from seeking our true happiness in God. In the "desire of the eyes," Wesley cautions, the imagination is gratified.[31] Wesley's wise counsel deserves sustained attention, but here I will only note that the sorts of objects that he identifies as idolatry belong chiefly to the realm of fancy. The idolatry he describes is not the product of a conscious awareness of the self in union with God but the mere consumption of sensory pleasures for personal indulgence.

The concern about idolatry brings a second worry into sharper focus: deception. While I have focused almost entirely on the creativity of the subject in producing works of imagination, we certainly should not neglect the potentially negative experience of consuming such creations. To be clear, entering into the imaginative world of the artist can be a profoundly positive and instructive experience. C. S. Lewis describes the salutary benefits of imaginative literature in his book *An Experiment in Criticism*: "in reading great literature," he says, "I become a thousand men and yet remain myself."[32] My much beloved colleague at Wheaton College, the late Roger Lundin, described the universal power of literature similarly: "We try on different ideas and identities. And we dream of ways that diseases might be cured, wounds healed, and enemies reconciled. And we do so with the hope that when Christ is fully revealed, we will be like him, for we will see him as he is."[33] In seeing the world through works of imagination, we see through new eyes and begin to understand ourselves in the process. Yet, even here, some might wish to pause, for this is precisely what worries some about literature and the arts. The idea that we so enter the world of the text that we don't just forget about the world around us—we embrace this new world. And once that happens, who knows what might follow? The British novelist Jeanette Winterson describes just this sort of anxiety when one of her characters bemoans the power of literature to inflict mayhem in our lives: "the trouble with a book," she says, "is that you never know what's in it, until it's too late."[34]

These challenges to an unbridled embrace of imagination, particularly in its most positive, optimistic forms, should lead the theologian to meditate on the impact of sin on the imaginative faculty. In fact, though Coleridge's later reflections on imagination are seldom discussed, he tends

---

31. Wesley, "Unity of the Divine Being," 534–35.

32. Lewis, *Experiment in Criticism*, 141.

33. Lundin, "Life of Culture and the Christian"; cf. Lundin, *Beginning with the Word*, 26.

34. Winterson, *Why Be Happy When You Could Be Normal?*, 33.

to de-emphasize the faculty of imagination in later writings in favor of other philosophical and theological concepts that allowed for the knowledge of God.[35] Sara Coleridge, the poet's daughter and his foremost nineteenth-century editor, claims that her father had "stroked out" the final clause of the definition of the primary imagination.[36] Many think Coleridge wanted to avoid highlighting his earlier embrace of pantheistic systems. But I think it is equally possible that his own experience of profound brokenness led him to question his earlier articulation. In fact, some scholars trace a lesser-known vision of the imagination in his later notebooks, in which Coleridge theorized that true imagination may only be found among those peoples who "have developed a sense of the reality and cosmic pervasiveness of evil."[37] More specifically, Coleridge theorizes that the recognition that things are not as they ought to be creates a tension within the finite individual. Rather than perceiving all reality in the unity of divine love, the individual risks continual apostasy in self-seeking delusion. The negative outcome of such brokenness is that, over against the positive assessment of imagination, we tend to create that which leads to chaos. Positively, Coleridge thinks such a state of discord may lead us to seek out the liberation we so desperately need: "this feeling of tornness, essentially a feeling of our privation or lack of actuality, causes us . . . to feel the need for redemption, a tenuous acknowledgement of our ultimate home within the actuality of divine grace."[38] This "negative romanticism" qualifies the optimistic view of imagination we rightly cherish in Coleridge's aesthetics and helps to explain why much of his own poetry seems unable to accomplish that which he intuits—"an epiphany never quite actualized."[39]

Sanctified Imagination

The theological assessment of imagination, with a recognition of sin, opens up new paths of reflection. In fact, through this extended meditation on the work of S. T. Coleridge and Julian of Norwich, I have suggested that Christian theology has something vital to contribute to the discussion of

---

35. In later publications such as *Aids to Reflection* (1825), Coleridge appealed less to imagination in favor of his well-known distinction between Reason and Understanding; cf. Evans, *Sublime Coleridge*, 108.

36. Namely, "and as a repetition . . . I AM" (*Biographia Literaria*, 1.304n3).

37. Anthony Harding, quoted in Reid, "Satanic Principle," 259; cf. Harding, "Imagination, Patriarchy, and Evil."

38. Reid, "Satanic Principle," 264, 267.

39. Reid, "Satanic Principle," 277.

contemporary aesthetics. For a theology of imagination not only captures the creativity of the human as bearer of the image of God but also articulates the need to address forms of imagination that are contrary to God's eschatological vision for the world.

Imagination, while a creative faculty, can go its own way. The problem is not merely the knowledge of good and evil, but the way such knowledge has reconfigured our perception of the world. We are all mis-formed not only as individuals but within our communities. Augustine makes this abundantly clear, but recent theologies addressing questions of race—a problem on which American Christians remain woefully under-reflective—have pointedly challenged the church to rethink fundamental conceptions of social identity and self-consciousness. Willie Jennings, for example, describes this as a "diseased social imagination" and asks whether Christian theology is even able to discern how "its intellectual and pedagogical performances reflect and fuel the problem."[40] Jennings challenges whether any discussion of God and wonder that fails to acknowledge the temptation to make God in our own racialized images can ever truly reflect the startling proclamation of the Bible. A sanctified theology of imagination must reorient our imaginations around a transformative grace that turns our eyes squarely on these problems in order that we might truly see God.[41]

Sanctifying the perception of reality will necessarily reorient our understanding of creativity and the arts. Protestants, in particular, have a long heritage of opposing images as idolatry. In turn, the loss of signs and symbols, the relation between the outward and inward, has been devastating to the formation of a robust Christian aesthetic in some quarters. A prioritization of the spoken word and distrust for culture have accompanied a sterilization of worship and the diminishment of imagination in the process. When we strip the spaces we inhabit of the signs of a larger story—visual markers of the sacred in the ordinary—we leave the people of God with few reminders of their place in the drama of salvation. Scorn for aesthetic presentations of our lives as they really are—broken, frail, and hurting—has diminished our ability to convey the gospel. Yet, to appeal to the work of John Walford at a Wheaton Theology Conference many years ago, a broken beauty may be true to the human condition in ways that idealized portraits of perfection are not: "a broken beauty can be a redemptive beauty, which acknowledges suffering while preserving hope."[42] Artists, in biblical and theological perspective, have the capacity to act prophetically by naming,

40. Jennings, *Christian Imagination*, 6–7.
41. Cf. Rah, "Sin of Racism."
42. Walford, "Case for a Broken Beauty," 87.

engaging, and challenging the brokenness of our lives and pointing to the redemptive grace in Christ that holds the healing of the entire cosmos.[43]

The Christian response to an apostatic imagination, then, is the reformation of imagination. Such a task belongs at the heart of the mission of the church. Not only while listening to the word but as we gather at the font and around the table, we discover grace that allows us to see rightly who we are and turn our eyes on the one who has made us all. The liturgy takes us as embodied people and forms us as a new community. Coleridge seems to recognize the individual aspect of this process in the *Biographia*: "We begin with the I know myself in order to end with the absolute I AM. We proceed from the self, in order to lose and find all self in God."[44] Yet, at that point, he lacked the fuller language of embodied community that has the potential to break down long-standing sources of division.[45]

The recovery of Julian of Norwich's Augustinian theology may actuate the sort of imaginative activity that we require in our own age. As I have already outlined, her *Revelations* move from the outward image to the interior self in a process of creative imagination that begins in what Coleridge denominates the "fancy" and ends in the poetic creativity of the imagination. She is everywhere at pains to redirect attention from herself to God as the source of truth and meaning: "God, of your goodness, give me yourself; you are enough for me, and anything less that I could ask for would not do you full honour."[46] Fixing her eyes on Christ allowed her to recognize her own self, and in finding herself she was able to gaze in wonder at God.

Moreover, Julian of Norwich writes fully aware of the deforming power of sin on the finite will. In a meditation before the final showing, Julian describes her own encounter with a wicked fiend who grinned at her with "a wicked expression."[47] The terror she faced threatens to disrupt her union with God, as torment gives way to fear. But here she repeats a claim that reflects not the dewy-eyed optimism of some later generations, for "He did not say, 'You shall not be tormented, you shall not be troubled, you shall not be grieved,'" but rather an eschatological hope that unites the self to God: "all shall be well."[48] Indeed, awe and wonder fill the *Revelations of Divine Love*, for she recognizes the greatness of God in comparison to her own

43. On such a vision, see Dyrness, *Poetic Theology*, 177–80.

44. Coleridge, *Biographia Literaria*, 1.283.

45. On Coleridge's philosophical exposition of the relationship between mother and child, a sensory experience that "primes the pump" of self-consciousness, see *Opus Maximum*, fragment 2.

46. Julian of Norwich, *Revelations of Divine Love*, 48 (LT 5).

47. Julian of Norwich, *Revelations of Divine Love*, 152 (LT 66).

48. Julian of Norwich, *Revelations of Divine Love*, 155 (LT 68).

finitude: "I beg you all for God's sake and advise you for your own advantage that you stop paying attention to the poor being to whom this vision was shown, and eagerly, attentively and humbly contemplate God, who in his gracious love and eternal goodness wanted the vision to be generally known to comfort us all."[49] Indeed, her entire work is just what she claimed—a visionary account of divine love.

The formation of a Christian theology of imagination, developed here with the assistance of two English theologians, has much to offer for both theology and its integration with literature and the arts. Christians have sometimes cried out, like a child in the night, fearful of the workings of the mind. Upon closer inspection, however, we may discover that light comes through participation in the life of the church, our fixation on outward things loosens, and the shadows flee away.

---

49. Julian of Norwich, *Revelations of Divine Love*, 53 (*LT* 8).

3

Children, Wonder, and the Work of Theology

EMILY HUNTER MCGOWIN

Six years ago, I was putting my then–six-year-old son to bed. Since bedtime closely follows our family's time of evening prayer, God is a regular subject of our conversations. That night, my son mused about God's love. Our conversation was so memorable, I wrote it down:

> William: "God's love must be infinity big. Like infinity plus a hundred. Or infinity plus a million."
>
> Me: "I think you're right. Probably even bigger than that because it includes the whole universe and any universes beyond that."
>
> William: "So how big is Satan?"
>
> Me: "It's hard to say for sure. The Bible doesn't say a lot about Satan. But he's definitely really small compared to God."
>
> William: "Oh, that makes sense! Because love is greater than hate. And the truth is greater than lies. And light is greater than dark. So, I bet every time Satan hates or lies, he just keeps getting smaller and smaller and darker and darker."
>
> Me: "That's a really cool way to think about it, buddy."
>
> William: "And I bet in the new heavens and new earth, God's love will be so big and so bright and powerful that Satan will

grow smaller and smaller and weaker and weaker . . . until he just disappears."

When William finished speaking, I found myself awed into silence. I don't know where he got that imagery, but it filled me with wonder. In the quiet twilight of my son's bedroom, I could see God's glorious future: the brilliant, blazing love of God expanding to fill and transfigure the entire universe, causing the chaos of evil to retreat, shrinking exponentially until it simply disappears.

During the same time period, I was serving as a pastor and mentor in our church's Godly Play program. Godly Play is an approach to children's religious instruction rooted in the Montessori philosophy of education. Jerome Berryman, the founder of Godly Play, says his approach offers "spiritual guidance" to children through carefully structured worship, which immerses children in sacred stories, parables, liturgical actions, and contemplative silence.[1] A key part of responding to sacred stories and parables in Godly Play is a time for children and mentors to "wonder" together. As with my son, there's no doubt I learned as much, if not more, from the children and their wondering as they did from me.

My experiences as a parent, pastor, and Godly Play mentor have nurtured a growing conviction: children are not simply Christians *in potentia*, or disciples in the making. Children, precisely as children, are recipients of grace and servants of God. Children know God and are known by God from birth. After all, Jesus points to children as models for receiving God's kingdom. This means we don't have to wait until they've reached adulthood to benefit from children's example and ministry.

Yet, in a time when theologians are rightly attending to and learning from a variety of historically marginalized voices, children remain, by and large, ignored. Globally, children from birth to fourteen years of age make up almost 26 percent of the total population—one quarter of the world.[2] In the US alone, children account for approximately 23 percent of the population.[3] Yet, in the words of one priest-theologian, "Theology remains the province of adults talking to and about other adults about the nature of the supreme adult who is God."[4] Do we really believe Jesus when he says the kingdom of God belongs to children? Perhaps not.

What does all this have to do with wonder? I argue in "Wonder and Theology" that wonder begins theology, sustains theology, and serves as

1. Berryman, *Spiritual Guidance of Children*, 3–4.
2. World Bank, as of 2019.
3. U.S. Census Bureau, "Projected Age Groups and Sex Composition, 2017–2060."
4. Asbridge, "What is a Child?," 20.

theology's ultimate end. But, as many of us know instinctively, wonder is also a crucial aspect of childhood. There are complicated reasons why we make this association—too many to detail here. Still, I think wonder can be understood to be a central part of the vocation of children. If this is true, then the church and theological academy alike ignore children to their detriment. Put positively, caring for and learning from children is a vital Christian practice, both for the church as a whole and for theologians in particular.

I should acknowledge, though, that I have not always thought of children as contributors to the work of theology. Often, I have been guilty of the opposite assumption. Due to their vulnerability and neediness, I have regularly seen children as a hindrance to my work. My first child was four months old when I entered a PhD program and our family continued to grow throughout my studies. Both then and today, I found myself fretting regularly about how much more I'd be able to accomplish if I weren't facing so many motherly demands. And yet, without denying the real challenges children pose in daily life (a challenge many of us are more acutely aware of due to the pandemic), I am compelled to offer an alternative perspective.

Children and Childhood in Christian Theology

For most people, the connection between wonder and children is not difficult to make. In the West, at least, we have a strong sense that the two go together. "Philosophy begins in wonder," Howard Parsons says, "but wonder begins in the child."[5] Why do we assume this is true? Many scholars think we have the Romantics to thank.[6] Indeed, some argue that the very notion of childhood—or at least the emotional and sentimental weight we associate with childhood—is a Romantic invention.[7] Whether or not this is the case, many of our notions of childhood coincide with a "renaissance of wonder" in the Romantics.[8] Yet, as I have noted, children and childhood remain underdeveloped in theology. Todd Whitmore's evaluation of the Catholic

---

5. Parsons, "Philosophy of Wonder," 101.

6. For discussion of the development of Romantic notions of childhood in Western literature, see Reinhard Kuhn, *Corruption in Paradise*. Arguably, two of the most influential figures on Western notions of childhood are Jean Jacques Rousseau and William Wordsworth.

7. There are competing narratives about this process beginning with the groundbreaking work of Aries, *Centuries of Childhood*. Helpful summaries are provided by Cunningham, *Invention of Childhood*, and Montgomery and Woodhead, *Understanding Childhood*.

8. Quinn, *Iris Exiled*, 251–74.

Church is true of all Christian communions: "For the most part, church teaching simply admonishes the parents to educate their children in the faith and for children to obey their parents."[9] What children are, to whom they belong, what they are owed, and what they are called to do and be in the world—these kinds of questions have only recently begun to be explored seriously by Christian theologians.

Theologically speaking, what is a child and childhood?[10] Answers to this question have varied in Christian theology since the earliest days of the church.[11] In what follows, I briefly sketch the New Testament's perspective on children, summarize the three majority perspectives in the Christian tradition, and then, in interaction with contemporary theologians, offer another point of view.

In the Gospels, children are chief among "the least of these" and recipients of the kingdom of God. Precisely because of their powerlessness and vulnerability, Jesus says God's kingdom is intended for them (Mark 10:13–16; Matt 19:13–15; Luke 18:15–17).[12] The Gospels further characterize children as models of receiving the kingdom of God (Mark 10:15).[13] Children never served as ideals for adults in Jewish literature, and to compare adults to children in the Greco-Roman setting was deeply offensive.[14] But Jesus says children demonstrate to adults how to enter God's kingdom. And Jesus so closely identifies himself with children that to welcome a "little one" is to welcome him (Mark 9:37; Matt 18:1–2, 4–5; Luke 9:46–48).

---

9. Whitmore with Winright, "Children."

10. Postmodern sociologists like Chris Jenks claim "child" and "childhood" are social constructs. There is no universal, natural identity "the child" that exists across all times and places. Rather, children and childhood take a variety of forms based upon their historical, social, and cultural contexts. I agree "child" and "childhood" should be problematized, but I also think there's value in deploying a kind of "strategic essentialism" (to use Serene Jones's language). In short, this means assuming a general, natural basis for child and childhood, while also being aware of the need to make decisions about the usefulness of such terminology in particular contexts. This is also the approach of Mercer, *Welcoming Children*, 18–19.

11. Some of the following builds upon my research in *Quivering Families*.

12. Gundry-Volf, "Least and the Greatest."

13. Willmer and White discuss the social and cultural context of first-century Judea, which helps make sense of Jesus' choice of the child as a sign of the humility (see *Entry Point*, 128–45).

14. Gundry-Volf, "Least and the Greatest," 39.

Figure 3. Lucas Cranach the Elder, *Christ Blessing the Children.*

The rest of the New Testament builds on Jesus' perspective, but does not substantively expand it.[15] When the epistles do speak of children, they enjoin children to obey their parents, and to do so "in the Lord" (Col 3:20–21; Eph 6:1–4). Thus, children are positioned alongside their parents under the rule of Jesus Christ. The fact that children are addressed directly with ethical instruction indicates their status in the household and the church as ones who possess their own agency and responsibility in Christ.[16] They have a role to play in the household of God.

Beyond the early church, Christian theologians through the centuries have generally thought of children in three major ways. First, children have been understood as sinners in need of restraint and discipline. Most influential in this regard is Augustine, who understood all human beings to be implicated in Adam's sin. His notion of original sin led him to conclude that even *in utero* the human person is thoroughly corrupted.[17] Children, therefore, are in desperate need of baptism and the unmerited grace it mediates, as well as adult instruction in Christian faith and practice.

---

15. I disagree with Berryman that Paul has a "low" estimate of children, but they certainly do not receive much of his attention. For Paul, childhood is something to grow out of (see Berryman, *Children and the Theologians*, 40–44).

16. Gundry-Volf, "Least and the Greatest," 56.

17. See Stortz, "Augustine on Childhood," 94.

The second way Christian theologians have conceived of children is as persons in the making in need of growth and instruction. Thomas Aquinas was perhaps the most eloquent proponent of this perspective. For Thomas, children do not have complete use of their rational faculties and are, therefore, incomplete.[18] So, the child is vulnerable, and adults have an urgent responsibility to care for and guide children into adulthood.[19] Childhood's significance, then, lies in the fact that it is eventually left behind as the child becomes a full person.[20]

The third major perspective of Christian theologians is to view children as innocents in need of protection and nurturance. Of course, the perceived innocence of children does not entail a denial of their status as sinful. Rather, the emphasis shifts to their vulnerability, dependence, and reasoning incapability relative to adults. This perspective is best represented by Horace Bushnell,[21] who wrote *Christian Nurture*, one of the first substantive inquiries into the religious lives of children.[22] Bushnell never denies the sinfulness of children, but he argues there is no good reason a child must resort to sin and wickedness if the child has been gently guided toward loving God.[23]

As I said previously, the three perspectives on children just sketched have rarely been foregrounded in theology.[24] When spoken of at all, children have been incidental to larger theological concerns. The major exceptions appear only in the twentieth century: Karl Rahner and Hans Urs Von Balthasar, both of whom offered short but substantive reflections on children and childhood in their later years.[25] Moreover, in the twenty-first century, several theologians and religious scholars, including Marcia Bunge, David

---

18. Aquinas, *Summa Theologiae*, II-II, q. 10, a. 12.

19. Jensen, *Graced Vulnerability*, 8.

20. Jensen, *Graced Vulnerability*, 9. Obviously, this perspective privileges reason as a core dimension of human life. Thomas's point of view seems to value children more for who they will one day become. In Jensen's words, "Children are on the way to personhood, and childhood is rapidly discarded along the way" (Jensen, *Graced Vulnerability*, 10).

21. Among the Romantics, Jean-Jacques Rousseau is especially notable. *Contra* Augustinian anthropology, Rousseau posits that everything in its "natural" state is inherently good (see further Rousseau, *Emile*).

22. Bushnell, *Christian Nurture*, 10.

23. Through careful nurturance in the home, he says, the child of a Christian family will find it "all but impossible" to forsake the Christian faith (Bushnell, *Christian Nurture*, 10). For more, see Margaret Bendroth, "Horace Bushnell's Christian Nurture."

24. For more discussion of the tension among the three perspectives, see my chapter, "Children and Childhood in the Full Quiver," in *Quivering Families*, 125–68.

25. Rahner, "Ideas for a Theology of Childhood"; Balthasar, *Unless You Become Like This Child*.

Jensen, Martin Marty, Joyce Ann Mercer, and Bonnie Miller-McLemore, have focused on children and childhood as distinct topics of theological reflection. Drawing especially upon Jensen and Marty, I would like to offer another perspective to what has been outlined earlier. Yes, the child is a sinner (as are all human beings), the child is developing into an adult, and the child is innocent with regard to experience and capability. But the child is also a mystery.

The child is a mystery in a theological and sacramental sense: a tangible thing in which something divine is revealed.[26] Christian faith confesses God became a child. To be more exact, the Word, the second person of the Trinity, became human and, as a human being, grew from infancy through childhood and into adulthood. In the womb of Mary, John Saward writes, "the Son took the way of childhood into the world, and thus united Himself to every child."[27] In addition, orthodox trinitarianism holds that even prior to the moment of the incarnation, the Word is eternally begotten of the Father. Thus, "before" his conception and birth, "before" his assumption of the human office of Son, Vigen Guroian says, "his divine hypostasis is related to the Father as Son and he 'occupies' the office of divine Sonship." So, "Childhood and sonship and daughterhood have a divine origin."[28] There is, then, childhood and child-ness in God.[29] George MacDonald puts it more simply: "Childhood belongs to the divine nature."[30] So, the child, by virtue of her identification with the Word—who is eternally, and also became temporally, a child—reveals something of God.

There is more to say, though. There are only two groups with whom Jesus so closely identifies that he claims to receive them is to receive him: the poor and children.[31] As MacDonald says, "[T]o receive a child in the name of Jesus is to receive Jesus; to receive Jesus is to receive God; therefore,

---

26. One of my favorite definitions of mystery comes from Jeremy Driscoll: "A concrete something that when you bump into it, it puts you in contact with a divine reality" (*What Happens at Mass?*, 3).

27. Saward, *Way of the Lamb*, 68.

28. Guroian, "Office of the Child in Christian Faith," 113.

29. Rahner describes it this way: "Childhood is only truly understood . . . when it is seen as based upon the foundation of the childhood of God" ("Ideas for a Theology of Childhood," 50). The term "childness" comes from Anderson and Johnson, *Regarding Children*, 7.

30. MacDonald, "Child in the Midst," 13.

31. I am using "the poor" to encompass all the groups mentioned in Matthew 25:31–46: the hungry, the thirsty, the stranger, the naked, the sick, and the imprisoned. "Truly I tell you," Jesus says, "whatever you did for one of the least of these brothers and sisters of mine, you did for me."

to receive the child is to receive God himself."[32] In other words, children reveal God to us. As sinful, limited, vulnerable, and innocent as they may be, children are living, breathing icons of the only-begotten Son of God, who fully reveals the Father because he has always known and loved the Father.

In addition to revealing something of God, the child-as-mystery also reveals what it means to be human. That is to say, the child precisely as a child, manifests all the glories and vulnerabilities of humanity. Jensen's theological dimensions of childhood are particularly insightful at this point. "To be a child," he says, "is . . . to be chosen by God . . . to be open and vulnerable to the grace that makes life possible . . . and . . . to be a pilgrim, oriented God-ward and toward the present."[33] Not only do these points indicate what it is to be a child, they also reveal what it means to be human. Children are icons of humanity, too. While we are accustomed to thinking of adults—typically, straight, white, male, able-bodied adults—as the archetype of humanity, it is, in fact, children, in all their variegated and contextual complexity, who most fully reveal what it means to be human.

As Jensen says, to be human is to be chosen by God, to be subjects of divine love. So, childhood is both preparation for and symbolic of the universal human station to which all are called: child of God.[34] Also, to be human is to be open and vulnerable, both to grace and to harm. As Jensen says, "The vulnerability of children . . . is a fact of the God-given relatedness into which all persons are born: though most visible in infancy, we never outgrow it."[35] Finally, to be human is to be on pilgrimage: to be attentive to the present while proceeding on a lifelong journey toward God.[36] While adults are not as adept as children in attentiveness to the present—indeed, we avail ourselves of books, workshops, and therapies to learn simply how to be in the present—human life is lived in the present and all are oriented toward a future in God (1 Cor 15:28).

In summary, then, children show us what it means to be human. In his research on children's spirituality, Robert Coles has been saying something similar for decades.[37] His comments from a 1993 interview are worth quoting at length:

32. MacDonald, "Child in the Midst," 9.
33. Jensen, *Graced Vulnerability*, 44.
34. Guroian, "Office of the Child in the Christian Faith," 120.
35. Jensen, *Graced Vulnerability*, 49.
36. For discussion of how children require imagination to make sense of their lifetimes, see Willmer and White, *Entry Point*, 93–94.
37. Robert Coles's five-volume series, *Children of Crisis*, which documents how children and their parents deal with change, won the Pulitzer Prize. Especially relevant for our purposes, though, is his later volume, *Spiritual Life of Children*.

> [W]e are all children, and thank God we are. The problem is we don't know it well enough. This is one of the things Jesus taught us—to struggle toward childhood and never forget it or outlive it. And to retain within ourselves whatever shred of innocence and trust and willingness to engage ourselves with the world in the yearning and unashamedly vulnerable way that children possess. This was one of his major lessons to us. And all this talk about being "mature" and growing up and progressing through stages and phases misses the point of how important it is to retain that connection—not to "the inner child" but to the sense of vulnerability and yearning that childhood is about. That's a big part of ourselves. Or it ought to be.[38]

To be clear, to say children reveal humanity is a claim still rooted in the Christology with which we began. Jesus Christ is the Son, the child, the true human being, who privileges children as revelatory of his person and kingdom. It is Christ who is the elect one, the vulnerable one, and the ultimate pilgrim on the way. When I say that children are a mystery, I am saying that children, through their relation to Christ and to all of us, are revelatory both of God and of humankind.

The Child's Vocation to Wonder

It is well and good to say a child is mystery, but what difference does that make to the topic of wonder and theology? As icons of Christ and humankind, wonder is a central part of the child's vocation. Through the waters of baptism, children are adopted into the eternal family of God. Unlike the biological family, which will eventually come to an end (Matt 22:30), God's household will endure forever.[39] If children belong to the church (and the church belongs to children), then children have a vocation in the Christian community.[40] We often speak of *adults* having vocations and children as "next generation" leaders. But, as my friend and longtime pastor, Mary Gonzalez, insists, "Children are *this* generation. They are leaders today!"[41] Indeed, if children are full members of the body of Christ, then they too have a divine service—a purpose, work, and a way of being in the world to which God calls them.

---

38. Coles, "Struggling Toward Childhood."

39. McGowin, *Quivering Families*, 164.

40. Certainly, one could argue that all children, by virtue of being made and known by God, have a vocation in the wider world, but that is not the focus of this essay.

41. Interview with Mary Gonzalez, January 7, 2021.

How might one characterize the divine service of children? Theologians Marcia Bunge and Vigen Guroian have described in their work different accounts of the vocation and office of the child.[42] Bunge, drawing upon Luther, finds in Scripture eight duties or responsibilities that children perform to benefit the family and the church.[43] Guroian, by contrast, opts for the language of office. He wants to avoid the subjective and individualistic connotations of vocation. "An office does not *belong* to someone," he says. "Rather it is a *station* into which a person is 'placed' or 'called.' The office of child does not belong to any particular child, but all children hold that office because they are children."[44] An office makes a claim upon us, denoting the performance of a task, with responsibility to others within a community.[45]

Whether we use the language of vocation or office, though, the point remains: children *as children* have divine purpose, responsibilities, and work to do. Of all the aspects of the child's vocation that Bunge proposes, three seem particularly significant for our purposes: to learn about and practice the faith; to play and be in the present; and to teach adults and serve as models of faith. Children do not need to grow up before fulfilling this divine service in God's household. Indeed, it is precisely because they are children that they be and do these things. This is especially true in the case of wonder. To learn and practice faith entails playing and being in the present, which then teaches adults and offers a model of faith to others. And wonder is a vital driving force in this interconnected work.

At this point, it helps to venture beyond the bounds of the discipline of theology for insight. Neuroscientists, philosophers, and educators agree that wonder and play are vital aspects of learning.[46] Einstein famously called the experience of the mysterious "the fundamental emotion which stands at the cradle of true art and science." Indeed, wonder is "the engine of all intellectual inquiry."[47] Throughout the educational and philosophical literature, a general consensus emerges that children are natural wonderers. This is in

42. Bunge, "Vocation of the Child," 35.

43. Of course, Bunge acknowledges her list is not exhaustive but lays the groundwork for a meaningful Christian understanding of the child's vocation.

44. Guroian, "Office of Child in the Christian Faith," 104.

45. Guroian, "Office of Child in the Christian Faith," 104–5. Of course, there's a sense in which all Christians share in the office of child since we never cease to be children of God. But the child *as child* is a particularly vital manifestation of the office of child, demonstrating "what kind of a person a Christian needs to become to inherit the kingdom of heaven" (105).

46. See, for example: Egan, Cant, and Judson, eds., *Wonder-full Education*; L'Ecuyer, "Wonder Approach to Learning"; Schinkel, "Education as Mediation between Child and World"; Kearns, "Subjects of Wonder."

47. Hadzigeorgiou, "Value of Wonder," 40.

large part due to their lack of experience with the world.[48] They also possess what appears to be an inherent humility and guilelessness, being accustomed to not knowing things and lacking control of their surroundings. Thus, philosopher Gareth Matthews has been insisting since the 1970s that children are particularly suited to the work of philosophy.[49] He says, "young children are much more likely than adults to raise philosophically interesting questions, make philosophically interesting observations, and engage, on their own, in philosophically interesting reasoning." Matthews calls philosophy "children's work," which "children show themselves to be very good at."[50]

Unfortunately, our education systems in the West often unwittingly educate wonder (not to mention humility) *out* of children. Many educators have noted with vexation that learning has gradually become equated with obtaining the right answers. In the words of Laura Piersol, "[Teachers] present the world as almost fully known; we have removed the mystery and turned the puzzles into simple ones that can be solved in a few neat steps.... It is rare that we collectively wander in thought anymore and so it becomes rare to wonder."[51] Now, I realize I am painting in broad brushstrokes, and this essay is not about reforming the education system. Suffice it to say that most educators are doing their best to figure out how to reinvigorate pedagogy and curriculum with wonder at all levels of education. What's important for my purpose is the fact that educators and philosophers agree that wonder is the natural purview of children. When we bring this insight into interaction with Scripture and the Christian tradition, it seems a special virtue of children, when given all the necessities of life, to wonder—at God, themselves, and the world. This penchant to wonder fuels their vocation to play, learn, and practice faith.[52]

---

48. Quinn offers some nuance on this point, saying, "[S]ome of what we call wonder in children is only curiosity and some of it is misplaced wonder since the child does not distinguish between mysteries and problems. But the very fact that children ask questions is evidence of their consciousness of ignorance" (*Iris Exiled*, 31).

49. Matthews, "Philosopher as Teacher." See further Matthews, *Dialogues with Children*; Matthews, *Philosophy of Childhood*.

50. Matthews, "Philosophy as Child's Play," 25.

51. Piersol, "Our Hearts Leap Up," 12.

52. In his chapter, "Creation," Keith White makes a distinction between childhood wonder and adult wonder. He says childhood wonder leads immediately to play. They are not pondering the meaning of creation but experiencing and interacting with it. In so doing, children are "developing a grasp of their own capabilities, senses, movement, control, and their bodies" (56). I'm not sure if the distinction needs to be so strong, nor do I think it holds universally. Still, it is worth considering in depth the ways in which the wonder of children and adults may be both similar and different.

Indeed, as they go about their vocation in the church, children are teaching the adults who interact with and care for them. It is for this reason that, in the Godly Play approach to religious education, Berryman insists that adults view themselves as mentors. Being a mentor means, among other things, placing oneself in the posture of one who accompanies and learns *with* a child. Thus, I am compelled to ask: what if theology, like philosophy, is children's work? And what if theologians saw themselves as co-wonderers with the children in their midst? And what if theologians made it a point to listen to, learn from, and do theology with our littlest sisters and brothers in Christ?

Doing Theology with Children

I have argued that wonder begins theology, sustains the work of theology, and serves as its *telos*. I have also contended that the child, though long neglected in Christian theology, is mysterious in a sacramental sense, and uniquely revelatory of both God and humanity. Moreover, wonder is a crucial aspect of the office of children in the church. If these claims are affirmed, then my final point follows naturally: caring for and learning from children is a vital Christian practice, both for the church as a whole and for theologians in particular. Given the centrality of wonder to the theological endeavor, the church and theological academy are at a serious loss without the contributions of children. In the words of another priest-theologian: "Without the participation of children, not simply their presence, the Church . . . is as incomplete as when it excludes the poor or the sick. Theology needs to be challenged by the vision, perspective, and experience of children."[53]

Of course, I am not the only theologian to make this claim. Jerome Berryman, Bonnie Miller-McLemore, and David Fitch, among others, have each made similar arguments in their respective projects.[54] But, I want to be clear: I am not simply saying caring for children is good for theologians at a personal level—though this is certainly true (even for those who don't consider themselves "kid people"). Attending to real children—wondering at and listening to God with them—will substantively transform our theological work for the better.

Before concluding, though, I need to offer an important caveat. In any discussion of children and childhood, we run the risk of romanticizing, fetishizing, or even idolizing children. Even as I uphold the vocation of the

53. Asbridge, "What is a Child?," 20.
54. Berryman, *Spiritual Guidance of Children*; Miller-McLemore, *In the Midst of Chaos*; Fitch, *Faithful Presence*.

child within the church, I must avoid the trap of thinking about children only, or even primarily, in terms of how *they* can help *us*. Indeed, the theologian "has to be open to the child and receive her without imposing preconditions on the encounter."[55] In other words, children must be permitted to be full persons with their own wants, needs, and agency.[56] And children must be allowed to remain *children*—vulnerable and dependent upon adult protection and advocacy. Any endeavor to do theology with children must be mindful to avoid harmful pitfalls.

How then do theologians undertake the theological task with children? I am eager to elaborate on the possibilities in future research. But I will venture this for now: the input, insight, and concerns of children must be allowed to inform every aspect of the theological endeavor, including the topics and questions we consider, the methods we use, the ways we construct our work, and the patterns of our lives.

Consider the last point, for example. For the most part, professional theologians spend the majority of their time with adults, considering the questions and concerns of adults, for the sake of adult audiences. Most of us are unwittingly insulated from face-to-face encounters with Jesus' "least of these," especially children. What would it mean to reconstruct our lives so that we are no longer shielded from the needs, concerns, and wonder of children? Certainly, I affirm the good that theologians do as teachers of adults in the church—I am one of them. But what if we took up positions as mentors and fellow learners among our church and neighborhood children? What if it was our regular practice *to tend to children* as part of our theological vocations?

The Child Theology Movement (CTM) and Child Theology have been trying to lead the way in this regard, seeking "to reform all theological reflection and enquiry" in light of the needs of the child.[57] They have been holding regular consultations since 2002 to discuss what child theology looks like. So far, two books have been produced out of their proceedings.[58]

CTM leaders acknowledge that the connection between theology and children can run in two directions. On the one hand, theology can provide

---

55. Pridmore, "Salvation," 191.

56. Robert Orsi's warning about notions of children's innocence holds in regard to wonder, too: "Ironically, the discourse of innocence puts children at the greatest risk because the emptiness of innocence creates a space into which adult desire can be projected." We must be vigilant to avoid this tendency (see Orsi, "Crisis about the Theology of Children," *Harvard Divinity Bulletin*, quoted by William Werpehowski, "In Search of Real Children," 63).

57. "About CTM," https://childtheologymovement.org/about-ctm/.

58. Willmer and White, *Entry Point*; and Collier, *Toddling to the Kingdom*.

grounding for the understanding and care of children. This is to go from theology to the child, producing theologies of childhood and advocacy for children. But, on the other hand, one can also go from child to theology. Moving in this direction means one's God-talk changes because the child has somehow influenced it, even if children are not directly mentioned.[59]

I believe both directions are needed—theology to child and child to theology—and can never be entirely separated. Theology from, with, for, and by children will take a variety of forms and address a range of questions. But my ultimate point comes down to this startling reality: Jesus placed *a child* in the midst of his disciples (Mark 9:36; Matt 18:2; Luke 9:46). Given all he could have said and done, all the people and things surrounding him in that moment, Jesus centered *the child* for his followers—and that includes those of us who are professional theologians. What if we took that moment as paradigmatic for the theological task? What would it mean for us to do theology with a child in the midst?[60] As we ponder the possibilities together, I think the words of poet Jane Clements begin to show us the way:

> Child, though I take your hand
> and walk in the snow;
> though we follow the track of the mouse together,
> though we try to unlock together the mystery
> of the printed word, and slowly discover
> why two and three makes five
> always, in an uncertain world—
>
> child, though I am meant to teach you much,
> what is it, in the end,
> except that together we are
> meant to be children
> of the same Father
> and I must unlearn
> all the adult structure
> and the cumbering years
>
> and you must teach me
> to look at the earth and the heaven
> with your fresh wonder.[61]

---

59. Willmer and White discuss these two directions in what they call child theology in *Entry Point*, 13–14.

60. The language of "doing theology with a child in the midst" comes from Willmer and White, *Entry Point*, 12–14.

61. Clements, "Child, Though I Take Your Hand."

4

Imagination, Knowing, and Supposing

Scott Cairns

In Xanadu did Kubla Khan
A stately pleasure dome decree:
Where Alph, the sacred river, ran
Through caverns measureless to man
    Down to a sunless sea.
So twice five miles of fertile ground
With walls and towers were girdled round:
And here were gardens bright with sinuous rills
Where blossomed many an incense-bearing tree;
And here were forests ancient as the hills,
Enfolding sunny spots of greenery.[1]

---

1. Coleridge, *Poems and Prose*, 11–13.

I want to begin my modest contribution to our discussion by stipulating a conviction that some readers may not entirely share. To wit, while there exists an objective reality—which undergirds an array of objective truths—none of us has comprehensive access to this objective reality, save through a variety of profoundly subjective apprehensions. This is the gap—between the real and our apprehensions of it—where the human imagination manifests its most efficacious purpose, which is to enable our supposing, our consciously constructing, and our thereafter sharing with others what I would call our modest paraphrases of the truth.

These paraphrases of the truth must be acknowledged, for our moment, as being provisional as well as being but paraphrases. They must never be mistaken as conclusive, nor ever be treated as replacements for the truth itself—which, as I say, is unavailable to our direct observation. Any effort to treat such provisional, subjective apprehensions as replacements for objective reality and expressed as comprehensive, objective truth must be recognized for what it is—a species of idolatry. So, to repeat: one must not receive *what appears to be* as a replacement for *what is*. With that stipulation in mind, I believe we might more safely engage in our speculations regarding the human imagination's place in the human endeavor to glimpse aspects of an enormity that we cannot now, nor will ever fully apprehend.

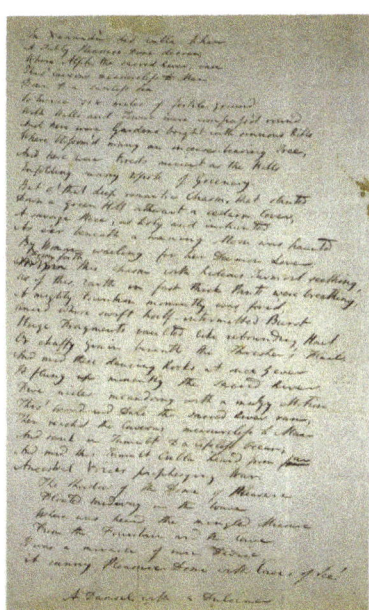

Figure 4. Draft of S. T. Coleridge's poem *Kubla Khan*.

I also believe that it would show very bad manners to begin any observations about what might pass for a Christian understanding of the imagination and its purposes without first touching base with the luminous parsings of the matter by Samuel Taylor Coleridge. And so, I have shared above the opening lines of what is perhaps Coleridge's most famous poem, "Kubla Khan." I expect to share the conclusion of that poem before my own conclusion here, and I hope to unpack along the way my reading of Coleridge's sometimes densely packed musings on the imagination.

Those musings are most readily encountered in his *Biographia Literaria*, a onetime staple of undergraduate literary education—if lately eclipsed by an array of latter-day reinventions of the wheel—but his obsessive framings and reframings of those musings are to be witnessed in virtually every line that he composed during his lifetime. This is because the imagination—its operation and its purpose—may be fairly appreciated as the central concern of his entire life's work. Famously, in one brief but—as I warned you—dense passage of the *Biographia*'s thirteenth chapter, Mr. Coleridge writes:

> The IMAGINATION then I consider either as primary or secondary. The primary IMAGINATION I hold to be the living Power and prime Agent of all human perception, and as a repetition in the finite mind of the eternal act of creation in the infinite I AM. The secondary I consider as an echo of the former, co-existing with the conscious will, yet still as identical with the primary in the *kind* of its agency, and differing only in *degree*, and in the *mode* of its operation. It dissolves, diffuses, dissipates, in order to re-create; or where this is rendered impossible, yet still at all events it struggles to idealize and to unify.[2]

Of course, Mr. Coleridge also speaks of *fancy* as the intellect's profoundly conscious manipulation of previously apprehended, aggregate matter—the rearrangement, say, of the building blocks we have collected and hold in our hands—but it is his initial parsing of primary and secondary imagination that I find most useful for what I'm about here.

For starters, let us agree that, in the Coleridgean scheme, the *primary imagination* is our common birthright. This "living Power and prime Agent of," as he attests, "*all human perception*" (italics mine) is an agency belonging to everyone who lifts eyes to witness the confusion of our surrounding appearances, and subconsciously makes sense of it, wrangling the chaos of appearances into something of an orderly construction, apprehensible; this is what Coleridge figures as a "repetition in the finite mind of the eternal act of creation in the infinite I AM." The primary imagination, then—as the

---

2. Coleridge, *Biographia Literaria*, 1:304.

finite mind's repetition of the creative act in the infinite I AM—is therefore to be appreciated as something of a communion. Moreover, we understand that we do as we are made to do, shaping our experience at every moment. Created in the image of the Creator, we inevitably create. This has become something of a cliché, but it is nonetheless a worthy characterization of who we are: co-creators with the infinite I AM.

Let us note, as well, that in this passage Coleridge holds that the act of creation—and the deep communion it involves—is eternal, which I take to mean ongoing, forever, without conclusion. Let us also stipulate that, in the Coleridgean scheme cited above, the artist is capable of echoing that subconscious agency with conscious activity. This is what Coleridge identifies as the *secondary imagination*, which "dissolves, diffuses, dissipates, in order to re-create." It is this secondary power of perception, creation, and re-creation—this essential artistic agency—that I hope to interrogate.

As a poet, I am most interested in our attending to what it is that the words we use have to do with this profound, re-creative echoing, and how those words, duly appreciated as matter, are sculpted into a pleasing, edifying, and meaningful form. In "The Author's Preface" to his 1825 production, *Aids to Reflection*, Coleridge cites clergyman Horne Tooke, quibbling both with Tooke and, as it happens, with Homer himself to make a special point about the agency of words, as such. Coleridge writes:

> Tooke entitled his celebrated work Ἔπεα πτερόεντα, Winged Words: or Language, not only the *Vehicle* of Thought but the *Wheels*. With my convictions and views, for ἔπεα I should substitute λόγοι, i.e., Words *select* and *determinate*, and for πτερόεντα ζώοντες, i.e., *living* Words. The *Wheels* of the Intellect I admit them to be; but such [wheels] as Ezekiel beheld in "the visions of God" as he sate among the Captives by the river of Chebar. "Whithersoever the Spirit was to go, the wheels went, and thither was their Spirit to go; *for the Spirit of the living creature was in the wheels also.*"[3]

When Coleridge writes, "*for the Spirit of the living creature was in the wheels also*," I see that he is indicating his conviction that *the Spirit's creative agency exists within the words themselves*. This is the very heart of my matter, both now and for the past three or so decades. Thereafter, Coleridge avers that words "are *living powers*, by which the things of most importance to humanity are actuated, combined, and humanized."[4] At the heart of any such dynamic view of language lies a disposition towards words that is as ancient

3. Coleridge, *Aids to Reflection*, 7.
4. Coleridge, *Aids to Reflection*, xix.

as the first chapter of Genesis, wherein The God is alleged to have spoken the cosmos into being.

Without doubt, Coleridge was among the most well-read persons of his generation; he may well have been the most well-read person of *any* generation. I think we might find some advantage in speculating how—aside from his own experience as a poet—he may have been led to this particularly dynamic view of language. He was—from the age of ten years and throughout his life—an uncommonly accomplished student of Hebrew, Latin, and Greek.[5] He pored over these languages, and he pored over their attendant cultures. His own English word choices bear witness to the degree to which he understood our English language to be haunted by an expansive cloud of etymological ghosts. He was profoundly aware of the generative capacities of such haunted terms, and this, as I see it, turns out to be an essentially Hebraic disposition. I have spoken and have written about this matter in the past—this Hebraic insight of language *mattering*—but I remain devoted to sharing the good news as often as I am provided a soap box to stand upon.[6]

In her book *The Slayers of Moses*, Susan Handelman quotes Hans Georg Gadamer as having articulated a very telling difference between certain Greek and Hebrew words for *word*, a distinction that reveals competing notions of what a word *is* and what it *does*.

> We must begin then, as usual, with the Greeks. And [quoting Gadamer,] "Greek philosophy more or less begins . . . with the insight that a word is only a name, i.e., that it does not represent true being." Indeed the Greek term for word, *onoma* [ὄνομα], is synonymous with name. By contrast, its Hebrew counterpart— *davar* [דָּבָר]—means not only word but also thing.[7]

Of course, Greek language offers, besides *onoma*, an array of terms that one might enlist in this discussion: *lexis* [λέξης], *epos* [ἔπος], *mythos* [μύθος], and the more familiar (to Christian Bible readers, at least) *logos* [λόγος]. Handelman's observation, however, applies without quibble to all but one of these cases; *lexis*, *epos*, and *mythos* all participate in this dichotomy of essence and substance; each is understood, in its activity, as a particular flavor of naming, that is, as an expression of prior matter. The final case, *logos*— understood to be the embodiment of an idea—actually provides an instructive complication of Handelman's contention, for it illustrates that, were it not for Christendom's onetime acutely Neoplatonic turn, general Christian attitudes towards words, even today, might have been far more suggestively

5. Holmes, *Coleridge*, 26–43.
6. Cairns, "Shaping What's Given."
7. Handelman, *Slayers of Moses*, 3–4.

Hebraic, and far less reductive, and our sense of a given word's activity would less likely be limited merely to naming, to denotative finger-pointing.

When the evangelist, theologian, and poet Saint John uttered *Logos* as his word for Word in the first chapter of his Gospel, he was making what I suspect to be a very Jewish point with a very Greek gesture. Until that moment, *logos* was generally consigned to the transcendent realm of Platonic Ideas, the realm of Real Things, of which the apparent world was supposed to be but a shadow. When Saint John wrested Logos from the ether and placed it in the muck among us, he was articulating a collision of realms, a collision whose concurrently disruptive and generative powers a good many Christians have all but forgotten, even if certain of the fathers and mothers of the church have tried, without much success, to keep us on track. When Tertullian utters his famous, "What has Athens to do with Jerusalem?," he attends to this matter precisely: the reductive effects of our applying systems, philosophical categories, and dichotomies upon the uncategorical mystery of the incarnation, and the trivializing effect that such a poor marriage has upon the reciprocal mystery of human divination, or, as we say at church, our *theosis* [θέοσις], our becoming what we are called to become, which is holy.

Whichever Greek word for Word we choose, its usage is similarly problematic; because the Neoplatonic notion of the *written word* assumes it to be a name merely; it is, in practice, perceived as a sorry substitute for the *spoken word*, which is itself a sorry substitute for the *thought*, which is a very sorry substitute for the very distant *Idea*—that objective reality to which we have no real access, save through this tortured ontology of diminishing returns, or by some act of transcendence, which skirts the matter at hand (and often discounts all matter in general) in favor of a purely intellectual apprehension of the allegedly real. This sadly gnostic model, of itself, poses no great hardship until one begins to suspect how it undermines the status, the intrinsic value, of whatever immediate body or body of text it's applied to. The human body, for instance, might be understood to be—as Plotinus understood it to be—naught but an unfortunate prison house for the human spirit; the earth itself becomes little more than the vehicle of some cosmic allegory. Back in the realm of text, the difficult poem in the hand becomes little more than an encrypted message whose code must be cracked if we are ever to get at the thing, the prior and preferred event it is able only to point toward, the thing it merely names, gestures in the direction of—and once that code is cracked, once the poem delivers its directions to the ballpark, the poem itself can be discarded, for its message has been received and put to proper use.

On the other hand, the Hebraic notion of the written word—*davar*—presumes the word itself to be a thing, and even to be a power, a thing with generative agency.[8] This perspective enables the consequent, Hebraic understanding of a text as *a made thing capable of further making*. This will serve, at least for now, as my definition of any art worth pursuing. The difference between such Neoplatonic and Hebraic dispositions is perhaps helpfully demonstrated by comparing conventional, admittedly Hellenized Christian habits of exegesis (whose tonal inflections are often strident, insistent, definitive, and whose purpose is something like certainty) with traditional rabbinic habits of narrative commentary (whose tonal inflections are more often playful, speculative, provisional, and whose purpose is to "open the text" in order to glimpse through that, opening further and unanticipated meaning). For instance, a great many rabbinic *midrashim* begin their observations with something very like "and another interpretation might be."

For the commonplace Christian exegete (and—since there may be some of these attending to these observations—please note that I'm not saying *every* Christian exegete), the Scripture is examined for the singular reality to which it allegedly points back; the text is pored over and explicated, often in great detail, but its words are most often perceived as the static names for prior things, and the resulting exposition (being made of words, and worse, of subsequent words, belated words) will always remain distinctly referential to Scripture, distinctly belated, and valuable, if at all, only to the degree to which it avails the decoding of the prior, the scriptural text, which is itself understood as something of a gloss of the transcendent Real, which lies some distance behind even that scriptural language.

So, let us hurry back to the more generous other hand: the rabbinic writer (as well as—I should add—the Semitic writer of early Eastern Christendom[9]) approaches the Torah as if its every word, its every letter, were a live and powerful thing, possessing live and powerful agency. As a possessor of live and powerful agency, each word, each letter of Torah is capable of provoking endless response, endless new production, which, by its nature, also partakes in the holy, the inexhaustible. And which, by its nature, also carries the germ of reproductive power, and therefore also bears live and powerful agency.

Imagine a column of Torah, a column of sacred text. Imagine a surrounding layer of exploratory commentary, inscribed in response to the provocations of that Scripture's suggestive phrases, words, letters. Over time, this outer layer itself provokes additional, subsequent, exploratory

---

8. Neusner, *Introduction to Rabbinic Literature*, 6.
9. A likely example of such would be the *madrashe* of Saint Ephraim the Syrian.

layering. Now, imagine this activity continuing until the generated power of Torah emanates outward, continuously infusing every layer of response with its own, original—one might say "germinating"—power to produce further text.

My own immediate interests, admittedly, have most to do with how poems work, with how poets employ their imaginations to read and to write. Still, I suspect that a more general truth lies waiting here. I suspect that the rabbinic model might reveal something of the collaborative way in which all art comes about, perhaps even something of the collaborative way in which an actual future is shaped. For the belated poet—the belated artist of any art, really—the Neoplatonic model can be as crippling as it is meager. It cripples the new writer by setting up chronological priority as chief virtue, and (as Harold Bloom has observed) by setting up whatever power one perceives in prior text—whatever power one receives from prior text—as a cause for anxiety and self-consciousness.[10] It locates literary power in the past, and it relegates the poet of the present to a point many removes from that original power. It is meager, for it locates significance also in the past, offstage (as it were), making of the new poem on the page a mere reference to the precursive moment and its original issue in event.

The Hebraic model, however, locates living, generative agency in the words themselves—"in the wheels also," as Mr. Coleridge has insisted—and therefore, in the present as well as in the past; it empowers the live poet with the self-same agency that his or her precursors enjoyed; and it provokes the giddy prospect that in even the newest work lies the seed of further—subsequent, but nonetheless dynamic—production. Just as with this habit of observing words as *things*, words as *powers* may call to mind the traditionally rabbinical disposition towards words—the Kabbalist's disposition towards even single letters. It may also bring to mind a range of latter-day attempts to trouble the Neoplatonic ontology that would understand words as mere *tokens* of what matters, mere shadows of a preferred reality—that privileged elsewhere, which the words can only point toward, but do not partake of.

George Santayana's understanding that our sense of words as *expression* must be attended by a concurrent sense of words as *evocation* strikes me as one attempt to trouble the Neoplatonic model. Santayana reminds us that, when we speak of poetry, in particular, "expression," in and of itself, is a misleading term, suggesting as it may, that a prior something, already experienced, already known, is subsequently, directly, and discretely expressed by the text. In his "The Elements and Functions of Poetry," Santayana writes, "[I]f we drop the limitation to verbal expression, and think of poetry as that subtle fire and

---

10. Bloom, *Anxiety of Influence*, 12–16.

inward light which seems at times to shine through the world and to touch the images in our minds with ineffable beauty, then poetry is a momentary harmony in the soul amid stagnation or conflict—a glimpse of the divine."[11]

How might one prepare for such a glimpse? How might one respond to such a glimpse? I have found that my having cultivated a taste for the vertiginous has proven to be of some assistance in these matters, and I have found that both poetry and apophatic theology continue to provide our most promising discourses for illumination.

The heart of the matter seems to me to be the heart itself, or, perhaps more nearly, the mind descending to the heart, or much more nearly what the fathers and mothers of the early church would have called the *nous* [νοῦς], the intellective aptitude of the heart. This is the faculty—intuitive, imaginative, visionary—that I have sought to develop over the course of some forty-plus years as a would-be poet. This is what I presume Coleridge to have been after, and also Santayana, as well as Saint Gregory of Nyssa, Saint Isaac the Syrian, Saint Maximus the Confessor, Julian of Norwich, George MacDonald, and Wheaton College's own, Saint Clive—the beloved C. S. Lewis. All of these employed their noetic imaginations in what can best be understood to be a dialogic relationship—by way of reception and response—with all that came before them, of all that lay before them, of all that came to mind *in the midst of* and *after* poring over all that delicious confusion of appearances. For most of my teaching career—now approaching forty years in duration—I have sought to share with my students the notion that both literary study and literary production depend upon just such a dialogic relationship. In fact, I have sought to share with them my perception that—for the poet—these are not separate endeavors at all.

For much of my writing life—most of my poems—I have commenced my writing day with reading. That is to say that when I am at my desk preparing to begin a writing session, I lift a book and I read. Admittedly, while I do attempt to keep up with new works by friends and admired writers who are living and continuing to produce, I must admit that, for purposes of my ongoing conversation, most often I stick to the beloved departed—those poets and other authors whose works rest in a stack on my desk. Other books come and go, but these remain ever at hand, and my conversation with them continues.

That stack holds the works of Saint Isaac of Syria, Saint Maximus the Confessor, Saint Gregory of Nyssa, Samuel Taylor Coleridge (of course), Emily Dickinson, Rainer Maria Rilke, W. H. Auden, Robert Frost, Wallace

---

11. Santayana, *Essential Santayana*, 280.

Stevens, Constantine Cavafy, and Elizabeth Bishop. On a given morning, I settle into the chair at my desk with a yellow legal pad, a sharp number two pencil, and a book pulled from the stack. I take and read. I am looking for what I had not seen before—though I have turned those very pages countless times—and I am inevitably rewarded with a new glimpse, a new provocation. When that happens, I mark my page, take up my pencil, and respond. Should I run out of gas, I simply turn back to the book, poring over its words until yet another provocation sparks response. This will happen, for, as you know by now, "the Spirit of the living creature [bides] in the wheels also." I am not alone in this disposition. In fact, I acquired this dialogic disposition by way of the very practice I describe—poring over "living words" and being awakened into new creation by the Spirit whose agency continues to operate within those living words.

I have already shared with you the opening lines of Coleridge's "Kubla Khan," and, as I've suggested, I will in short order share with you that poem's final lines in hopes that those lines will further illustrate my sense of things. Just now, however, I would like to share some key lines from Wallace Stevens's similarly illustrative poem, "The Idea of Order at Key West." The poem opens, famously enough, with a strophe that will, I trust, assist my argument:

> She sang beyond the genius of the sea.
> The water never formed to mind or voice,
> Like a body wholly body, fluttering
> Its empty sleeves; and yet its mimic motion
> Made constant cry, caused constantly a cry,
> That was not ours although we understood,
> Inhuman, of the veritable ocean.[12]

While there is much here to unpack, I would first draw your attention to the dialogical dynamic offered by the curious phrase that inhabits the midpoint of the strophe: "and yet its mimic motion / Made constant cry, caused constantly a cry."

I trust that when we come upon "mimic motion," we are reminded of Coleridge's characterization of the primary imagination as a "repetition in the finite mind of the eternal act of creation in the infinite I AM," and also of his characterization of the secondary imagination "as an echo" of that primary repetition. Still, the subsequent assertion regarding that mimic motion's agency is what most attracts me: it "made constant cry" and also "caused constantly a cry." This is where the essential dialogical relationship is first introduced in the poem.

12. Stevens, *Wallace Stevens*, 128.

Made constant cry. *Caused* constantly a cry.

Attend with me to the dynamics of the aural exchange that the poem images.

> The sea was not a mask. No more was she.
> The song and water were not medleyed sound
> Even if what she sang was what she heard,
> Since what she sang was uttered word by word.
> It may be that in all her phrases stirred
> The grinding water and the gasping wind;
> But it was she and not the sea we heard.
>
> For she was the maker of the song she sang.
> The ever-hooded, tragic-gestured sea
> Was merely a place by which she walked to sing.
> Whose spirit is this? we said, because we knew
> It was the spirit that we sought and knew
> That we should ask this often as she sang.
>
> If it was only the dark voice of the sea
> That rose, or even colored by many waves;
> If it was only the outer voice of sky
> And cloud, of the sunken coral water-walled,
> However clear, it would have been deep air,
> The heaving speech of air, a summer sound
> Repeated in a summer without end
> And sound alone. But it was more than that,
> More even than her voice, and ours, among
> The meaningless plungings of water and the wind,
> Theatrical distances, bronze shadows heaped
> On high horizons, mountainous atmospheres
> Of sky and sea.[13]

As you can hear, the dynamics of dialogue—of call and response—are implicated throughout the lines that follow the opening strophe, but I would draw your attention to the poem's penultimate move:

> It was her voice that made
> The sky acutest at its vanishing.
> She measured to the hour its solitude.
> She was the single artificer of the world
> In which she sang. And when she sang, the sea,
> Whatever self it had, became the self

---

13. Stevens, *Wallace Stevens*, 128–29 (emphasis mine).

> That was her song, for she was the maker. Then we,
> As we beheld her striding there alone,
> Knew that there never was a world for her
> Except the one she sang and, singing, made.[14]

One of the great pleasures of verse poetry lies in the way that (what I would call) *the stichic sense*—the sense offered by a discrete line—complicates the sense offered by overall syntax, which may span many lines. Intelligent lining can supplement, complicate, multiply, or even contradict what might otherwise be received as the singular utterance of the sentence, *per se*. For instance, while the sentence above—taken as a simple sentence—observes that "[i]t was her voice that made the sky acutest at its vanishing," the line break allows our privileging and emphasizing—if only for a moment—the profound assertion that "It was her voice that *made*." In a similar subversion of what would prove otherwise to be a relatively meager syntactical sense, when we come upon the sentence that concludes "for she was the maker," the lining—the stichic sense—allows us to diminish the effects of the end punctuation in order to witness a species of ideational enjambment that yields "for she was the maker. *Then we*." For the brief duration of that line break, we are able to see that we, too, are in this moment "the maker"—albeit one inspired by our reception of what the "she" has sung within our hearing.

Keeping in mind this dialogical dynamic—which is, in my estimation the imaginative engine that powers all art reception and art production—let's return to Mr. Coleridge and his haunting poem, "Kubla Khan." In the poem's final move, a muse figure not unlike that of Stevens's "She [who] sang beyond the genius of the sea," appears to similarly endow the speaker of the poem with the power to receive the vision, to respond in kind, and thereby to endow others with power to see, and thereafter to say—perhaps to say more.

> A damsel with a dulcimer
> In a vision once I saw:
> It was an Abyssinian maid,
> And on her dulcimer she played,
> Singing of Mouth Abora.
> Could I revive within me
> Her symphony and song,
> To such deep delight 'twould win me,
> That with music loud and long
> I would build that dome in air,
> That sunny dome! those caves of ice!

---

14. Stevens, *Wallace Stevens*, 129–30.

> And all who heard should see them there,
> And all should cry, Beware! Beware!
> His flashing eyes, his floating hair!
> Weave a circle round him thrice,
> And close your eyes with holy dread,
> For he on honey-dew hath fed,
> And drunk the milk of Paradise.[15]

And we? Should we lift the manna from the dew and partake, should we lift the cup and drink, we too will be obliged to build, to shape, to make.

The imagination—specifically, the duly prepared noetic imagination—becomes the organ of our most intimate engagement, our communion, with all that we behold, all that we but glimpse, and all that we are thereby led to suppose; the noetic imagination becomes the means by which we enter into conversation—generative conversation—with the Creator and his creation. It becomes the agency of our collaboration with our Creator as we shape the very future—which, I insist, has yet to be written.

---

15. Coleridge, *Poems and Prose*, 12–13.

PART II

Wonder and Creation

Second canto | Karen An-hwei Lee

The illumination of beloved statutes, Psalm 119:129–30

Your laws are wonderful.
No wonder I obey them!
The teaching of your word

gives light,
so even the simple
can understand.

Let us spread your love and light
to the far ends of the earth, the lamp
of your word yielding warmth,

reconciling all nations to you,
restoring our broken and wounded hearts
through the Holy Spirit—

may your beloved laws and statutes
glorify your wonderful nature,
your justice tempered with mercy.

"Four Cantos on Wonder." Performed by the New Arts Trio to music composed by Misook Kim for the Wheaton Theology Conference (April 2021). Italicized verses: New Living Translation of the Bible (2015) by Tyndale House.

5

Making as an Act of Longing and Lament

Tish Harrison Warren

One of my favorite memoirs is Mary Karr's *Lit*, which recalls the breakup of her marriage, her struggle with alcoholism, and her conversion to Roman Catholicism. She tells NPR though that "embracing the meditative and spiritual aspects of Catholicism didn't make the writing process any easier." In her interview, she says writing *Lit* was "horrible":

> I threw this book away twice . . . I walked around in my bathrobe for three days and made obscene gestures at the rafters. And there are a couple people I call at such times, sort of the way the president would push the red button. I'd call these people. So I called [the novelist] Don DeLillo, and DeLillo sends me a postcard that says "write or die." . . . I think I sent him one back that said "write *and* die."[1]

DeLillo and Karr are both right. The task of "making" is always situated in the "already-not yet" of reality—and by "making" here I specifically mean artmaking, but I take a generous view of that. I mean everything from writing a book or poem or a song to making a loaf of sourdough or knitting a scarf for a friend.

---

1. Gross, "Mary Karr, Remembering the Years She Spent 'Lit.'"

Eschatological Longing

Don DeLillo's card, "write or die," is perhaps more true than he realizes. The act of labor and artmaking—as terrible as it feels at times—is an attempt to grasp the ineffable and transcendent. It is an ordinary way that we reach toward beauty and glory, a way of reaching toward the eschaton, the place (or time or dimension) of beauty and glory. Every note on a guitar or delicious turn of phrase or quilt quilted is part of Jesus' work in making all things new. Even though the completion of Jesus' work lies in the future, it is already established through his life, death, and resurrection. Jesus' resurrection was our first glimpse of the new heavens and new earth, where death and the power of death, dies. As N. T. Wright has written, the resurrection of Jesus means "not the *redefinition* or *redescription* of death . . . but the *reversal* or *undoing* or *defeat* of death."[2] As Christians, our acts of making are an embodied proclamation that the curses of Genesis 3 are not the final word. They point to our telos when makers will "long enjoy the work of our hands."[3] Art making calls forth the future, rendering the eschaton present in the here and now.

We see this at times through an overt representation of the future in art itself. Jeremy Begbie discusses how Indonesian artist Nyoman Darsane paints his hometown of Bali. "He paints the fertility of that lush place he knows so well," but, he says, "not even Bali looks that good." Darsane paints his home but with such gorgeousness that he is intentionally pointing to what Begbie calls his capital-H home. It's Darsane's attempt at glimpsing the glory of the new heavens and new earth through the stuff of earth—both his paint and brush but also his place, his hometown, and his imagination.[4] But even when we aren't specifically representing the restoration, there are moments when the experience of art calls forth the overwhelming goodness of being in such a potent way that it overwhelms us.

Annie Dillard's *Pilgrim at Tinker Creek* tells stories in which people who were born blind receive immediate sight through medical intervention. Dillard describes the inherent struggle and awe that comes from a sudden new vision of the world. One young girl was so overwhelmed by her first sight of an ordinary tree, leaves glinting in the breeze, that she spoke about "the tree with the lights in it." For Dillard this was an epiphany, or even better, an icon showing the interior nature of things, the pulsing glory hidden in the heart of reality:

2. Wright, *Resurrection of the Son of God*, 201.
3. As Isaiah says in 65:22; see also Micah 4:1–4.
4. Begbie, "Sense of an Ending," 230.

It was for this tree I searched through the peach orchards of summer, in the forests of fall and down winter and spring for years. Then one day I was walking along Tinker Creek thinking of nothing at all and saw the tree with the lights in it. I saw the backyard cedar where the mourning doves roost charged and transfigured, each cell buzzing with flame. I stood on the grass with the lights in it, grass that was wholly fire, utterly focused and utterly dreamed. It was less like seeing than like being for the first time seen, knocked breathless by a powerful glance. The flood of fire abated, but I'm still spending the power.[5]

We also have this experience as artists. Through the act of making—in blessed moments—we feel that we are touching on a goodness, truth, and beauty that is beyond us and our own ability to produce. Through making, we touch a kind of hyperreality where it feels the wind is at our back. We are participating in heaven. This is sometimes called the "flow," when art pours out of you. But we do not only experience transcendence in the ecstatic moments of our work, but because of the nature of art itself. Artmaking or any encounter with beauty points us to that which is *beyond and greater* than ourselves. Madeline L'Engle writes, "When the artist is truly the servant of the work, the work is better than the artist; Shakespeare knew how to listen to his work, and so he often wrote better than he could write; Bach composed more deeply, more truly than he knew; Rembrandt's brush put more of the human spirit on canvas than Rembrandt could comprehend."[6] Through our work of making, it feels we are touching on "the more" of reality.

Making art is therefore a practice in watching for the kingdom coming. "At the moment we see something beautiful," wrote literature scholar Elaine Scarry, "we undergo a radical decentering."[7] According to Simone Weil, beauty requires us to "give up our imaginary position as the center."[8] This is true of ourselves as individuals, but this encounter with beauty also decenters our moment in time as well. Beauty—and works of art—are a sort of timelessness in time. This is because as we as individuals are decentered by beauty, the world as it currently stands is also decentered. We see that this world is not all that there is. Things are not simply as they are. Beauty introduces the idea that things can be more and better than they are—that perhaps there is something true and real about our longing for a world that is whole and good.

5. Dillard, *Pilgrim at Tinker Creek*, 30–31.
6. L'Engle, *Walking on Water*, 14.
7. Scarry, *On Beauty and Being Just*, 111.
8. Weil, *Waiting for God*, 159.

In his great discussion of the relationship between beauty and justice, Nicholas Wolterstorff points out how beauty (and specifically the goodness inherent in the physical world) is part of Jesus' showing forth the kingdom of God: "Shalom incorporates our right relationship to—and more than that, our delight in—the physical. As a sign of God's kingdom of Shalom, Jesus did not just forgive sins and relieve religious anxiety; he healed bodily infirmities. Such healing was consonant with the prophetic vision of shalom, which included banquets with rich, red wine. And surely the wine of which the prophets spoke was no more some sort of nonmaterial, spiritual wine than the bodies that Jesus healed were nonmaterial, spiritual bodies." The craft of good wine (like all well-done craft) is a way to literally taste and see shalom. It is part of the announcement that the kingdom of God is at hand.[9]

I write in my recent book, *Prayer in the Night*, about a year of sorrow, a year when my father died, I lost two sons to miscarriage, and I moved across the country from Austin to Pittsburgh. About six months into this hard year, I found it really difficult to pray. I write that during this time, "I began to intensely crave beauty and wonder. The old saying is true: hunger is the best condiment. As I endured the mystery of loss, any picture of beauty, moral or physical, was like manna."[10] I would go to Phipps Conservatory in Pittsburgh as often as I could, sometimes multiple times in a week. Phipps is an Edenic oasis of warmth and color. It is a botanical garden in an enormous glass greenhouse. The instant you walk in the earthy sweetness of herbs and flowers greets you like incense rising to heaven. The lush green is at first too much to take in. I pause and take a deep breath. My body relaxes and my eyes adjust to the depth of color. I begin to notice various shades of green, lighter and darker. I notice colors, flowers, trees, cacti, koi, waterfalls. I needed this in that hard year. It kept me alive as much as food and water did. Not only because beauty is by nature a comfort to the grieving. But also because it tutored me about the hope of glory. The year had shown me again and again that things are not as they should be. But Phipps reminded me through my body—through the physical world—that things may not always be so, that although darkness is all around us, as Hopkins's "God's Grandeur" reminds us, "there lives the dearest freshness deep down things; / And though the last lights off the black West went, / Oh, morning, at the brown brink eastward, springs."[11]

In other words, this beauty decentered my own moment of suffering by situating it within an eternal kingdom. The beauty of a cultivated garden

---

9. Wolterstorff, *Until Justice and Peace Embrace*, 130.
10. Warren, *Prayer in the Night*, 62.
11. Hopkins, *Selected Poems of Gerard Manley Hopkins*, 20.

testified to the truth of what is coming. It was the cock's crow proclaiming that darkness will end. In this way, our work—and the wonder that births it and sustains it—are a foretaste of the solid promise of the coming kingdom. Our creative acts are therefore made from a posture of expectancy and longing.

In the Tolkien classic *Leaf by Niggle* (required reading for anyone interested in artmaking), we meet Niggle, an artist, whose passion is to paint a particular scene, which begins in his mind as a leaf and continues to grow—stretching across more and more canvas—into a whole landscape. It is some great country that Niggle sees in his head and more beautiful than anything he's actually seen or could paint. Reflecting on this story, Alonzo McDonald claims that Tolkien suggests through it that, "on occasion, God may give man the gift of envisioning a sudden glimpse of the underlying reality or truth."[12] Niggle is pulled along by the vision. This painting captures the longing of his soul.

In my own work as a writer, I identify with this longing. I feel like Niggle often. When I'm drawn to a new project, it feels like seeing a distant but beautiful glow—the details of which I can't always make out. But there is a deep draw, attraction, and ache for something more beautiful, more glorious than I know that I can do. It feels like a dare. Can I reach toward that distant glory that I cannot quite grasp?

A Taste of the Fall

If the posture of artmaking is longing, it is also one of longing unfulfilled. If, through beauty, we are decentered from ourselves and if we are called forward into the future (timeless) eschaton, then we are also called back to the reality of the fall. In our act of making, we experience the power of death. Mary Karr wrote back to her friend—with her dark and wonderful sense of humor—"write and die." And she's right. Artmaking as glorious as it can be does not rescue us from death and sin. Despite our making, or artistic success or failure, we still experience the power of death in our lives. We still die. Moreover, we experience the power of death in and through artmaking itself.

Although I begin a new project with this alluring vision of distant beauty that dares me on, inevitably, there is also frustration and confusion that comes with this blessed dare. In my mind, I hear and see more beauty that I can't get on paper. There's always a remainder in my imagination, something I cannot nail down. My work regularly takes me into the

---

12. McDonald, "Introduction," 8.

expansive power of words but I unavoidably run into the end of their ability to capture reality. Or, at least, my own ability to wield them. I wonder if this is the reality that led Aquinas, after a lifetime of writing, to give up the habit, shockingly leaving his last book unfinished with only the enigmatic words, "I can write no more. All that I have written seems like straw."[13]

Artmaking is a way we reach toward the eschaton. Yet, compared to the glory of what is to be, it feels like straw. We experience making then—to some extent, constantly—as a place of futility and incompletion. We experience hope and longing in our work but also depression, frustration, sorrow.

In his advice to young artists, Ira Glass gestures toward the frustration inevitable in making: "Most people I know who do interesting, creative work went through years of this. We know that our work doesn't have the special thing that we want it to have. We all go through this."[14] He says this can be overcome through time and work, but Aquinas's experience and Mary Karr's obscene gestures at the rafters lead me to wonder. Of course, we can grow as artists. We practice and improve. Yet, part of the vulnerability of the artistic task—always, this side of heaven—is the willingness to enter into an endeavor that will be beyond our grasp. In other words, part of our own vulnerability as makers is that we *willingly take up tasks where we bump up against our own limitations*. Therefore, grief is part of the experience of making. It is a normal and inevitable byproduct of making. This may be part of why so many artists end up depressive and addicted, but it is also part of how the act of making can be sanctifying.

Embracing the inevitable grief inherent in the practice of "making" is a way of taking up our cross and entering into the suffering and vulnerability of Jesus. And that sounds very lofty and spiritual, but the reality of it feels terrible. This is why we have that oft-repeated adage, "Writing is easy. All you have to do is open a vein and bleed" or that "writers hate writing, but we like having written." A. G. Sertillanges notes the pain of his intellectual work, saying, "All workers bewail the moments of depression that break in on the hours of ardor and threaten to bring their results to nothing . . . What danger there is of giving up when you are in this distressing state of mind!"[15]

Not only do we taste our own limitations and the fallenness of labor through the act of making, but art itself is ephemeral. The kingdom flashes forth in artmaking but disappears just as quickly. Art touches on the timeless but art itself—most art anyway—will not be timeless. Books go out of print. Paintings gather dust in basements. Songs eventually fall silent. I think

---

13. Tugwell, "Introduction," 266.
14. *This American Life*, "Ira Glass on Storytelling."
15. Sertillanges, *Intellectual Life*, 218.

of the dramatic image in Kurt Vonnegut's *Bluebeard*, when the celebrated abstract expressionist painter Rabo Karabekian—famous for his works *The Temptation of Saint Anthony* and *Windsor Blue Number Seventeen*—suffers catastrophe when these great works are corrupted because the highly touted paint that he uses, Sateen Dura-Luxe, disintegrates, leaving an empty canvas and destroying his reputation. For Karabekian, the bogus "postwar miracle" of Sateen Dura-Luxe is emblematic.[16] This is a gesture toward how all of our endeavors—however successful—are vanity, vanity.

Our only hope then in the sorrow of making is the redemption that God himself brings. In *Signs amid the Rubble*, Lesslie Newbigin writes:

> Our faith as Christians is that just as God raised up Jesus from the dead, so will He raise up us from the dead. And that just as all that Jesus had done in the days of His flesh seemed on Easter Saturday to be buried in final failure and oblivion, yet was by God's power raised to new life and power again, so *all the faithful labor of God's servants which time seems to bury in the dust of failure, will be raised up, will be found to be there, transfigured, in the new Kingdom*. Every faithful act of service, every honest labor to make the world a better place, which seemed to have been forever lost and forgotten in the rubble of history, will be seen on that day to have contributed to the perfect fellowship of God's Kingdom. As Christ, who committed Himself to God and was faithful even when all ended in utter failure and rejection, was by God raised up so that all that He had done was found to be not lost, but alive and powerful, so *all who have committed their work in faithfulness to God will be by Him raised up to share in the new age, and will find that their labor was not lost*, but that it has found its place in the completed Kingdom.[17]

I cannot say what this will precisely look like metaphysically, but Newbigin's suggestion that good work is made eternal in Christ offers us hope. It hints at the fulfillment of Isaiah's promise that God's people "will not labor in vain" (Isa 65:23).

We glimpse this reality in *Leaf by Niggle* as well. Niggle experiences constant frustration in his work. He is interrupted. He is distracted. He finds his picture "wholly unsatisfactory, and yet very lovely."[18] Ultimately, he doesn't finish his work before he dies. Yet (after a brief time in a kind of purgatorial hospital/workhouse), Niggle arrives in a new country and sees

---

16. Vonnegut, *Bluebeard*, 21.
17. Newbigin, *Signs amidst the Rubble*, 47 (emphasis mine).
18. Tolkien, *Leaf by Niggle*, 19.

it. *His tree. His mountains. His landscape.* The one on which he worked so haphazardly and imperfectly: "Niggle looked up, and fell off his bicycle. Before him stood the Tree, his Tree, finished. If you could say that of a Tree that was alive, its leaves opening, its branches growing and bending in the wind that Niggle had so often felt or guessed, and had so often failed to catch. He gazed at his tree, and slowly lifted his arms and opened them wide. 'It's a gift' he said." The story goes on, "All of the leaves he had ever laboured at were there, as he had imagined them rather than as he had made them, and there were others that had only budded in his mind, and many that might have budded if only he had had time."[19] Niggle's own work was ephemeral. In fact, it is only because Niggle releases its ultimacy and willingly leaves his work unfinished to go help a fairly annoying neighbor in need that he then receives the fruit of his work back in the resurrection. Niggle's work is incomplete and fairly shabby. But God makes it real and permanent.

There's a great mystery here. What does this mean? How will our work and labor and art be made alive and whole in the resurrection? I have no idea how this happens. But it is our hope: our labor is not in vain, not because of our own success or ability but because God takes even our labor and raises it up on the last, eternal day. It's a gift.

But now, as artists, we live in the meantime. We constantly experience both longing hope and painful lament in our making. Through the objects, stories, or songs we make, we proclaim: "How Long, O Lord?" Through embracing and inhabiting these postures of longing and lament, we inscribe these emotional realities into our work—into our art—allowing it to become a reflection of eternity.

Our work and our lives themselves must hold together both the realities of darkness and light, fall and glory, or we will fall into either a despair and cynicism that denies the eternal truth of beauty or a kind of saccharine sentimentality that denies the reality of sin and death. Begbie discusses the need for what he calls "Easter" art—but also notes that art not only participates in the resurrection but also passes through Good Friday. He writes, "The dissociation of sentimentality and beauty is only possible inasmuch as we interpret both through the narrative of the church's *triduum*: Good Friday, Holy Saturday, and Easter Day." Sentimentality is an attempt to prematurely grasp Easter morning. We rush too quickly to the news of victory over evil, without honoring the truth of darkness and death. A Christian "counter-sentimentality" depends on witnesses to the cross—the sorrow

---

19. Tolkien, *Leaf by Niggle*, 29–30.

and sin of the world—as well as the resurrection. If we belittle one, we inevitably belittle the other.[20]

Embodied Practices of Longing and Lament

So how do we learn to be Christian makers who faithfully embody both Good Friday and Easter Sunday? Artmaking is an experience in time. Yet artmaking simultaneously calls us out of present time into the future restoration and into the past catastrophe of the fall. In a similar way, Christian practices bring us into a timelessness (even as we continue to live in time). The posture of holding the dark reality of the fall on one hand and the hope of restoration on the other is not only the posture of artmaking, but also the posture of the whole Christian life. I want to look at specific Christian practices that teach us as artists how to inhabit these postures of longing and lament.

First, through the regular practice of silence and contemplation, we learn to yearn for and watch for the eternal—the transcendent—in our world and therefore in our art. Silence, like beauty, decenters us. It calls us out of performance and productivity to recall God's presence and power. It also reminds us that what we have to say (through writing or painting or baking or singing) is not the most important thing to be said. Richard Hooker called silence "our safest eloquence" because it reminds us that God's "greatness [is] above our capacity to reach."[21] God is the longing of our souls and of our making. In this way, silence calls us out of our timebound moment into the eternal presence of God. A noisy and busy life numbs us both to hope of the eschaton and to the sorrow of the fall, preoccupying us instead with a kind of distracted low-grade anxiety. This is not the abundant life—abundant with both grief and joy that we see in Jesus—but the anesthetized frenzy of contemporary life. Thomas Merton said that if a sermon isn't born of silence, it's "a waste of time."[22] The same can be said of everything we make and create.[23] This is particularly a challenge for me with the siren song of social media (which is a demand of my writing life) and also with the reality of raising small children. But a life lived lamenting the fall and longing for the eschaton is inevitably a contemplative life. This kind of life has to be cultivated like the cultivation of the artistic craft itself.

20. Begbie, "Beauty, Sentimentality, and the Arts," 61.
21. Hooker, *Richard Hooker*, 201 (I.ii.3).
22. Merton, *Entering the Silence*, 649.
23. Merton, *Sign of Jonas*, 266.

Second, as artists we embrace the dual Christian practices of lament and celebration. Through the pouring out of our own disappointments artistically and otherwise—to God and our community—we learn to lament. Lament is the most common form of psalm in the Psalter. Through meditation on the Psalms, we learn to lament—learn how to embrace the brutal honesty we find there. Through the Psalms we wrestle with the horrifying gap between the promises of God—joy, peace, deliverance—and the experiences of pain and feeling of Godforsakenness in our lives and work.

Along with lament, we embrace celebration. This too is alive and well in the Psalter. We intentionally celebrate every little milestone in our own work as makers. We celebrate the ways God uses these things we make, even in their imperfection. I have spent time around people who work with those experiencing homelessness and addiction. One thing that strikes me about these friends is that they are very honest about the brokenness of the world. They don't settle for pat answers or calls to look on the bright side. They pull no punches. These are people who regularly see death and darkness up close. But at the same time, they embrace celebration. They see every day of sobriety, every person who is helped, every cause for joy as a moment to stop and notice. In the same way, as makers, through our work and lives, we intentionally take up practices not only of lament but also of celebration. In our lament and in our celebration—perhaps particularly in the reading of the Psalms—we join the millennia-long chorus of the church in lament and celebration. Our own calls of "How long, O Lord?" and "Hallelujah" are part of a long conversation between God and his people.

Practices of lament and celebration are a kind of emotional discipleship, which inevitably shapes us as artists. We learn to resist sentimentality or triteness as well as despair and cynicism. When we learn to notice and to honestly name the joy and sorrow in life and work, our work itself becomes more truthful.

Lastly, the chief spiritual practices that hold together both lament and celebration are the sacraments themselves. Baptism and the Eucharist contend against sentimentality and despair. They hold death and life together, admitting both unflinchingly, in a proclamation of the already and the not yet. The Eucharist is a meal of sorrow and joy. On one hand, it is a meal of sacrifice. A meal of death. A body broken. Blood flowing. It recalls Jesus' last meal on earth. When we take this meal, we participate in his final night on earth, when he wept in the garden, when he sweat blood alone as his friends fell asleep. By taking this meal, we proclaim that things are not as they are meant to be. Yet, this meal is also a taste of a wedding feast, a palpable declaration that God's love overcomes every power of death. It is a meal where we remember that we are going home and receive the presence of Christ even now. In the same way, baptism is a witness to and reminder of death—the death of Christ and ours in him. We are buried with Christ in baptism. It's a funeral. Yet, we are witnessing resurrection. We are raised with him to new life. The central practices of the church—our sacraments—can only be understood as practices that hold together the tension of relentless human vulnerability and the enduring love of God. They tell us, again and again, generation after generation, through our very bodies, that all of human joy and sorrow are caught up into the love of God and, there, made new.

The sacraments proclaim the fall, the eschaton, and indeed the entire story of redemptive history. They take place in time but are practices that draw us into *kairos*, the fullness of time. We taste in them the future resurrection of the saints, the wedding feast of the lamb, but also the crucifixion of Jesus. Through the practice of the sacraments, we learn to approach the rest of life—including the work we do—sacramentally. We learn to see this stuff of earth as pregnant with God's presence. Yet, in this stuff of earth we glimpse both death and life. These practices send us back into the world differently. We enter our work as people who do not deny the darkness in the world, who admit it and lament it. But we also have glimpsed—however imperfectly and distantly—the hope of all things being made new. Even us. Even our work of making.

6

The Artistry of Place

Andrew Peterson

I forget exactly when it happened, but at some point in the last decade I came to the realization that I had visited all fifty of these United States. I got out a map and tested myself to be certain. I'd put my finger on California and conjure up a specific memory from there: *I played in Hollywood at the Hard Rock Café, opening for Caedmon's Call; I drove north through the Klamath Mountains, alone.* I'd slide it over to Minnesota: *I walked the streets of Ely in the winter and discovered that though the Canadian border was only a few miles across the boundary waters, it would take five hours to drive there.* On it went, until I was sure it was true. Thanks to twenty-five years as a performing songwriter, it's safe to say I've set foot in more of this country than most. (I'll admit I don't have a clear memory of North Dakota, but I'm certain I was there in 1992. Trust me.) To be sure, that doesn't make me an expert on much of anything besides how to change guitar strings or which items on a Taco Bell menu are best to eat at 3 AM. My experience was often limited to a day or two at a time, usually in the context of a concert at an evangelical Protestant church (though you might be surprised just how varied that context is, depending on the denomination, the size of the church or city, and the decade I was there). But I did learn a thing or two.

Over the years, thanks to literally thousands of shows, I developed a routine. If we were playing in a town or city I'd never heard of, I'd look it up on Wikipedia and read about its demographics, its local history, and its notable residents, if any. If there was time, while the band was setting up I'd sneak out for a solitary walk (hoping to find a used bookstore, but happy to wander for a few hours either way). Most often, however—especially in the eastern half of the country—there would be no place to walk because there *was* no town. No city. No countryside. Just suburbs. Mile after mile of neighborhoods and sidewalks that led to nowhere in particular. The same box stores, the same fast food. To be fair, wherever we toured the people I interacted with were great and the churches were almost always hospitable and generous. But now and then we'd find ourselves in a wonderful place—a *Place*—that was unique and vibrant and full of stories, but of course the exception proved the rule. Soon the thrill of travel (though not performing) faded and I began to recognize a ubiquity, a *placelessness* in almost every corner of the country. After spending significant time in other countries, I always returned home with a head full of questions about America. How did we get here? What am I, as a songwriter and novelist, supposed to do about it? Is there any way to escape the morass of this suburban blandness in my own neighborhood? Are there theological implications to the way we build roads, sidewalks, neighborhoods? Do infrastructure and zoning affect the way we behave toward one another? When we pray that God's kingdom would come on earth as it is in heaven, does that mean the church has a responsibility to shape our villages, towns, and cities to reflect that coming kingdom, where every people, tongue, nation, and tribe care for the earth and each other as priests and stewards of creation? In short, what can we do, right now, to tell a better story?

Wilderness vs. Culture

When I was a kid I watched Bob Ross on a regular basis. His show, *The Joy of Painting*, was on the local PBS channel every weekday after school, so we'd bounce from Bob to *Speed Racer* to whatever weird televangelist was in vogue at the time and then back to Bob Ross to see what progress he'd made on his painting of happy little trees where the happy little squirrels lived. We loved the way he giggled when he cleaned his brushes on the leg of the easel. Bob was most definitely uncool, with his big hair and his hippie shirts and his whispery way of talking, but I think every child of the eighties and nineties secretly admired him. When a commercial interrupted whatever hijinks Tom and Jerry were up to and we switched back to Bob as he lovingly scratched burnt umber tree branches into existence on an underpainting of phthalo blue, all of us Peterson kids were in silent agreement that he was the man.

There was, however, one thing I didn't like about Bob Ross's clichéd landscapes. At some point about halfway through each painting, he would step back and inspect the snowy mountain lake overhung with firs, think for a moment, then lean in with his knife and add the roofline of a happy little cabin.

"Not the cabin, Bob!" I would groan inwardly. "Why can't it just be mountains, without sullying things up with human settlement? Aren't landscapes enough?" As a kid I had big ideas, passionately held, about the untainted West. Nothing sounded more romantic to me than riding a horse through Montana with nary a cabin in sight, a notion informed by films like *Dances with Wolves* and *Lonesome Dove*. Wherever humans came in contact with nature, I believed, chaos ensued. Since I had spent my youth in Illinois and Florida, two of the flattest places in North America (you may be surprised to learn that Florida is *the* flattest state in the union), nothing stirred my longing for adventure like the thought of mountains.

When many of us go to a state park, that's what we're after, right? Pristine nature. Wilderness. An absence of billboard blight. Vistas without power lines. And when we go on a hike in that state park, we bring a backpack full of granola bars, a bottle of water, and zero expectation of encountering any meaningful civilization. We're heading into the wilderness, so we have to stock up. Goodbye exile, hello Eden!

I get the appeal of what I've just described. Though I've never been one for weeklong backcountry hikes thanks to an inherited set of unreliable knees, I do love a good tromp through the forest. If there are waterfalls, all the better. Maybe, like me, you've done it: you drive an hour to the trailhead, lock the car, apply the bug spray, take a deep breath, then plunge into the forest for the next few hours, eventually backtracking to your car and the weary drive home to your computer and the righteous feeling of having taken in some nature. Verily, trees are good medicine—so is silence, and wonder, and an intentional pilgrimage to the vastness of the wilderness. I think we'd all agree that people would be better off with a bit more hiking and a lot less screen time. But over the years I've come to see the wisdom of Bob Ross, and what his predilection for happy little cabins has come to represent.

People weren't meant for wilderness. We were meant for a garden. As much as I hate litter, we weren't meant to "leave no trace." Indeed, Andy Crouch argues that human beings, made in God's image, are here specifically to make something of the world.[1] I'm drawn to the romantic ideal of untouched creation, but, taken too far, it misses the fact that God gave

---

1. Crouch, *Culture Making*, 23.

us creation specifically to *be* touched, to be cultivated, to be dwelt in and shaped, to be encountered and loved and honored by his image-bearing children. It goes without saying that we've made quite a mess of things, which is why state parks are so precious and so necessary. I hope they last forever. But if you think about it, a visit to a gorgeous place like Yellowstone is only possible because of human culture: highways, roadside dives, filling stations, nature centers, and the tireless work of people clearing all those footpaths and building the boardwalks and bridges that keep us from being boiled alive in the hot springs. In order to even lay eyes on that wilderness, we have to make something of it. Someone has to set its boundaries. Someone has to name it. Someone has to financially support it to keep it working so we can see those herds of elk grazing in the preserve. In fact, the very idea of "wilderness" as we know it is a fairly modern invention.

Before the nineteenth century, the word *wilderness* had a pejorative ring to it. It wasn't where people went on holiday, but rather where Israelites wandered, where Jesus was tempted, where Adam and Eve were exiled. Eden was a garden and exile was wilderness. Wilderness was a place of disconnection. But something changed. The writings of Henry David Thoreau and John Muir (as well as the romantic poets) are evidence of reversal in the way people thought about nature, extolling the virtues of the wilderness as a place where it was possible to escape the mundane and experience wonder, meaning, and even the presence of God. Thoreau wrote that "in Wildness is the preservation of the world." Muir described the wilderness as a picture of heaven itself.[2] People had begun to think of cities as places of disconnection and even corruption,[3] and wilderness was the antidote. Wilderness was now sacred, which suggested that cities, towns, and human culture were by nature spoiled. If the goal is unspoiled nature, though, the answer is to avoid spoiling it. And the way to do that is to responsibly engage with creation, to integrate it into our lives, to make a way for the next generation to fall in love with it. If they love it, maybe they'll care enough to steward it well.

I hate to be the bearer of bad news, but the United States, on the whole, hasn't stewarded it well. And I don't just mean that from an environmental standpoint, though that's certainly true. I mean towns. Cities. Infrastructure. The *places* where human beings live out their humanness. We tend to live in places that are sequestered from nature, so that most of us work in cities or suburbs with flimsy, half-baked versions of nature and culture ("no-places," according to journalist James Howard Kunstler[4]) all week long, then

2. Cronon, "Trouble with Wilderness."
3. Miller, "Faith in the Suburbs," 125.
4. Kunstler, *Geography of Nowhere*, 136.

we plan occasional trips to the state parks to try to stir up some wonder and balance things out. Central Park is lovely, but it's a good picture of what I'm talking about.

If you've ever been to Manhattan, you know it: Central Park is miraculous, with its rolling hills, huge granite boulders, old trees, and ponds. Meandering walkways wind serenely beneath the gaze of all those skyscrapers, and it's possible, ironically, to feel the peace of the deep woods even when surrounded by one of the busiest cities in the world. It could be argued that Olmsted, who designed the park, rescued New York City from itself. I honestly don't know how New Yorkers would survive the sheer mass of urbanity without Central Park's peaceful green presence right there in the heart of it all. It's marvelous. I've heard New Yorkers say that just knowing it exists keeps them from going crazy, whether they visit or not.

And yet, it's sequestered, bordered by stone barriers and lovely iron gates. Seen from above, it's a rectangular strip of green, beautifully incongruous among all those tall, gray structures, separated from the city only by herds of yellow taxis. One second, you're in the chaos of the Big Apple, and, as Marjorie Kinnan Rawlings wrote about Florida, by stepping through the gate you leave one world and enter the mysterious heart of another.[5] Trees welcome you like monks in a monastery and bid you to lay down your heavy burden. Walkers, joggers, bikers, and pigeon-feeders abound.

I'm so glad Central Park exists. As I said, I'm glad parks exist, period. They're symbols of our need for silence, our need to be in the presence of growing things, and our need for rest and play. On the other hand, I wonder if they've added to the American idea that human life happens on one side of the street, while nature's life happens on the other, and never the twain shall meet. Isn't it odd that in order to experience the glory of nature we Americans have to get in a metal car with an internal combustion engine and drive somewhere just to walk in a big loop for a few hours and then come home to our screens? Some might argue that the suburbs provide an answer to this, what with our subdivisions on the edge of town, complete with lawns and sidewalks and impractically small front porches. Isn't that a decent integration of culture and nature? Sadly, suburban America is merely another "no-place" that neither honors where we live, nor the humans who live there.

We have three kinds of places in the United States: the city, the country, and large swaths of that murky in-between called "the suburbs." In the 1600s the Puritans brought with them ideas of what towns should be: a house and barn, along with kitchen gardens and plenty of fruit trees. Their

---

5. Rawlings, *Cross Creek*, 8.

farmland lay just outside the village. The center of civic life was the church building, which was used for town meetings, various social gatherings, and occasionally for the storage of crops. Most of the towns were near a water source, and everyone pretty much stayed put. Nature and culture were intertwined. There were natural limits that everyone agreed to, more or less. But by the end of the 1600s, disgruntled by the meddling restrictions of distant England, colonists began to spread out. After all, it's at least one of the things that brought them to America in the first place: individualism.[6]

If you've ever been frustrated by, say, sidewalks that lead to nowhere in particular; the unsightly tangle of power lines overhead; the ubiquitous sprawl of McDonald's restaurants, shopping malls, and gas stations; by the decrepit state of many of our town squares; or by the general blandness of so many houses built in the seventies, take heart—you're not crazy. Things could have been so much better, but greed, racism, the automobile, and the sense that America is so big that we've got land to burn and no real reason to slow down and invest in places—*real* places, as opposed to no-places—shaped life as we know it.

One of the major factors was our country's idea, after the displacement of Native Americans, that "land was first and foremost a commodity for capital gain."[7] Land wasn't first and foremost God's precious gift for us to steward, a garden to tend, a foundation of our communities tied directly to our flourishing as human beings—but rather was a way to get rich. Kunstler writes, "The commercial transfer of property would become the basis of American land-use planning, which is to say hardly any planning at all. Somebody would buy a large tract of land and subdivide it into smaller parcels at a profit—a process that continues in our time . . . Nearly eradicated in the rush to profit was the concept of stewardship of land as a public trust: that we who are alive now are responsible for taking proper care of the landscape so that future generations can dwell in it in safety and happiness."[8]

This rush to profit, kicked into high gear by the invention of the automobile, led to the hasty planning of towns and cities, often with little thought given to either architectural aesthetics or the simple, practical, lovely things (like cafés, trees, farmer's markets, shopping districts, and functional walkways) people need in order to flourish in community as God meant for us to. Eventually, for a whole host of reasons, the United States became a land of urban sprawl and subdivisions. By doing so, we cut ourselves off, not just from the vast natural beauty of this continent, but also from the vaster

---

6. Kunstler, *Geography of Nowhere*, 22.
7. Kunstler, *Geography of Nowhere*, 26.
8. Kunstler, *Geography of Nowhere*, 26.

beauty of community. We got our lawns, our two-car garages, our flat-screen televisions, and our quiet neighborhoods thirty minutes from town; all we had to do was give up any hope of permanently settling down in a place we could learn to love for the rest of our lives, our connection to the earth God made for us, and our life-giving reliance on each other.[9]

There is, of course, a theological component to all of this. Eric O. Jacobsen, a pastor in Tacoma, Washington, got his PhD in Theology and the Built Environment (it makes me so happy that one can get a doctorate in that) dug into these issues in a book called *Sidewalks in the Kingdom*. He writes, "In the Christian imagination, where you live gets equal billing with what you believe. Geography and theology are biblical bedfellows. Everything that the creator God does, and therefore everything that we do, since we are his creatures and can hardly do anything in any other way, is in place."[10] *Place matters.* Where we live, and how we live there, affects us spiritually and shapes our understanding of what it means to be children of God.

Individualism vs. Interdependence

Our country is nothing if not individualistic. I have a healthy dose of it myself. Before I built my little writing cottage, the Chapter House, I had to go to downtown Nashville and sit in the waiting room of the metro planning offices for hours at a time to get the proper approval. The individualist in me was grumpy. It's *my* property. Why can't I build whatever I want there? When I was getting final approval from the inspectors there was a laundry list of goofy little things I had to fix, like ridge vents on the roof and the exact height of the front steps (I was an inch off). It rankled me to the core. A beautiful building might cost more (which is bad for my bottom line), but it also ennobles its environment and blesses every eye that sees it for many

---

9. Willie James Jennings argues for the historical and theological connection between European Christian colonization and our disassociation from the land. In "Overcoming Racial Faith," he says, "[European Christians] renamed the land, reorganized common life, and reformed the ecologies of native peoples. At the heart of this transformation was a world-altering reconfiguration of the relationship between land and identity.... These European settlers viewed people as separate from land and viewed land for its development potential as private property. Europeans taught the peoples of the new world that they carry their identities completely on their body, detached from any specific land or animals or agriculture or place. Lands and landscape were captured and transformed into inert segments of space that may be turned toward any use its owners desired—that is, private property.... [The land and its animals] became our tools and resources, and we became geographically adrift in the world, seeing places and spaces as undeveloped dirt or sites in transition to becoming something else" (7–8).

10. Jacobsen, *Sidewalks in the Kingdom*, 9.

years to come (which is good for the community). What's good for business right now might not be good for your children's children when there's a parking lot where there might have been a grove of towering white oaks.

But Jacobsen suggests a biblical alternative to individualism: interdependence.[11] We need each other, and we need to be needed. I was grouchy about the codes I had to adhere to with the Chapter House until I imagined my neighbor building something wacky right next to our property line. While designing the look of the building I was also acutely conscious of what my neighbors would think, what they'd have to look at every time they passed my property. I wanted them to be glad the Chapter House is here; I wanted it to make their lives better (not to mention the lives of future generations), and the building codes were there to help me do that. Restrictions, as any songwriter or poet will tell you, can be good. They drive creativity. But certain other restrictions, specifically the zoning sort, have gutted communities of some of the best things community has to offer.

Here's what I mean.

There's a subdivision near us called Mill Run. By a stroke of good luck, the planners decided to line the streets with silver maples instead of those trees from the pit of Gehenna known as Bradford pears. (Bradford pears, by the way, are an abomination. I'm not using that word flippantly. They were engineered in the 1960s and because they cross-pollinate with every other kind of pear tree, their prolific offspring is destroying forests faster than kudzu. I think of them as a tree version of the velociraptors in *Jurassic Park*. They're preferred by developers because they're cheap, they grow fast, and they produce malodorous but pretty white flowers in the spring, which happens to be when most home sales happen. But after the developers leave, the trees require regular pruning, a gust of wind can split them in half, and they're producing an inhospitable forest of non-native offspring that's riddled with thorns. Left unchecked, they'll soon overtake all the lovely oaks, maples, sycamores, and ashes that are native to our part of the world. Take my word for it: they're awful. If you have one in your yard, for goodness sake, *cut it down* and spend $25 on a maple at Lowe's.[12]) Mill Run is a nice place, complete with a greenway that follows the bends of Mill Creek and houses that rise on the shoulder of a gentle hill. Coming around the bend on the feeder road you can see Mill Creek glistening in the valley, and above the creek, the subdivision houses are clustered in what looks like a quaint village, especially at dusk when the house lights are aglow. Truly, it's a beautiful sight. But there's something missing.

---

11. Jacobsen, *Sidewalks in the Kingdom*, 25.
12. Hurley, "Detested Bradford Pear is Coming to a Forest Near You."

After my first few visits to Europe and the United Kingdom, where towns are older than the United States by a thousand years, I came home to culture shock. There, I had grown used to cities that came of age long before cars were invented, villages that were built when most people walked everywhere. The towns across the pond have narrow streets and shops with display windows, and if there's a river or a creek nearby, then you can actually *see* it, because the houses were built right up to the banks, for practical as well as aesthetic reasons. The houses were often built of stone, brick, or huge timbers—or if they were of more modern wooden construction, they were built to last more than a generation or two. In every village, town, and city, there's an old church, any number of cafés or coffeehouses, and a shopping district. The ones in England all have at least one village pub. In other words, there's commerce, a reason to go outside once in a while, a situation in which it's possible for you to bump into your neighbors.

Humans want more than merely to live in a house. We want to be a part of the life of a community. American subdivisions, zoned as strictly residential, allow nothing but houses. That means that unless you drive somewhere, there's no place to eat. No place to gather with your friends in a cozy nook next to a fireplace. No place of worship to beautify the landscape or provide a place for worship. No integration with the nearby creek so that you'd actually know it's there if you didn't go looking for it. And here's the thing: most American subdivisions are about the size—in population and area—of those little villages so many of us pine for. If I could change one thing about American subdivisions, I'd require them all to have a café, a little grocer selling local produce and baked goods, a coffeehouse, and (because I love hobbits) a village pub. If I couldn't get all of the above, I'd settle for the pub. Or a used bookstore. Or both. Who wouldn't want to go for an evening stroll and have a slice of pie at the local baker's, where you might bump into a neighbor or two whom you haven't seen for a few days? Everybody in town would want to live in that neighborhood.

In the sixties, an unassuming New Yorker named Jane Jacobs stood up to city mogul Robert Moses's attempt to tear down Greenwich Village in the name of progress.[13] Years ago I played a show in the Village at the Bitter End, a little hole-in-the-wall club with a deep musical history. The wall near the stage boasts names like Bob Dylan, Jackson Browne, Billy Crystal, and James Taylor, and let me tell you I felt way out of my league—but I also felt the vibrant history of the place, and I loved it. It was a *place*. A few years after that, my album *The Far Country* was mixed in Greenwich Village, which meant my producer Ben and I had several wonderful days to wander the

---

13. Consider the account of land use in Flint, *Wrestling with Moses*.

city while we waited to approve mixes, and I'm here to tell you that the world would be a poorer place without the Village and its quirky energy. It's hard to imagine what New York would have been like if Robert Moses had gotten his way. Greenwich Village is an artsy neighborhood, crammed with cafés, coffeehouses, old trees, and—because it's in New York City—pedestrians everywhere. Part of the thrill of Manhattan is the array of people from every nation, tongue, and tribe, and there are few better places in the world to people-watch.

Get this. The first hundred pages of Jacobs's book *The Death and Life of Great American Cities* is dedicated purely to sidewalks.[14] That's right: *sidewalks*, an aspect of community life that we seldom think about, but which she argues is crucial to what makes for a good city. Sidewalks give us a healthy balance between privacy and human contact. This is a shocker to folks living in a subdivision, but the presence of strangers is a good thing, augmenting the very life of the place. In a city, we expect to see strangers in the neighborhood, thanks to the commerce, and yet we aren't at all surprised to see familiar faces. That shared life gives us a way to know people without the burden of any expectation that we'll be best friends. There's a beauty in the fact that we're rubbing elbows with people who are very, very different from ourselves, in every way imaginable. Meanwhile in the suburbs, we've zoned out the commerce, and at the same time, because most of the houses cost the same, we've gotten rid of any real diversity of income. This, of course, has racial and ethnic implications as well. When the suburbs boomed onto the scene near the turn of the twentieth century, they were a way to escape "otherness," which meant neighborhoods were largely segregated. Even after the 1968 Housing Act made that sort of discrimination illegal, according to sociologist Brian J. Miller, "suburbs resorted to other options to keep out 'less desirable residents,' including a lack of enforcement of housing laws, exclusionary zoning practices, limiting certain kinds of development, and not welcoming new religious groups."[15] With all commerce zoned out, there's no reason for strangers. When strangers become cause for concern, anyone who seems like they don't belong gets reported on the local Nextdoor message board. We learn to live in suspicion, and sometimes outright fear. The irony is, people feel safer in crowds. If you're walking on a busy street, then you turn down one with no one in sight, wouldn't you feel uneasy? Crime actually goes up where the sidewalks are empty.[16]

---

14. Jacobs, *Death and Life of Great American Cities*, 29.
15. Miller, "Faith in the Suburbs," 124.
16. Jacobs, *Death and Life of Great American Cities*, 31.

There's another, subtler factor at work, which I experienced back when we lived in a Nashville subdivision. Subdivisions come with an unreasonable expectation of what Jacobs calls, with an almost audible groan, "togetherness," a feeling that we're all supposed to be friends, intimately involved in each other's lives.[17] It's unreasonable because that's just not the way humans work and live together in public. We don't have the time or emotional bandwidth to keep it up, so we end up pulling away into our bonus rooms and Facebook accounts, never really knowing anyone because it's either all or nothing. In the public sphere, however, diverse human contact should be balanced with privacy, which is what a community with a healthy sidewalk life provides.

Creation and Culture

One day we got enough rain that Mill Creek looked high enough to kayak. On a whim, I drove to the nearest Walmart and bought a plastic kayak for $100, then got my wife to drop me off upstream. As I floated serenely down the creek, I realized that in all the years I'd lived here, I'd never considered the hidden world that lay just out of sight. The little boy version of myself was wide awake. Great herons laboriously took wing as I approached. Startled turtles dived from where they were sunning on fallen trees. Kingfishers swooped from branch to branch. Little falls of spring water fell musically from the steep banks. I saw towering sycamores, cottonwoods, pin oaks, sugar maples, black locusts, and green ashes. Families of ducks winged downstream until I reached them, then quacked and flew off again to wait for me. To my dismay, I also saw plenty of discarded tires and rusty washing machines. Occasionally, through the brush I heard people on the greenway not twenty feet away and was frustrated all over again that whoever planned the footpath cut them off from all this beauty. How hard would it have been? And if the people in the neighborhood knew how wondrous this ancient waterway was, would it be treated as a garbage bin for tires and old appliances? I doubt it.

Granted, I'm thankful to have a greenway near the house and I love to bike and jog on it, but after experiencing older cultures where walking along a pleasing creek is integrated into everyday life as a way of getting from *here* to *there*, I'm exasperated every single time I'm out there because it's so sequestered. Here is the place where we jog. And over there is the place where we go to work. And over there, in the other part of town, is the place where we shop. In short, our whole way of life hinges on cars. Imagine how many more people would know the trees, the creek, and their neighbors if the

---

17. Jacobs, *Death and Life of Great American Cities*, 62.

places we lived were built more with humans in mind than cars. Jacobsen, speaking theologically, writes, "It's time that we call into question the assumption that the needs of the automobile should be met above all else. We need to build cities and neighborhoods that allow us to get out of our cars and get to know one another by paying attention to the age-old conception of public space."[18] Yes, yes, yes.

Now that I've gone off on all the problems, let me say that I do see some signs of change on the horizon. Not far from the end of the greenway, about a mile through yet another neighborhood, there's a place called Lennox Village. The community was designed with storefronts below and apartments above, integrated in just the way I'm describing. At the other end of the greenway, about four miles away, there's a walking bridge that crosses Mill Creek and connects our neighborhood to a park with six beautiful soccer fields. On any given Saturday you'll see a wide diversity of people of out there having the time of their lives. It is most definitely a cultural good. It's called Orchard Bend Park because at one end of the fields there's a stand of apple, pear, and peach trees a farmer must have planted many moons ago, and in a blessed moment of clarity, whoever was in charge of the park thought to keep them. The city went to the trouble of planting all manner of native trees along the path, and though they're only saplings now, in twenty years the tree-lined walkway will be a gorgeous thing to see. Thank you, Nashville. Still, I won't be truly satisfied until there's a place to buy ice cream for the grandkids.

My favorite city in the South (excluding Nashville, of course) is Greenville, South Carolina. Right there in the heart of downtown the Reedy River courses noisily between boulders before cascading into one of the most beautiful city parks you can imagine. A suspension bridge made just for walkers spans the falls, and below you see paved footpaths meandering their way down to grassy lawns bordered by all manner of flowers. At the foot of the falls the trail follows the river into the dark embrace of a vale of tall trees, where the ruins of a century-old mill hunker on the banks. If that were all, it wouldn't be so different from many parks that show off waterfalls: a beautiful destination, but with nothing much to do but look around and maybe have a picnic. But as I said, the river courses right through the center of downtown, and the planners integrated all that natural beauty with the city itself—proving that if it's wonder you want, you don't have to drive to it.

I've joked with my family for years that the true measure of a city's greatness is the number of park benches it can boast. In that sense, Greenville is a truly great city. Everywhere you walk, someone was thoughtful enough to provide a bench, situated just so, allowing you to take a load off,

---

18. Jacobsen, *Sidewalks in the Kingdom*, 80.

people-watch, write a poem, or contemplate how glad you are that there's a coffeehouse a five-minute stroll away. And there aren't just coffeehouses, either. Clustered around the river you'll find cafés, bookstores, hotels, and, yes, ice cream shops. Even the office buildings in the older part of downtown are beautiful, overlooking streets lined with stately trees, all strung with lights that make the evening walk back to the parking lot delightful. A few years ago I was there in the early spring and wrote this sonnet:

> To sit by a river and think is good.
> If that river is singing over stones,
> Even better. If it's in a green wood
> In the springtime, as the sun warms your bones,
> Then you have to give thanks. You have no choice
> But to praise the Lord of Earth and Heaven,
> And lean against a stone wall and give voice
> To gladness by writing a poem. Even
> Better than that is when glade and river
> Vein through the heart of a good city. Then,
> things could hardly be better. The Giver
> of the world is pleased when in a garden glen
> His children know the holy place where rest
> And beauty meet. Then God and man are blessed.

To be clear, I'm not talking about gentrification. Every neighborhood should have organic ways for neighbors of varying incomes, races, ethnicities, and religions to interact, which could lead to friendship, empathy, goodwill, and solidarity. Not only that, but every neighborhood should also be a *place*, distinct from other places, built to integrate with its natural features. If there's an old orchard, *save* it. If there's a creek, keep it visible and clean, and allow the structures to frame it like a painting, to complement what God has already made. (Whatever you do, don't plant Bradford pears—which God *didn't* make, strictly speaking.) Creation doesn't have to be devoid of human contact to be beautiful, as Bob Ross demonstrated with his clichéd little cabins. Whenever I'm in the United Kingdom, I'm less moved by the natural landscape than by its integration with the cultural one. Britain has had—and continues to have—its share of ecological missteps, but centuries of human interaction somehow managed to adorn the countryside with narrow roads, stone walls, castle ruins, functional farmsteads, and thousand-year-old pubs set gracefully within a verdant landscape. What we make of the world can serve to make the painting more pleasing, not less.

I realize there are valid objections. In some ways, the life I'm describing is more likely to happen in the new creation than in the twenty-first century. I'm still just as flawed as everyone else, and the decisions I make every day have unintended consequences on my community as well as the ground under my feet. No matter how walkable and pleasing a city is, a mighty brokenness plagues us all. Jacobsen admits as much:

> The church cannot, and never could, rely on external forms of either ecclesial or civic institutions to guarantee the success of its mission. We need to be constantly reminded by the private Christians that our fundamental task continues to be evangelism of individuals through direct relationships. Despite my deep affection for urban charm, I have to concede that I would rather have tract homes and strip malls where the gospel is being openly shared and received than even the most engaging urban setting where it is not.[19]

All this dreaming can certainly morph into a naïve nostalgia for the elder days, when things were simpler and everybody had a horse and lived off their own land. But the truth is, our forebears' lives were brutal—just look at the photographs of haggard farmers in the late nineteenth century, or for that matter, the photographs of the people they enslaved. No doubt they would have been grateful beyond measure for a Sunday drive to the shopping mall. I'm not looking back, but forward. By integrating our many technological goods, cultural institutions, and even business ventures with a godly stewardship of creation and community, we could be that much closer to a vision of what God intended for humankind. Indeed, we're inviting the new creation into this present darkness. We're practicing resurrection, painting pictures of the kingdom as it will be in its fullness, un-desecrating what was already sacred.

N. T. Wright, in his magnificent book *Surprised by Hope*, wrote that

> the church that takes sacred space seriously not as a retreat from the world but as a bridgehead into it will go straight from worshipping in the sanctuary to debating in the council chamber—discussing matters of town planning, of harmonizing and humanizing beauty in architecture, in green spaces, in road traffic schemes, and . . . in environmental work, creative and healthy farming methods, and proper use of resources. If it is true, as I have argued, that the whole world is now God's holy land, we must not rest as long as that land is spoiled and defaced. This is not an extra to the church's mission. It is central.[20]

---

19. Jacobsen, *Sidewalks in the Kingdom*, 159.
20. Wright, *Surprised by Hope*, 265.

We won't see that divine integration complete until, as the old hymn says, "Jesus who died is satisfied, and earth and heav'n are one." Yet even now, as I write these words, I'm reminded that this is my Father's world—*this* one that we've tarnished with injustice, broken communities, and its grayscape of asphalt. I long to see the Father's kingdom come on earth as it is in heaven, a kingdom that isn't just a spiritual reality, but a physical one—as physical as Jesus' resurrected body. And the church's business is heralding that kingdom by putting our talents to work. That means loving our neighbors, our cities, our places; it means stewarding our time, widening our imaginations, and tending to nature and culture responsibly, in his name, for his glory, until the master of the house returns. In doing so, we make room for wonder—not just the wonder of wild places, but the wonder of cultivated ones.

I have hiked into the Grand Canyon. I have stood on peaks in Colorado. I've explored caves deep underground and flown on airplanes high above the earth. I've even been to North Dakota, though I can't exactly remember it. I have known the wonder of wild places and give thanks for them. After all, the earth is the Lord's and the fullness thereof. But it's the small wonders that I delight in the most, the places where creation and culture lock arms: the slow changes of seasons outside my window; the laughter of friends gathered around a hearth fire; kayaking the creek that flows through the neighborhood; waving hello to neighbors at the farmer's market; a walk to the local bakery; the wide diversity of the people cheering at the soccer fields down the street; the pleasure I see on peoples' faces when they taste the honey gathered by my bees. As much as I love state parks for their grandeur, I wouldn't want to live in one, far from the life of a community. And as much as I love life in a community it's difficult to live in one where creation isn't flourishing alongside us and among us in peace. God is glorified by creation rightly stewarded and humanity rightly loved. I long for the day when every subdivision becomes a village, when every suburb becomes a community, when every house becomes a home, when every sidewalk leads somewhere, when every no-place is given a story again, when every soul on every street is welcomed and wanted, when the farm and the symphony hall and the high, green mountain are all seen as God's gifts to his people. I don't know how to get there, but a garden is a good place to start. A restaurant by the creek wouldn't hurt, either. May we widen our imaginations and live toward that coming city, even here, even now.

Yes, Lord, establish the work of our hands.

7

Placed Wonder through the Arts

JENNIFER ALLEN CRAFT

"All really inhabited space," the philosopher Gaston Bachelard writes, "bears the essence of the notion of home."[1] Bachelard's central assumption is that to be human is to long for home. A desire for home, he suggests, acts as a compass for the rest of our actions in places. In other words, our sense of place and our actions within it build on an innate longing for home, which reflects the phenomenological shape and telos of human life. This, of course, is not just a modern philosophical question, but also one that bookends the Christian narrative of creation and redemption. In their book *Beyond Homelessness*, Steven Bouma-Prediger and Brian Walsh identify humans as creatures called to be "homemaking gardeners," made in the

---

1. Bachelard, *Poetics of Space*, 5. There is divergence in the way writers use the terms *space* and *place* within broader literature. French phenomenologists, of which Bachelard is indicative (see also LeFebvre, *Production of Space*), tend to use the term *space*, though in this excerpt from Bachelard the meaning is much the same as what other authors indicate by the term *place*. In general, however, *space* tends to be characterized by the universal, abstract, and open experiences of freedom, while *place* indicates the particular, localized, and that which carries embodied meaning and experience. Here, I will use the term *place* throughout to indicate this more lived experience in physical locales which carry both individual and communal meaning, story, and identity. Many authors suggest that places are made from spaces in an ontological sense, but that place precedes space in a phenomenological sense (for examples, see Edward Casey who prioritizes our relationship to "place" in lived experience).

image of a "homemaking and garden-planting God."[2] This vocation defines our embodied existence in the world today, along with the eschatological nature of our being in the world as creatures oriented toward a final home. We long for a home that is "not yet" while being called, in participation with the Holy Spirit, to begin the homemaking work of new creation in our current places.

While our teleological and phenomenological orientation ought to be oriented toward emplacement, our current state of being—life in a global pandemic—might better be described as a profound state of homelessness, an existential and often physical detachment from our places and communities. We find ourselves seeking out a renewed sense of wonder in place, asking what it means to live well in our places and to meet God and one another within them.

For most, even when viewed through the most ideal lens, place is a complex matrix of feelings, practices, and experiences that conveys a longing yet to be fulfilled. Indeed, rarely is our sense of place and making of home within our places uncomplicated. For many, their current sense of home is anxious and unsettled. Rather than provoking rest and belonging, home can symbolize violence and terror.[3] The problem of sin further separates us from our places: our disordered state of being results in repeated patterns of exile. No wonder we feel a sense of disenchantment with the world. Nevertheless, we are not eternally placeless, nor are we bound to such feelings as a necessary state of being. Patterns of belonging are possible, though they exist in a constant state of transition and, indeed, making.

In order to cultivate a true sense of belonging and home, we must engage in habits of placemaking on a regular and repeated basis. I believe that theological reflection on wonder and the arts can expand our ways of understanding these patterns of making place in the world today. Wonder, I will argue, is best understood in relation to place; wonder allows us to transcend our place while, at the same time, deeply grounding us within it. By "placing" wonder in this way and understanding the arts as a primary vehicle to such experiences of wonder, we might better develop a truly Christian sense of place, which balances the "this-worldly" realities of placemaking within its eschatological framework. Developing our experience of placed wonder through the arts, then, might help better enable us for our theological vocation of making home.

2. Bouma-Prediger and Walsh, *Beyond Homelessness*, 15.

3. Consider, for example, cases of domestic violence that characterize some experiences of "home" or, more recently, racial unrest during the COVID-19 pandemic, which has clarified society's understanding of the African American experience of home on a corporate, social level as one of violence and terror.

Placing Wonder

To attach the disposition of wonder to place is somewhat paradoxical. For some philosophers, wonder is an experience that "un-homes" us and is "related to a kind of homesickness."[4] Wonder, in such a view, has a *dislocating* character, uprooting us from our expectations and conceptions of the way things should be. Drawing on Hannah Arendt's notion of homesickness and meaning, philosopher Anders Schinkel writes, "Wonder can therefore jolt us out of our 'home,' our forgetfulness, and make us question what we took for granted."[5] This assessment parallels the thinking of Josef Pieper, who maintains that wonder shocks the person out of their sense of the way things are. Speaking of the experience of wonder, he writes, "all that he had taken for granted as being natural and self-evident loses its compact solidarity and obviousness; *he is literally dislocated and no longer knows where he is.*"[6] These thinkers argue that wonder becomes an operative disposition for locating meaning as it disrupts our normal modes of perception. It puzzles and bewilders and pushes us to an experience of that which is "other" to us. It reassures us of our own ignorance, opposing our rationalist tendencies to attempt to understand the world as fact, and rather seeks to ground us in the abundant mystery of the world. Pieper thus argues, "And so, to wonder is not to know, not to know fully, not to be able to conceive. To conceive a thing, to possess comprehensive and exhaustive knowledge of a thing, is to cease to wonder."[7]

While wonder may dislocate us conceptually, this mystery and ignorance, however, should not be read as a surrender to dislocatedness. Wendell Berry, a helpful guide in these matters, assures readers that, on the one hand, ignorance helps us to avoid falling prey to the tendency to think we can rule over a place. "Praise ignorance," he declares, "for what man has not encountered he has not destroyed."[8] Ignorance provides a path to care, for that which we have never accessed cannot be pillaged for industrial use.[9] On the other hand, though, Berry's praise of ignorance calls

---

4. Schinkel, "Wonder, Mystery, and Meaning," 300.
5. Schinkel, "Wonder, Mystery, and Meaning," 303.
6. Pieper, *Leisure*, 114 (emphasis mine).
7. Pieper, *Leisure*, 116.
8. Berry, *Selected Poems*, 88.
9. While Berry is often critical of the "industrial economy" (for example, see his essay "Two Economies"), his larger point is that such economies often take the position of dominion rather than servant-like, responsible use. Berry's wider oeuvre reveals his belief in the responsible making of (or making-with) places, rather than the possessive mastery of places and their resources. Relatedly, it might be argued, to the contrary, that

us into a deeper knowledge and understanding of place, and he recognizes the role of wonder in developing such attention. Ignorance, he writes, is "a way of acknowledging the uniqueness of every individual creature, deserving respect, and the uniqueness of every moment, deserving wonder."[10] In Berry's wider system of thought, self-reflective ignorance accompanied by open attention and wonder, is thus the prerequisite for true hospitality, community, and responsible placemaking. Berry, in other words, relates his praise of ignorance and the disposition of wonder to the wider experience of knowing and loving our places. To live well within place, we must walk in both ignorance and understanding. To experience wonder, we must be both rooted and unrooted, open to new insight and experience while locating oneself properly within a given moment.

The relationship between ignorance and knowledge that is definitive of our experience of wonder according to Berry, then, may reveal the way that wonder operates in relation to place more generally.[11] Wonder "un-homes" us, but it does so precisely by drawing us into a placed encounter. Wonder deepens our sense that the meaning of things is never *fully* understood, but presses us to lean into them, drawing our hearts and minds simultaneously toward objects of wonder, while keeping us at a measured distance from them. I use the term *placed wonder*, then, to emphasize a central paradox. In an experience of wonder, we are invited into the mystery and ongoing story of a place that is never fully known, while at the same time called to cultivate a new knowledge that unfolds over time and invites belonging and care.

Mike Cosper, for example, tells a story of his encounter with frost flowers in the opening chapter of *Recapturing the Wonder*. While out running on a trail, he encountered a phenomenon that appeared like "pulled taffy... curled, white, and translucent," which stopped him in his tracks and bewildered his understanding.[12] It was a profound moment of beauty that captured his imagination and provoked a sense of wonder and attention. While he would later find the scientific explanation for frost flowers, in that moment of placed attention, they became a signal to the abundant mystery

---

ignorance breeds hate—it "others" people and places and therefore separates us from them, enabling our destructive and alienating tendencies. Berry lists several different types of ignorance, calling this one "fearful ignorance," though this is not the type of ignorance for which he generally advocates (Berry, *Way of Ignorance*, 54–55).

10. Berry, *Way of Ignorance*, 67.

11. The biblical theologian William P. Brown suggests a similar relationship between mystery and understanding within the disposition of wonder, arguing that rather than abolishing knowledge altogether, wonder is indeed where mystery and understanding meet (*Seven Pillars of Creation*, 5).

12. Cosper, *Recapturing the Wonder*, 20.

and beauty of the world, which the scientific fact could not adequately define. He reflects on the way the moment of placed wonder gave a deeper sense of truth of the world than the scientific knowledge later conveyed.

Similarly, a friend of mine once told a story about her experience of encountering thousands of spider webs that covered a large field at her family farm. Looking out over the field covered in such delicate tapestries of silk, she was startled with awe. The field that she had known for years was no longer what she expected. In that moment, she was further grounded in the beauty of the physical place, knowing it better than she had before. It was an experience, no doubt, of placed wonder.

In both of these examples, the experience of placed wonder thrives on an intentional dwelling in or attention to a place in order to achieve the deepening of both mystery and knowledge. As the mechanism for locating both deeper meaning and understanding, placed wonder becomes a force for cultivating a sense of home in the world by drawing us into repeated liturgies of both longing and love that produce a sense of *be*longing and placed identity. Placed wonder thus offers us both roots and wings, calling us out of our existing sense of place only to return us more fully to it. To apply the oft-referenced line of T. S. Eliot's "Little Gidding," in *Four Quartets*, in un-homing us wonder allows us to "arrive where we started and know the place for the first time."[13]

Our making of place in the world today, then, is definitively shaped by the experience of wonder. While the experience of wonder may allow us to "seek higher ground," it nevertheless understands groundedness as its end. It seeks not to dismiss emplacement but rather deepens the possibilities for our understanding of and action within places. Without wonder, places and our relations within them are flattened, becoming mere objects of dominion. But wonder invites us further into the work of placemaking and deepens our understanding of what it really means to be made in the image of a "homemaking God" who invites our careful co-laboring in the patterns of creation and redemption.

Experiencing Placed Wonder through the Arts

How, then, might we be better enabled to experience placed wonder that fosters our making of home in the world? In what ways can we seek a more wonder-filled dwelling in our places? Wonder cannot just be drummed up. There is not a formula to be exercised at will. It is the very nature of wonder to surprise and surpass expectations. Often wonder is not oriented toward

13. Eliot, *Four Quartets*, 59.

an object at all, but rather signifies a mode of being that casts its light on the subject as they experience new meaning. Wonder entails a transformation or *metanoia*, whereby we approach the world anew. However, wonder does tend to break through in certain types of practices. For instance, we are unlikely to wonder at the abundant beauty of the world without taking time to sit and pay attention to it. We cannot look with wonder on a person or place if we have not made ourselves available to look at all. Considering this, I believe that the arts are one context where we are likely to experience placed wonder.

Cecelia González-Andrieu understands art as integral to the experience of revelatory wonder. She writes that the arts "[make] experiences of overpowering wonder possible, purposely and concretely so."[14] They both "engender wonder and are also witnesses to someone else's state of wonder."[15] Several points of González-Andrieu's wider argument are relevant here for understanding art's relation to wonder more broadly, and, as I will argue, how we might understand both art and wonder as tied up in our making of place. First, she claims that wonder is experienced in concrete practice. It is not a transcendent, intellectual experience devoid of embodied particularity. The arts are uniquely capable of evoking wonder because they themselves are grounded in embodied experience that draw us in as participants and onlookers. Second, she suggests that the "otherness of art" is central: "In this radical otherness of the art from ourselves," she contends, "is the promise of surprise and wonder, which can only happen when we are open to a 'radical receptivity.'"[16] In our encounter with art, we must stand open to it, willing to be transformed by its meaning, and motivated to change in response to our placed encounter. We must accept its otherness as a necessary condition and learn how to attend to it fully in its otherness. Third, art engages us in revelatory wonder through beauty or, as González-Andrieu also notes, "its heartbreaking absence," and can therefore reveal both fundamental truth and goodness.[17] Finally, as a corollary to the third point, through cultivating wonder art moves us to insight on the brokenness of the world.[18] In doing so, the evocative wonder of the arts acknowledges that things are not "the way they're supposed to be" and thus hints at the potential for a redeemed future.

I would like to extend these basic points described by González-Andrieu in order to suggest that the arts, in their relation to what I am

14. González-Andrieu, *Bridge to Wonder*, 29.
15. González-Andrieu, *Bridge to Wonder*, 26.
16. González-Andrieu, *Bridge to Wonder*, 68.
17. González-Andrieu, *Bridge to Wonder*, 23.
18. González-Andrieu, *Bridge to Wonder*, 37.

calling placed wonder, embody the central and most important features of Christian placemaking practice. While this may seem surprising given the cultural detachment of the arts from our everyday lives, upon further reflection we will find that the types of practices and dispositions required for the making of place are often encompassed within both the processes and products of human artistry. The four features we have outlined here—their concrete embodiment, their acknowledgement of otherness, their relation to beauty, and their engagement with brokenness—are integral features of how the arts cultivate wonder *in* place and *for* placemaking so that we may experience a true sense of home in the world.

Concrete Embodiment

Placemaking is an architecture of action. It requires intentional practices concretely realized and enacted over time. We make our places through physically embodying our emotional, intellectual, and spiritual desires, and so construct a vision of the self in relation to the world. As particular expressions of both the world and their makers, the arts can become contexts in which to witness the placemaking practices of the artist, while also serving to model a vision of place that we might then imitate. The arts can, therefore, become both theological and practical paradigms for our own construction of home in the world, acting as sites where our own wonder may find a placed expression.

Patrick Sherry provides a robust theological account of the arts and beauty that potentially reveals this dynamic, proposing that the "wonder and admiration which artistic inspiration evokes may be seen as part of our wonder at the manifoldness of creation and at the continued activity of the Holy Spirit in the world."[19] Sherry grounds his theological aesthetic in the ways that the Holy Spirit enables our engagement with the created world, inspiring a sense of transcendence and awe at the depth of God's presence in and engagement with the entire cosmos. Part of our theological calling is to imitate the care of God for and presence within his creation—a God who wonderfully plants gardens (Gen 2), journeys to the springs of the sea (Job 38), and knows the number of hairs on our heads (Luke 12:7). Our theological vocation is modeled after God's attentive and loving presence and, therefore, thrives on our own wonder-filled response to God's good creative work. Everyday things, in turn, may then become vehicles of God's love for the world and a reflection of its mysterious meaning.

---

19. Sherry, *Spirit and Beauty*, 132.

The arts can provide opportunities to experience the wonder of everyday creation upon which our wider placemaking practices are built. California-based artist Kari Dunham provides a good example of how the arts can cultivate placed wonder in several series that chronicle the everyday realities of life at home. Here she produces works that convey the subtle beauty and wonder of our placed experience. For instance, in *40 Days of Trees and Ordinary Things* (2020), a project completed during her first two months of COVID-19 quarantine, she devotes her attention to the everyday moments of her life at home, shifting our perspective to experience the everyday wonder of a grapefruit or a lamppost.[20] She attends to the features of home that are often lost or overlooked and in so doing ascribes them deeper meaning. Wonder is not about the sensational, as Pieper describes, but rather offers a relationship to a quieter existence.[21] Dunham's images become a concrete record of our everyday, quiet life in place. They return our attention to the ways that our making of home is built not primarily on the big events but the small ones, the ways that we dwell in place through small, concrete actions that cultivate a sense of home and belonging over time.

Figure 5. Kari Dunham, *March 20 / Grapefruit with Dish.*

20. See the artist's website: https://karidunham.com.
21. Pieper, *Leisure*, 112.

Other works in her oeuvre reveal what she describes as the "comforts and discomforts" of home. A sink full of dirty dishes, women doing laundry, or people gathered around a table. *Come to the Table* (2014) offers an image of communion centered on hospitable homemaking practices. Men and women gather around a dining table to eat and drink, sharing conversation and connection. A woman clears dishes by herself as conversation unfolds, her service given for the sake of the other. The tone of this painting is joyful overall, even while the artist shows the mundane and often sacrificial practices that accompany moments of communion. In *We are Like Hired Hands* (2012), we see a more complicated picture of home and the woman's place within it, though. Three female figures fold laundry on the furniture, detailing the domestic work that often falls on the shoulders of women, their free time given in large part to the unthanked but expected tasks of domestic life. Throughout her work, Dunham engages viewers in a sense of placed wonder that initiates reflection on the impact of our homemaking practices both in the domestic spaces of the house and the wider creation. In Dunham's images, we concretely encounter the attentive care that the artist brings to her own life in place and are therefore motivated to discover our own places and practices in new and often rehabituated ways.

Otherness

While our modern sense of home has become increasingly interior, the biblical vision of home is more outward-focused—expressed not in personal comfort but in communal responsibility. The way we treat the "other" is a marked feature of the biblical notion of place, and when we fail to do so adequately, our sense of creation as a whole ultimately suffers.[22] Our making of place, then, must adequately learn to recognize the "other" while responding with hospitality and an invitation to belonging. The permeable boundaries of place provide a path for the radical recognition of the other without coercing the other to lose their distinctive identity.

The arts provide a place to understand this otherness while inciting wonder at the beauty and diversity of the other without becoming spectacle. Art allows us to linger in a space that is profoundly different from our normal modes of experience, and in doing so, cultivates an imagination

---

22. See Craig Bartholomew, *Where Mortals Dwell*, for a longer discussion of a biblical theology of place. On the communal features of a biblical notion of home, see Jen Pollock Michel, *Keeping Place*. See also my more detailed discussion of the responsibilities included in a biblical notion of home and place in chapter 3 of Jennifer Allen Craft, *Placemaking and the Arts*.

which sees the depth of meaning in experiences outside of our own. The amazement and puzzlement we experience through the artwork's evocation of wonder is grounded in a placed experience, calling us out of our own placed experience before returning us ultimately to it. The reciprocity and dialogic character of our dislocating experiences of wonder train us in the practice of homemaking, which offers hospitable communion to the other. In doing so, we can transcend boundaries and differences without dissolving them altogether.

One example of this can be witnessed in a series of works by Austin-based artist Scott Erickson, where he recontextualizes Jesus in a time of segregation. Jesus is placed on the back of a public bus, in a segregated swimming pool, or at a lunch counter with angry white onlookers at his back.[23] Erickson notes that "[o]bviously Jesus wasn't white," imagining situations in which Jesus would have been excluded—both culturally and personally—as "other."[24] Erickson seeks to draw our attention to the incongruous ways Christians preach Jesus' message while ignoring the ways his actions would challenge the dominant social imagination. While we may live in a post-segregationist world, we continue to "other" racialized minorities in a dominantly white society. Erickson thus "de-homes" Jesus from certain cultural expectations for action, while attempting to dislocate viewers from a racial imagining that contradicts a biblical picture of our life together in place.

Many of Erickson's other works reveal unexpected ways of imagining theological ideas, as in his *Honest Advent* series, which surprises viewers by imaging holiness and divine presence in the everyday realities of pregnancy, childbirth, and infancy.[25] These images evoke wonder at a God with us in place and encourage us to reimagine what places of divine presence look like for our wider communities.

We find that the placemaking practices found in the arts, whereby the artist "makes room" for a subject that might otherwise evade our glance or notice, un-homes us for a brief moment in time and causes us to reflect on the meaning of such un-homing experiences. Upon our return to "real life," we may find that we have been permanently moved—that our sense of place has become permanently dislodged and requires new and rehabituated making. Having learned from the aesthetic encounter how better to pay attention to, interact with, and experience otherness (whether in the art object itself or its depiction of a subject), our making of a home in the world

---

23. See the artist's website: https://www.scottericksonart.com/.

24. See his description of the pieces on his Instagram: https://www.instagram.com/p/CLZbAPWphH6/.

25. Erickson, *Honest Advent*.

integrates those practices and dispositions into a new and hopefully more hospitable way of being.

Beauty

Beauty is also a key component of how we experience placed wonder through the arts. Contemporary society often trains us to operate in a mode of disenchantment. We fail to understand the mystery and presence of God around us as we go about our everyday lives. But in experiences of beauty through the arts, we can be shocked out of our expectations for the way we think the world is and empowered to join together that which the world seeks to separate. Beauty can, therefore motivate us to reframe (or perhaps de-frame) our expectations for people and places and to understand the deeper truths of the world to which beauty speaks.

Massachusetts-based painter Bruce Herman exemplifies this way of imagining beauty in both his painting and writing. In his essay "Wounds and Beauty," Herman dismisses the Platonic notion of the beautiful as transcendent, which he argues "diminishes the value of domestic reality."[26] Instead, he seeks a beauty that finds meaning through communal intimacy and that embraces the wounds that come from relationships maintained and experienced over time. This type of beauty includes woundedness, dismisses sentimentality, and locates beauty in hope. Beauty offers us a true sense of home, Herman argues, as it acknowledges "the best is yet to come," while placing eschatological hope in the context of our current wounded experience.[27] Herman's *Woman* series reveals a "deeper form of beauty," which shows the possibility of material transcendence through a deeply embedded physicality.[28] Attention to the realistic detail of a woman's face and form are set alongside a context of abstraction, drawing us into deeper contemplation of the women themselves as they invite wonder at their depth of being and presence.

Herman's work instigates what Elaine Scarry calls an "unselfing" in his viewers by challenging cultural notions of beauty through the evocation of wonder.[29] Scarry writes that beauty allows us to perceive our own error, and

---

26. Herman, "Wounds and Beauty," 114.
27. Herman, "Wounds and Beauty," 115.
28. See the artist's website, https://www.bruceherman.com/gallery/woman/. Platonic transcendence understood through dualism is replaced here with a vision of the transcendent found precisely within the physical world.
29. Scarry, *On Beauty and Being Just*, 26.

it "pressures us to distribution."[30] The experience of attending to a beautiful thing, in other words, results not in an inward movement but an outward one. It is primarily kenotic, emptying the self in order to inhabit something outside the self. This is the reason that Scarry links beauty with justice.

While all art is not bound to engage us in an experience of beauty, art that *does* invite us into this type of "unselfing" through beauty can perform a prophetic function, calling us to re-evaluate our perception and relationship to the world and thus make it anew. The women in these portraits are "unplaced" in their abstraction, but at the same time the images reveal the ways that our Western notions of female beauty—conceptualized primarily as an object of desire—must be "unplaced" as well. Herman understands beauty not as an object of desire but as an act of discipleship and loving presence. As we re-evaluate our expectations for seeing beauty, we are, therefore, invited into a deeper presence in the world. Art can, in other words, recast our expectations for both beauty and place, highlighting the ways that our practices and perceptions require further discipleship and an openness to join together that which we have divided.

Brokenness

If beauty is integral to our experience of place, then, so also is our acknowledgement and interaction with brokenness. A vision of beauty divorced from brokenness becomes sentimentality, and a failure to recognize brokenness in our relation to the world results in further alienation from it, which turns our back on both hospitality and justice. Theologically, beauty and brokenness find their most complete expression in the cross, and it is there that we can understand the relation between beauty and suffering, which also sheds light on our placemaking practice. In the cross, we find a beauty that does not reject suffering and brokenness or move too quickly beyond it, but rather lingers and makes its home in the brokenness, even if that home is impermanent. Christ on the cross fully takes on suffering for the sake of redeeming beauty and thus transfigures brokenness by dwelling fully within it.

In understanding our relationships to place, I believe we might embrace a similar dynamic—one that does not eschew either beauty or suffering in their totality but seeks to understand them together. For it is only in identifying with the lost, the broken, and the displaced that Christ makes a place for the redemption of all. When we make our home in the world in such a way as to dismiss those communities for the sake of a limited

---

30. Scarry, *On Beauty and Being Just*, 108.

understanding of beauty or an easier path to redemption, we will likely fall victim to the same modes of homelessness we seek to reject.

Artistry is a practice that is uniquely capable of fleshing out both the wonder and tensions in these relationships, between beauty and brokenness, and in doing so teaches us something about what it means to make our home in both. Many artists know how to make a home in the midst of suffering and pain.[31] They teach us how to dwell in brokenness fully and fruitfully without giving up the hope that it will one day be made new. In doing so, art cultivates a placed wonder *within* the brokenness, allowing us a vision of healing place without ignoring the tensions of what our homes look like now.

One example of this dynamic may be found in the work of Chuck Hemard, a Southern art photographer based in Auburn, Alabama. Hemard works in medium and large format photography and his series of work, *The Pines* (2017), represents the tensions of beauty's relation to suffering as well as how both are integral parts of our experience and making of home. *The Pines* focuses on the sense of place innate to the southeastern pine forest and how the health and beauty of the native longleaf pine ecosystem depends on the practice of prescribed fire, an ecological land management technique that sets fire to the land in order to cultivate its health, vitality, and sustainable growth. Without fire, it is unable to regenerate, and native species get pushed out by biodiversity-threatening and invasive overgrowth.

Figure 6. Chuck Hemard, *#1 (burn) Okaloosa County, Florida 2012.*

31. See Fujimura, *Art and Faith*, on artists' role in the midst of suffering and their call to the work of mending.

Hemard chronicles these patterns and shows the ways that beauty grows from suffering, as in "#1 (burn) Okaloosa County, Florida 2012."[32] Here the ground is charred black and shows evidence of the cleansing fire that has been put to the ground only hours before. Ethereal smoke lingers in the background as evidence of the apocalyptic scene that has just passed. While prescribed fire has a destructive quality in the moment, in this ecosystem it ultimately fosters a more hospitable environment for creatures to make their home. The fire stands as a metaphor of homemaking practices in the natural world, as we learn how to interact with our environment in ways that produce beauty out of brokenness, while also acquainting us with practices that foster resurrection and health in our native places.[33] The fire-kissed landscape shows us a way to "practice resurrection" as Wendell Berry describes, promising the beauty of new creation born from suffering.[34]

Placed Wonder, the Arts, and New Creation

The eschatological nature of both artistry and our making of place has been a consistent thread throughout this investigation. In both, we catch glimpses of new creation as we practice the making of a place that dwells in what N. T. Wright calls the "overlapping and interlocking" of heaven and earth.[35] The glimpses we see of new creation are often born in longing, in the desire we have for home or beauty or connectedness, but which we cannot seem to grasp fully. Our sense of home is often born in homelessness, our desire for beauty forged in its absence or its distorted representations. These realities only make sense through the lens of new creation.

Artists and poets are integral to the task of making these connections, acting as "heralds of the New," as Makoto Fujimura describes in his theology of making, drawing us into dispositions and practices of hope, wonder, and attentive love that foreshadow our ultimate homemaking in new creation.[36] Patrick Sherry similarly suggests, "The arts, in their highest achievements, glimpse eternal beauty, and anticipate and give a foretaste of the reality

---

32. See Hemard, *Pines*, 24–31.

33. Crispin Sartwell describes fire as having its corollary in home and the apocalypse (*Six Names of Beauty*, 54–55).

34. Berry, *Selected Poems*, 87.

35. Wright, *Simply Christian*, Part One (*passim*).

36. Fujimura, *Art and Faith*, 58.

beyond, which is to come."³⁷ In beauty, he writes, "we glimpse the future transfiguration of the cosmos."³⁸

I have argued that art is uniquely capable of this new creation work: as it embeds us further in our concrete embodiment in places; as it orients toward the other and collapses inhospitable boundaries; as it expands our notions of beauty, wonder, and meaning; and as it calls attention to the brokenness of the places in which we are called nevertheless to make our home. Given these characteristics, it is unsurprising that the arts seem to produce in us what Ben Quash describes as the feeling of "vertiginous at-home-ness," a state of being that results from being simultaneously placed and displaced in the act of attending to a thing. This term, he says, "captures the paradox of dazzled wonderment," and conveys the manner in which we come to be bonded to and at home in the world even while recognizing its radical otherness.³⁹ This state of being conveys the eschatological paradox of being at home in God's kingdom made present to us here and yet longing for the new Jerusalem, which is "not yet," our true home made manifest in the age to come.

Quash clarifies that the Holy Spirit is central in the practice of "fitting us to our environment," and, I think, in cultivating our experiences of placed wonder through the arts.⁴⁰ The Spirit guides our insights and stirs our making in place, "making things more what they are, concretizing them rather than homogenizing them."⁴¹ The Spirit, in other words, draws us more deeply into our place—its otherness, beauty, and brokenness—magnifying the ways that we are called to be at home in the world while also reminding us of our perpetual state of homelessness this side of new creation. As the Spirit inspires and sanctifies our creative practice, our making in places resounds with the echoes of new creation.

In the end, God makes his home with us (Rev 21:3). What then does that mean for our homemaking practices in the here and now, as they call God into our places and prepare us for our own future dwelling in God's presence? And what ultimately does this mean for a theology of the arts? In imagining new creation, John returns us to the attitude of wonder: "And in the spirit he carried me away to a great, high mountain and showed me the holy city Jerusalem coming down out of heaven from God. It has the glory of God and a radiance like a very rare jewel, like jasper, clear as crystal" (Rev

37. Sherry, *Spirit and Beauty*, 159.
38. Sherry, *Spirit and Beauty*, 156.
39. Quash, *Found Theology*, 240.
40. Quash, *Found Theology*, 262.
41. Quash, *Found Theology*, 276.

21:10–11). This vision of heaven on earth places the writer of Revelation in a state of perplexed wonder as the glory of God encompasses the whole of creation. This wonder is not oriented simply toward the transcendent presence of God, though; it does not remove us from the earthly creation in which we have been called to work. Rather, the wonder of new creation invites us to rest in the home we have always longed for. It offers us the rooted place in creation that we have been seeking all along.

If the arts are a central avenue through which wonder is cultivated and experienced on this side of new creation, then we might begin to recognize them as an avenue for higher theological reflection, particularly when it comes to our making of and longing for place. Artists can help satisfy our theological longing for place by drawing us into the patterns of new creation. The arts signal our dwelling in a state of in-betweenness, in the margins between being at home and living in exile. By seeking to establish more intentional engagements with the arts in our places, we can navigate our placemaking with the attention, love, and wonder that such a vocation requires. The arts may indeed even help us to embody the prayer "thy kingdom come on earth as it is in heaven" more fully and more faithfully.

PART III
Wonder and Wisdom

Third canto | Karen An-hwei Lee

The field of radiant awe, Acts 4:30

Stretch out your hand
with healing power;
may miraculous

signs and wonders
be done through the name
of your holy servant Jesus.

May the hem of your cloak
and the apostle's kerchief
mend all flesh in your name—

flushed with new life
in your field of radiant awe,
blessed as water to wine,

men healed of blindness,
fishermen walking on the sea,
sleeping girls wakened to life.

"Four Cantos on Wonder." Performed by the New Arts Trio to music composed by Misook Kim for the Wheaton Theology Conference (April 2021). Italicized verses: New Living Translation of the Bible (2015) by Tyndale House.

8

Encountering the Uncontainable in the Arts

JEREMY BEGBIE

If anyone should not find himself astonished and filled with wonder when he becomes involved in one way or another with theology, he would be well advised to consider once more, from a certain remoteness and without prejudice, what is involved in this undertaking. The same holds true for anyone who should have accomplished the feat of *no longer* being astonished, instead of becoming continually *more* astonished all the time that he concerns himself with the subject.[1]

—KARL BARTH

"*Thanks be to God* for his inexpressible gift!" (2 Cor 9:15). Whatever else it is, this outburst from the apostle Paul in his second letter to the Corinthians is an exclamation of wonder.[2] It comes after a lengthy section dealing with a thoroughly down-to-earth business: raising money for the saints in Jerusalem. Quite why Paul should be so full of wonder lies at the core of

1. Barth, *Evangelical Theology*, 63–64.

2. Other oft-quoted Pauline verses and passages redolent of wonder, spilling into doxology, include Romans 9:5; 11:33–36; 1 Timothy 6:14.

what I want to explore in this essay. "A quite *specific astonishment* stands at the beginning of every theological perception, inquiry, and thought," writes Karl Barth, "in fact at the root of every theological word."[3] What is this "specific astonishment," and what might it have to do with the arts?

As a way into the topic, let me identify two broad convictions that seem to be common in many of the current theology and arts conversations. The first is that the experience of wonder has been on the wane in modern and late modern Western society, and that this ought to be a matter of considerable concern. A pervasive cultural shift going under various names—"secularization," "desacralization," "disenchantment"—has diminished our natural inclination to wonder, bringing woeful consequences, not least for the church. The second conviction is that the artistic imagination is uniquely placed to help us recover a sense of wonder, and that this presents the church with a golden opportunity. These convictions can call on much to support them, and I am broadly sympathetic to both. However, in what follows I argue that we would be wise to exercise some caution in the face of them, lest we fail to take note of the distinctive form of wonder that the gospel itself generates, the kind evinced by Paul in the verse just quoted. If we are persuaded that the arts do have a role in generating a much-needed wonder in our cultural moment, much will depend on being clear about what kind of wonder we think this might be.

Wonder and the Uncontainable

The term *wonder* has taken on a huge variety of senses in history,[4] but as understood in modernity it seems to be marked by a number of key features. At the very least, wonder is a reaction or response to something that arrests our attention. It cannot be self-generated. It also involves a large measure of surprise: it comes upon us with unbidden force, unexpectedly.[5] And it entails being pulled in by something intensely attractive: it is characterized by what one writer calls an "ecstasy of interest."[6] True as all this might be, considering that our interests here concern *God and Wonder: Theology, Imagination, and the Arts*, we are bound to be especially interested in wonder that has a metaphysical or theological dimension to it. With this in

---

3. Barth, *Evangelical Theology*, 64 (my italics added for "specific").

4. For useful overviews, see Quinn, *Iris Exiled*; Knox, "Introduction"; Deckard and Losonczi, *Philosophy Begins in Wonder*.

5. René Descartes could speak of it as "a sudden surprise of the soul," as cited in Knox, "Introduction," 2.

6. Lichtmann, "'Ecstasy of Interest.'"

mind, I want to highlight another feature that seems to be common to many experiences of wonder, and it is one that I believe can help us make some important connections between wonder, the arts, and God. I am speaking of a sense of *uncontainability*—"moreness," we might call it—and I want to distinguish between two broad types of wonder (by no means the only two) where this awareness is especially evident.

The first arises when we are faced with a reality beyond ourselves *whose significance is felt as far exceeding what can be contained by that reality*. We sense there is more to what we perceive than a quick glance could suggest, more than could be captured by bare description, more than is evident at this particular moment. We see a rainbow, and yet we see much more than a colorful arrangement of water droplets: we see beauty. When we gaze at our infant son or daughter asleep, we see more than a young, warm-blooded animal: we see the child we helped to make, a person of measureless value with a potentially rich future.

When this kind of wonder arises in response to the world as a whole, we are almost inevitably led in a theological direction. A painter once came to visit me in Vancouver. He claimed no particular religious belief but had been sitting in on some lectures I was giving. He told me that when walking home the previous day, gazing at the spectacular scenery surrounding him, he was suddenly gripped by the thought that (as he put it) "none of this had to be; everything I was gawping at didn't have to exist, and didn't have to exist in this form." He wanted to know what the Christian faith might have to say about this. He was experiencing one of the most primordial forms of wonder, much celebrated by philosophers and poets: wonder that there is something rather than nothing, that there *is* a world, and that the world appears to be contingent (that is, not to contain its own explanation). This kind of experience naturally presses us to ask if the world has a significance and origin that lies beyond itself—in an extra-worldly agency, such as God. And if we do take that step into theology, we may in due course be seized by that most exalted form of wonder, wonder in the face of *God's* uncontainability: that God is infinite (immense and eternal), and as such God cannot be contained (squeezed into or conditioned) by the finite.

A second type of wonder (often going with the first) arises through an intense sense of our own limitations, specifically when we are faced with a reality beyond ourselves and become acutely aware *it cannot be contained by our systems of representation, especially by our thought and language*. We ponder the vastness of the universe and say, "I can't get my head around it."[7]

[7]. This overlaps with what Immanuel Kant called the "mathematical" sublime: when we are overwhelmed by something of immense size and are acutely confronted with the limits of our sense perception (Kant, *Critique of the Power of Judgment*, 131–39).

Or we find ourselves astounded by someone's generosity to us. Clutching the unexpected check, we say, "I'm at a loss for words." With regard to God, this form of wonder translates into wonder at God's incomprehensibility—that our mental apparatus can never come close to encompassing God; or wonder at God's ineffability—that our language is always outstripped by the divine.[8] There is always more to God than we could ever think or say.

Secularity and Containment

The reason for highlighting the notion of uncontainability in this way is because it casts light on one of the more obvious features of the secular imagination: namely, its inability to cope with the uncontainable. And this, I believe, goes some of the way to explaining why wonder may have fallen on such hard times in modernity.

My interest here is not in the sociological phenomenon of "secularization"—exemplified in a drop in church affiliation, the modern separation of church and state, and so on.[9] Rather I have in mind an imagination of the world that in its extreme form is usually termed *naturalism*. On the negative side, naturalism rejects all otherworldly realities, the most obvious example of which is God, and on the positive side, it holds that natural science is the ultimate arbiter of all claims to truth and knowledge: the hard sciences (in principle) can provide an exhaustive account of all that is.[10] The key point is this: naturalism is a *containing* vision *par excellence*. It tells us the universe contains its own explanation. To ask why it is there—its "final cause"—is simply a non-question. It just *is*, without any rhyme or reason beyond its own closed existence.

It is not hard to see how this encourages a drive towards containment on *our* part; in other words, towards control and mastery. From the early modern era onwards, science has given us unprecedented power to name,

---

However, although the sublime may occasion wonder, it can also bring fear and terror, and so should not be equated with the theological sense of wonder I am expounding here. For further discussion, see Begbie, *Redeeming Transcendence in the Arts*, ch. 2.

8. Here I am not using "incomprehensibility" in its strong sense, meaning completely beyond understanding; only in the sense of something being ungraspable in its wholeness. Likewise, "ineffability" is not being understood to mean wholly unspeakable, but ungraspable in its completeness by speech.

9. The literature on secularism/secularization/secularism is by now vast. For some perceptive recent studies, see references in Yelle and Trein, *Narratives of Disenchantment and Secularization*.

10. For an exceptionally clear account of hard-line ontological naturalism, see Baker, *Naturalism and the First-Person Perspective*, esp. ch. 1.

grasp, and command the physical world, and this has led some to believe it offers an all-encompassing quasi-divine view of the world as it really is. When allied to the conviction that an object is no more than the sum of its parts (so that in manipulating the parts we can manipulate the whole), it is hardly surprising that we find technocratic, pragmatic, and instrumental attitudes being applied to virtually any reality we encounter, from planet earth to the person next door.

I am jumping over myriad details and qualifications here, of course, and I am very aware that this kind of bleached naturalism is a vision that goes far beyond what *bona fide* science requires or presumes. I am also aware that many will rightly point to signs of a less hard-line, "postsecular" mood in our emerging late-modern culture. My point here is simply that insofar as naturalism does represent strong sensibilities that have shaped and still shape the West, it is strongly marked by an ethos of containment, and we should hardly be surprised if wonder withers in its wake, if mystery turns into mastery.[11]

The Arts as Allies of Wonder

Enter the artist—uniquely poised, she believes, to counter this debilitating ethos of containment. Wave after wave of artistic energy has gone into opposing the closed, naturalist mindset we have sketched: from the early German, English, and American Romantics through Ruskin, Hopkins, and Kandinsky, to Anthony Gormley, Dorothea Tanning, and very recently, Marilynne Robinson, whose own resistance to naturalism is pungently set out in her book *Absence of Mind*.[12] To be sure, many in this stream have little time for orthodox Christian faith. Indeed, Charles Taylor proposes that for large parts of the population today, the world of the arts offers an alternative not only to bleak, godless naturalism but also to full-blooded religious commitment. The arts open up a postsecular spirituality where we can revel in

---

11. Admittedly, even very naturalistically inclined scientists can still speak of wonder. One of the most famous, Richard Dawkins, can even write a book about himself entitled *An Appetite for Wonder: The Making of a Scientist*. He is insistent that his own science does not undermine a sense of wonder: "I wish I could meet Keats or Blake to persuade them that mysteries don't lose their poetry because they are solved. Quite the contrary. The solution often turns out more beautiful than the puzzle, and anyway the solution uncovers deeper mystery. The rainbow's dissection into light of different wavelengths leads on to Maxwell's equations, and eventually to special relativity" (Dawkins, "Science, Delusion, and the Appetite for Wonder"). But as we might expect, this is a wonder shorn of any hint of metaphysics or theology.

12. Robinson, *Absence of Mind*.

wonder but without the shackles of institutionalized dogma.[13] Whatever the truth of that, Eugene Peterson sums up succinctly the potential many see in the arts: "artists," he says, "rescue us from a life from which the wonder has leaked out."[14]

And if this is so, we could well ask: how might they do this? What might it be about the arts that makes them such natural allies of wonder? Without attempting any kind of comprehensive answer, I want to explore just one pervasive feature of the way the arts appear to operate that seems especially relevant here, and, significantly, it has to do with uncontainability: their capacity to be multiply allusive, to generate an uncontainable wealth of meaning. The driving dynamic here, I believe, is what we typically find in the phenomenon of metaphor. A linguistic metaphor involves "figuring one object or event through another,"[15] or perhaps better, seeing one thing "through an *unexpected* other."[16] If I say "Jennifer Craft has a mind on fire," I am pressing you to think of Jennifer's mind through an unexpected other—a fire. What gives this metaphor its force is the incongruity in this combination of terms. And yet it still makes sense. (We don't assume Jennifer's brain has spontaneously combusted.)

This kind of incongruity would appear in one way or another to run through the *modus operandi* of much of what we have come to call art.[17] A frequent result, especially in the case of art with a high degree of "realistic" representation, is that something familiar is made unfamiliar, defamiliarized. The term "defamiliarization" was made famous by the Russian formalist critic, Viktor Shklovsky (1893–1984), who spoke about art "making [things] strange."[18] He lamented the way in everyday speech we increasingly rely on secondhand, off-the-shelf phrases and expressions that become dull with overuse, desensitizing us to the world we experience. An art like poetry pushes ordinary language out of shape—through metaphorical or figurative speech, and through metaphor-like artificial devices (rhyme, alliteration, assonance). The world is thus re-freshed, made strange. But it is also perceived more truthfully in the process, for relations are pointed up between things, relations we might otherwise never discover. Essentially the same point is made by Rowan Williams in his Gifford Lectures, *The Edge of*

---

13. Taylor, *Secular Age*, 352–61.
14. As quoted in Foerger, "Artists Rescue Us when the Wonder Has Leaked Out."
15. Taylor, *Language Animal*, 139.
16. Williams, *Edge of Words*, 133 (emphasis mine).
17. For fuller discussion, see Begbie, *Voicing Creation's Praise*, 233–55.
18. Shklovsky, "Art, as Device." For discussion, see Gunn, "Making Art Strange"; Chernavin and Yampolskaya, "'Estrangement' in Aesthetics and Beyond."

Words, where he considers what he calls "excessive speech" (he is thinking of poetry and fiction in particular).[19] Realistic fiction obliges us "to see what we thought we knew *as if for the first time*"[20] because it makes us perceive things together we might not otherwise connect, disclosing relations hitherto unnoticed. In Van Gogh's famous painting of a farmer's shoes, we are made to see more in shoes than we ever could before, previously unseen connections and resonances. And so we come not just to recognize shoes, but *re*-cognize, re-know them.

Consider another example: in the theater show *Stomp*,[21] commonly ignored domestic objects—trash cans, wooden poles, hammer handles, old newspapers, and the like—are composed into a scintillating festivity of percussion, dance, and visual comedy. The first item in the show is a virtuosic dance using domestic brushes. We are made to perceive more in brushes than we could before, as well as made to see what they can become. We arrive home after the show and glance at the brush in the corner of the closet: the familiar suddenly becomes unfamiliar. Consider yet another example: the Irish poet Seamus Heaney's singular skill at making the common uncommon. Through a complex array of poetic techniques Heaney endows the qualities of, say, a farmer's pitchfork, with extravagantly woven associations, reaching into territory that is unmistakably metaphysical.[22]

The result of such "uncommon" perceptions, then, is that we are opened up to the multiple meanings, connotations, and associations of things, and these by their nature can never be fully specified. A poem like Heaney's "The Pitchfork" generates a vast range of meanings that we could never fully spell out. This is empathically *not* to say that such art is vague, amorphous, or wholly indeterminate (that it can take on any meaning at all). It is to say we will never get to the end of it: there is always more to it, and always more that could be said and thought about it. And the same applies to what is presented *through* art of this sort. At its best, art makes us realize that things are more than they seem to be here, more than they seem to be now, more valuable than their being useful to me here and now. Art, in other words, subverts a reductive, one-size-fits-all, one-language-fits-all reading of the world, and with it any notion that we can finally control and master the world. And this, I am proposing, is one of the principal reasons why the arts so often engender wonder.

19. Williams, *Edge of Words*, ch. 5.

20. Williams, *Edge of Words*, 136; my italics. We recall the classic paradigm of wonder: the gaze of a child. See Quinn, *Iris Exiled*, 29–37.

21. https://www.stomp.co.uk/.

22. Heaney, "Pitchfork."

As I said before, a strong sense of uncontainability can carry us very naturally into theological terrain. So it is more than understandable if Christians should be excited by art's capacities in this respect, especially Christians who have felt the chill of the icy winds of reductive naturalism. For what if the pressure towards uncontainability in the arts were a profound intimation of something that characterizes the world as a whole, a presence in and to the world that always exceeds the world's grasp, an abundance of meaning that by its very nature will always resist any containment by the world? And what would this uncontainable, meaningful presence be except God? In music and dance, painting and poetry, do we not have a heaven-made opportunity to help restore theological wonder in a culture so bereft of a sense of the divine?

What Is This Uncontainable Infinite?

This kind of reasoning has great force and appeal. But it is just here that caution is needed. For there are some dangers that can hardly be overlooked. Most obviously, we could forget that art can generate kinds of wonder that never get beyond gawping at the spectacular, that never issue in anything fruitful, or that may even involve the demonic.[23] (The aesthetic displays at the Nazi Nuremberg rallies in the 1930s would be a case in point.) But there is a subtler hazard for Christians in enthusiastically aligning the infinite we sense through the arts with the divine. I have in mind the danger of assuming that any intuition of infinity through the arts will lead us naturally and unproblematically in the direction of the Christian God—that the arts will naturally carve out a boundless space for us into which the God of Jesus Christ can effortlessly be accommodated. I am not of course implying that all intuitions of the divine among non-Christians will be idolatrous through and through. Nor am I denying that for many the arts can serve to crack open modernity's secularizing shell, its "immanent frame" (Charles Taylor): this is surely something to be thankful for. But at some stage one is going to have to ask: "crack open to what?" I am reminded of the chain store, Bed Bath & Beyond, where the "Beyond" remains tantalizingly elusive. What or who, we may ask, is the God Beyond?

Why do we need to press this question? Because if we don't, we will easily fall prey to one (or all) of three problematic assumptions. The first is that this God Beyond can only be thought about from the perspective of the limits of our finite experience—God is beyond what we can now know here and now. The trap here is that we will project some feature of our worldly

23. For discussion, see Ward, *True Religion*.

experience inappropriately onto God, even if only by negation ("God is not changeable," "God is not physical," etc.). But what if the uncontainable God Beyond decided to meet us not at the limit of our experiences, but at the center, in order to thwart just this danger of projection? Presumably, we would need to think hard about what we were wondering at. Second, there is the assumption that we already possess an innate and intact ability to respond faithfully to this God Beyond. But what if that ability had been damaged, compromised? What if the uncontainable God Beyond needed to restore, re-create this capacity? Again, would we not need to ask questions about how apt our wonder actually is? Third, there is the assumption that this uncontainable God Beyond is an undifferentiated, uniform spirit—that for all intents and purposes, the Trinity is no more than Christian icing on a monotheistic cake, and will make no appreciable difference to the way we imagine God's uncontainability. But suppose the uncontainable God Beyond were inherently threefold, might that not do something to a wonder that claims to be theologically attuned?[24]

The irony is that all three of these assumptions have had something of a heyday in modernity. This does not in itself make them false, but we might at least ask how wise it is to resist modernity's secularity employing norms that are so basic to the modern ethos. Surveying some recent theological attempts to retrieve wonder through the arts, Matthew Milliner comments: "the underlying metaphysics assumed by such accounts still feel, to me, lingeringly modern. Which is to say that . . . such publications, brilliant as they frequently tend to be, borrow materials from previously constructed religious bridges, but do so (in my reading, at least) to modify the same wobbling, secular frame."[25]

If we *are* keen to recover wonder through the arts, then, it seems important to ask first: what kind of wonder is it that we want to promote? And to the extent we believe wonder *is* a response to the uncontainable, and, ultimately, to the uncontainability of God, we need to ask: what is distinctive about the uncontainability of the Christian God and how might this affect the way we conceive wonder? In the New Testament, I suggest, the uncontainability of the God of Jesus Christ is (whatever else it is) the uncontainability of *love-in-action*, a dynamic that belongs to the very identity and being of God, and which finds its supreme expression in the disturbing and stark figure of a crucified Messiah. In thinking about wonder, what would happen if we were attuned to this before anything else, and let our talk about

24. These common assumptions, and an associated one about divine agency in the world, are discussed at length in Begbie, *Redeeming Transcendence in the Arts*, esp. 57–76.

25. Milliner, "Enchantment of Lightning."

recovering wonder through the arts radiate out from this center? This is what I would like to explore—all too briefly—in the remainder of this essay.

The Uncontainability of Self-Giving Love, In—and By—Creation

"Thanks be to God for his inexpressible gift!" It is hard to tell precisely what Paul had in mind by "gift" here, since he has been talking about so many kinds of gift—including the giving of Christians to each other, the gift of Christ, the gift of money. But the ambiguity is surely significant, since the context makes it clear that he regards all these gifts as redolent of the generosity of the supreme Giver, God himself.

Near the start I spoke of two types of wonder, the first occurring when we are faced with something whose significance seems uncontainable, when we sense "there's more to this than meets the eye" here and now. Polish Nobel laureate Czesław Miłosz comments, "When a thing is truly seen, seen intensely, it remains with us forever and astonishes us, even though it would appear there is nothing astonishing about it."[26] In a theological register, the same sentiment is very evident in words from the Roman Catholic philosopher Jacques Maritain: "*Things are not only what they are. They ceaselessly pass beyond themselves, and give more than they have, because from all sides they are permeated by the activating influx of the Prime Cause.*"[27] And for Maritain, the arts are especially adept at bringing just this "excessive" momentum to light. Whatever hesitations we may have about Maritain's metaphysics, if the world is indeed brought into being and sustained by a God whose own life is one of eternal giving, then the notion that the things

---

26. For a recent, very engaging discussion of this quality of attention, see Miłosz, as quoted in Cording, *Finding the World's Fullness*, 27.

27. Maritain, *Creative Intuition in Art and Poetry*, 127 (my emphasis). As Trapani explains, "in the depths of its subjectivity, the Self enters into a 'mutual entanglement' with that other vast and inexhaustible sea of splendor and intelligibility, the universe of created beings and relations, things that have their own objective, independent existence. It is these that Maritain simply calls 'the Self' and 'the *Things*' ... The 'Things' are causally sustained in existence through their participation in an act-of-existing as radiated by the *Ipsum Esse Subsistens* [the self-subsisting act of existing, namely God]. Through this participation, all created beings receive not only their very existence, but their aspect of mirroring and reflecting the in-scrutable, unfathomable, and ineffable ocean of Divine Intelligibility" (Trapani, *Poetry, Beauty, and Contemplation*, 66–67). The complexities of Maritain's aesthetics are considerable and cannot be entered in detail here. While I am very sympathetic to his account of the "excess" belonging to finite particulars, I am not convinced that this is best supported by a metaphysics so strongly tied to the classical transcendentals (especially to Aquinas's understanding of beauty).

of this world "give more than they have," more than they can contain, will surely begin to ring true. For it would resonate with a kind of love that does not seek to possess, but gives and gives, and has its fullness of being *in* and *through* this giving. On this account, it is God's loving commitment to the world (as other than himself) that enables the world itself to become generative, ever *more* than it is here and now. The poet Malcolm Guite catches this well, echoing Maritain in words addressed directly to God:

> Even the things within the world you make
> Give more than all they have for they are more
> Than all they are. Gifts given for the sake
> Of love keep giving[28]

Indeed, the world's very existence can be seen in this light. Recall my Vancouver friend walking home, suddenly seized by wonder at the fact there is something rather than nothing, that there *is* a world with its own integrity but which does not contain its own explanation. The Christian may well respond, this is because the world is created by God. True enough; but there is much more to wonder at here. Indeed, if we are not careful we will easily slip into thinking of the creation of the world as no more than an act of sovereign might. In a Christian account, the world is created through a particular kind of power, power redolent of love, a love that is by its nature not possessing or enclosing but ecstatic, outgoing. Classical theology speaks of an eternal self-giving within God, a ceaseless generativity, the Father's begetting of the Son, a momentum of generating and sustaining a divine other. And it is this momentum of self-giving that has been turned "outwards" in the creation of the world. God, without need or compulsion, creates and sustains a reality that is not God but is eternally loved *by* God. Words from the poet Rod Jellema are apt here: planet earth is "a hurtling planet . . . swung from a thread / of light and saved by nothing but grace."[29] Now we can wonder at the world not merely as "nature" but as creation,[30] for it is the result of God's love-in-action, his desire to share his love with another.[31]

---

28. Guite, *Parable and Paradox*, 47.
29. Jellema, *Slender Grace of Poems*, 33.
30. For an excellent discussion of this, see Wirzba, *From Nature to Creation*.
31. Does not something of the same apply to the making of art as well? Many artists have spoken about a willingness to honor the otherness of the medium they work with, or the otherness of, say, the characters they fashion in fictional literature. In other words, there often seems to be a sort of self-dispossession in artmaking. Maritain's resistance to a certain kind of instrumentalism that circles around the artist's will is especially relevant here—as when artistic creativity is seen as essentially about the expression of inner feeling, or is driven by the desire to promote a moral virtue or spread propaganda. He insists that the making of art is opposed to any such impulse to control or manipulate

We went on to speak of God's uncontainability: the infinite God cannot be encompassed, held by the finite world. But to speak of God's infinity is not *primarily* to speak in negative terms of a quality the world does not have (the property of unboundedness), but to speak positively of a life of love, climactically revealed in Christ, that cannot be changed, diminished, or controlled by anything external to it. We recall Moses at the burning bush confronted with "I AM WHO I AM" (Exod 3:14)—this is a declaration of uncontainable freedom if ever there were one. But as the context makes clear, this is not the bare freedom of "I can do anything" but the freedom of the covenant God who will liberate Israel from slavery.[32] The wonder of Moses is the wonder of someone overawed by a positive love-in-action, by a God who will not let go of his people. The scene is wonderfully portrayed by the Israeli artist Jordana Klein, in a fire of myriad colors blazing and bursting beyond the picture frame.[33]

The point can be expanded. In the Exodus passage, God's faithfulness is not only revealed as uncontainable by the finitude of the world, but as uncontainable by the world's fallenness, by the forces of sin and death (of which slavery, of course, is one outcome). God is always more potent than whatever opposes him. Yet this is not simply the superior potency of brute dominance but the power of loving faithfulness, inexhaustible generosity. So when it comes to God's ultimate battle with evil enacted in Christ, God's goodness shows its true colors in acts that by their nature are excessively generous. Hence the surplus of wine at the wedding at Cana (John 2:1–11) when all Mary needed was a bottle or two; the promise of living water for the Samaritan woman, water that will never run dry (John 4:14); the leftovers at

---

("egoism is the natural enemy of poetical activity"); it is properly engaged "for the sake of the work" (Maritain, *Creative Intuition in Art and Poetry*, 144, 43). It is undertaken in relation to concrete realities, moving with the grain of the "stuff" encountered. In this way it can disclose and generate a form of what is already there in things, relations and dimensions otherwise inaccessible to our habitual perception. On this, see Williams, *Grace and Necessity*, ch. 1, esp. 25–31.

32. In this connection, it is worth mentioning another passage where wonder rises to the surface and is just as easy to misread. In Romans 11:33–36 Paul marvels at the ways of the God who elects. But here Paul is not, as is so often thought, celebrating an arbitrary divine will that chooses by whim, but rather the will of the covenant God whose loving desire is that both Jew and Gentile will come to belong to the people of God.

33. https://www.jordanaklein.com/product-page/burning-bush-3. In this connection, it is worth noting that our language of "presence" may well need to be rethought in this light. There is much said about "presence" in relation to the arts these days, out of a proper concern to rehabilitate wonder in the face of the uncontainable presence of God. But it is worth remembering that divine presence in Scripture is presence that makes a difference, and catches us up in transformative acts; it is not, so to speak, simply to be stared at.

the feeding of the four thousand (Mark 8:8; cp. John 6:12). God defeats evil not with an equal and opposite force, not by meeting it on its own twisted terms, but with a love that, climactically on Good Friday, reaches into its extremities and outlives it, outpowers it with an infinite surplus of goodness. And on the third day, we witness the fallen, dying matter of the body of Jesus not simply resuscitated but re-created into something beyond all calculation and expectation, a body that cannot be held (Mary is told *"Noli me tangere"*), a body of superabundant beauty: a new creation, no less. The New Testament scholar Richard Bauckham gives this eloquent poetic expression:

"Four Women and a Tomb"

After so much slow sorrow,
emptied of feeling,
drained dry of hope,
still their love led them.

At the third cockcrow
on the third morning
they gathered,
heads cloaked and baskets
weighty with fragrance.

Out of love's fullness
he poured himself, emptied,
an offering,
sweet-scented as April
in the garden of God.

That spring of all loving
that never runs dry
poured a deep draught for them,
quenching their emptiness
—an emptied tomb
and wonder, heart-whelming wonder.[34]

In this way the very idea of uncontainability is not only enlarged but set on a radically new footing, the footing of grace—what Bauckham calls "love's fullness." The same goes for the wonder it provokes. Numerous artistic possibilities for giving voice to this fullness of grace come to mind: from the lavish, coiling swirls of the ninth-century Book of Kells,[35] to the generosity

34. Unpublished poem, used by kind permission of the author.
35. https://digitalcollections.tcd.ie/concern/folios/8g84mm373?locale=en.

of an over-the-top and unexpected dinner in the film *Babette's Feast*, to the remarkable interweaving of human pain and God's extravagance in the art of Steve Prince, which typically bursts with symbolism and overshoots its own borders.[36]

We should also not miss the eschatological flavor of this excessive momentum and its implications for the arts. For things are "more than they are" at this moment in time: they are *on their way* to a future. N. T. Wright asks: "How can art, Christian art, Christian music be both utterly realistic about the appalling state the world is in and utterly hopeful about the way it will be?" Wright echoes the New Testament's resolve that a pledge of a final new creation has been ratified in Christ, and through the Spirit we can begin to share in that hope now.

> The Christian contribution to the arts must lie along the line of listening to the longing and groaning of creation, a longing which is itself multi-dimensional because it is the evidence of the Spirit's groaning and longing within the world, and expressing and portraying that longing both in its present agony and in its certain hope.[37]

A Christian celebration of the arts is thus "the sign and celebration, within the world of shame and sin and death, of the triumph of the Lamb as a past event and of the ultimate future victory of God over all the powers of evil."[38]

The Uncontainability of Love by Thought and Word

What of the second type of wonder we highlighted: when we become acutely aware of a reality that cannot be contained by our systems of representation, especially by our thought and language? This of course applies supremely to God. "Thanks be to God for his *inexpressible* gift!," writes Paul. Here of course he has language in mind, and for reasons of space, this is where we will focus our comments (bearing in mind most of what we say here about language can be said of thought as well). The word rendered "inexpressible" (*diēgētō*) has the sense of uncircumscribable, "unwraparoundable." God's generosity, his love-in-action, is ineffable, not in the sense that it is entirely unspeakable, but in the sense that it will constantly resist our idolatrous desire to encompass and grasp it in speech.

---

36. As in, e.g., "Second Line: Rebirth," https://imagejournal.org/artist/steve-prince/.
37. Wright, "They Sing a New Song."
38. Wright, "They Sing a New Song."

This pushes to the surface something that has been only implicit in what we have said so far, something especially pertinent when we are thinking about the limits of our language. Wonder, in the sense we are exploring here, can be deeply disturbing. For to be dispossessed of the notion we can get some kind of fix or "hold" on the divine is to be stripped of one of our most cherished illusions. We should thus be suspicious of theological accounts of wonder that give the impression God wants to give us an experience of uninterrupted ecstasy. To borrow words from Bernard Sawicki, if wonder really is caught up in the life of God there will be rupture as well as rapture.[39] And this is surely what we would expect of a God who wins the world back through a crucifixion as well as a resurrection. Wonder will inevitably bring some sense of God's judgment on our speech: habits of language will have to be undone, unlearned as well as relearned; indeed, it may be that at times we will simply need to be silent.

Much could be said about how the arts can be caught up in this process—at times holding at bay our compulsion to speak, at other times prizing open and holding open the language that we do use—in order that our dealings with God never become routine, humdrum, drained of wonder. Music, I suggest, is especially potent in this respect. For, to state the obvious, it is the most resistant to expression in the kind of language we use when we want to direct someone's attention to something precisely and unambiguously. Its "aboutness" is irritatingly elusive. Philosophers have long wrestled with the fact that for most of us music is profoundly meaningful yet clearly does not "mean" in the way a straightforward assertion means. It is impossible to say "this is a table" in music; or sum up "the meaning" of a song in referential speech of this sort.

There is a wealth of writing now to suggest that this is because music relies upon—and brings to our awareness perhaps more than any other art form—the inarticulate, pre-theoretical background of meanings that are entailed in inhabiting the world as embodied creatures, a background that by its very nature can never be exhaustively specified.[40] As such music can remind us not only of our rootedness in particular patterns of order in the physical world and our engagement with them, but also of the fact that the physical world we inhabit always exceeds our representations of it.

What is true of the physical world here is of course infinitely more true of God. When taken into the realm of "God-talk," music can give powerful witness to the fact that such language, even the most specific and precise we

---

39. Sawicki, "Between Rapture and Rupture."

40. Begbie, "Word Refreshed" 363–65, *et passim*. For perhaps the best known discussion of this tacit background dimension, see Polanyi, *Tacit Dimension*.

use, can never enclose or circumscribe the divine dynamic of love of which it ultimately speaks and in which it is caught up. Indeed, music can serve to hold that language open, keep at bay our inclination to think we can get a total grasp of the divine. What happens when we sing "Amazing Grace" as opposed to merely say it? What happens when J. S. Bach writes a vast fugue to plead with God: *Dona Nobis Pacem*? What happens when a Pentecostal congregation bursts into singing in tongues at the end of a hymn? Language is being opened and held open. Not repudiated,[41] but enabled to become a medium through which we are made aware of myriad dimensions of meaning surrounding these words, meanings which music—just by the way it operates—helps us sense are uncontainable, inexhaustible.[42] And insofar as that happens, I submit, wonder will never be far behind.

"Thanks be to God for his inexpressible gift!" It is no surprise that Paul's wonder slides into thanksgiving. In fact, one could say it is this more than anything else that makes Christian wonder so distinctive. Most of us cannot help falling into wonder at the sight of a rainbow. But those who are overwhelmed by the uncontainability of God's love-in-action cannot but help fall into gratitude as well.

---

41. When Paul writes "Thanks be to God for his inexpressible gift!" he could hardly be implying: "therefore never say anything about it." Inadequacy should not be confused with falsity.

42. In the example of singing in tongues I cited, the opening up of the words of the hymn will of course happen retrospectively, not concurrently.

9

The Doxological Apostle

NIJAY K. GUPTA

What does the apostle Paul have to teach us about God and wonder? The answer might seem obvious. Paul is widely acknowledged as the church's first and greatest teacher of Christian theology.[1] One cannot help, of course, but be impressed by Paul's sharp intellect, the way he argues incisively for the centrality of the self-giving death of Christ, for the beauty of the "diverse unity" of the church, for the mysterious and powerful work of the Spirit, and so forth. James Dunn has argued that the most appropriate way we should recognize the vocation and impact of Paul is through his favored term, "apostle."[2] Seeing and reading Paul through this interpretive lens is apropos because it keeps the focus on Paul's calling and mission as one whom God sent to bring the good news of Jesus Christ to the Gentiles, the nations. This helps to account for his travels to regions across the Roman Empire, to which he dispatched numerous theological letters giving comfort and exhortation to fledgling churches.

But there is a common danger in the traditional ways that Christians "use" Paul in the church throughout the centuries and today. We have a tendency to recognize Paul as a *teacher*, but perhaps at the expense of looking at the Christian lessons presented by his life and lifestyle.[3] Paul was more than

---

1. See, e.g., Dunn, *Theology of Paul*; Keck, *Christ's First Theologian*.
2. Dunn, *Theology of Paul*, xvii.
3. There are some excellent works of historical fiction that paint a picture of Paul's

only a writer. I suggest that, if we pay careful attention to Paul's epistolary writings, we catch important glimpses of Paul *as* worshipper of God. This requires us to see *behind* the ink and paper of these letters to a real, flesh-and-blood person who had a vibrant relationship with God through Jesus Christ.[4] We can look through Paul's eyes at a God worthy of our wonder and worship.

Of course, Paul offers some great teachings *about* the church's devotion to God, some formal dynamics related to how worship should be conducted in 1 Corinthians 11–12, for example. Those are important for understanding Christian worship, but that is not what I am talking about here. There are ways in which the worship *life* of Paul appears in his letters, revealing his liturgical *soul*, as it were. *That* is what I am interested in. In order to do so, we could launch right into areas in his writings where this might be evident. We will do that further below. But in order to get us thinking in fresh ways about Paul modeling worship of God, I wanted to start off with something more creative. If we use a bit of imagination, we can contemplate what it might have looked like to "follow" Paul around and see how he lived, how he carried out his ministry, and how he worshipped God in the midst of the din of life. So, I wrote a short piece of historical fiction to paint a picture of the "doxological apostle" Paul in a snapshot of "normal life," in the hustle and bustle of what might be a regular day. This hopefully offers a bit of inspiration before we open up the pages of his letters to look for Paul in praise and wondrous awe.

A Devoted Life: A Short Story from the World of Paul[5]

Aquila was intently reading a letter when he was startled by a loud knock on the door. He instinctively looked over at the door, as if he could see through it; obviously he couldn't. Before he could ask, *Who is it?*, the answer came from the other side, "It's Alexander! Get off your butt and unlock the door!" Aquila furled his brow and looked over at Priscilla, who smiled back at him, as if to say, *Have fun*. Aquila sighed and went to unlock the door.

Alexander burst in, "Aquila, my friend, what are you doing inside on a nice day like this? Stop reading, you're always reading. You need to have fun

---

life; see Wright, *Paul*, and Witherington, *Week in the Life of Corinth*.

4. The book of Acts plays an important role in shaping our understanding of Paul, but there we see Paul through the lens of Luke. My interest in this essay is seeing Paul through his own words.

5. I will not comment on the details behind some of the assumptions made about ancient worship in the narrative, because I want to keep that section free from distraction for the reader; but, for reference, see Barton, "Dislocating and Relocating Holiness"; Gupta, "'They Are Not Gods!'"; Gupta, *Worship That Makes Sense to Paul*; Hurtado, *Destroyer of the Gods*.

sometimes. Here I brought you some figs." He plopped a satchel in Aquila's hands while trying to steal a glance at what Aquila was reading. "Oh hi, Priscilla."

"Aren't you going to offer Alexander something to drink, Aquila?" Priscilla asked as she began to tidy up the room. "Yes, of course," Aquila said, in a dutiful tone. "Alexander, would you like some water? Alexander?"

Alexander was nosy, which had him wandering around the room looking at the knickknacks and decorations; he'd been here many times, but he was a curious person by nature. At this moment it wasn't a knickknack that captured his attention, but rather a person in the other room, kneeling on the ground and talking loudly.

"Who's that . . . and what is he doing?"

Aquila, realizing that his houseguest was visible, attempted a quick explanation: "That's our friend Paul. He's staying with us for a while. . . . He's loud."

"Who is he talking to?" Alexander asked, moving closer to Paul in search of another person.

Aquila explained, "He's praying; he does that a lot. Why are you here again?" ("Aquila, that's rude!" Priscilla mouthed to him.)

Alexander ignored the question at first. "Where is his god?" Alexander was looking for a statue to signal cult devotion. Paul seemed like he was just . . . talking to himself.

"We do not have images," Priscilla explained. "We pray anytime, anywhere, God hears us from heaven," she added, while pointing and looking upwards.

"Oh," Alexander grunted, clearly unimpressed. "He's one of you. I gotta say, I never would have believed it if I hadn't seen it with my own eyes. Praying without an image seems like praying to an empty room."

"Oh look, it's dinner time," Aquila interjected. "I'll see you tomorrow at the guild meeting." Aquila was moving uncomfortably close to Alexander, as if to shoo him away.

"Aquila, friend, I wanted to see if you were going to the Artemis festival."

"It's not my thing," Aquila added abruptly.

"Don't be a sourpuss. I'm not asking you to make a sacrifice. It's a party. There are dancers. They decorated the temple just for today." Alexander's tone changed from warm invitation to irritated insistence: "You're doing nothing; just come for a bit."

Aquila was obviously about to make an unconvincing excuse, when a voice blurted out: "I'll go." Everyone's heads turned to Paul, who was walking into the room. Alexander and Aquila both looked at each other with surprise. "I like this guy," Alexander said. Before Priscilla and Aquila could say goodbye, or anything else, Paul grabbed his shawl by the door and they were off.

They turned onto a main road moving towards the noise and bustle of the day's commotion.

Alexander began to make polite conversation: "Is this your first time to our great city of Ephesus? It is wonderful, no?"

"I am enjoying it very much," Paul said with a warm smile.

"Have you visited our glorious Artemis temple before? People come from all over the world to pay respect to our great divinity. Her temple is twice the size of the Parthenon! Your god lives in Israel?"

Paul wanted to correct Alexander without being impolite: "Our God doesn't live in a temple. He is Spirit and does not need a home, but you might say heaven and earth belong to him."

With a little chuckle, Alexander said, "How can you prove the glory and power of an invisible God with no palace or image? A sucker like you I could pay with invisible money! I'm kidding, my friend."

Paul wasn't offended. He had this conversation with people . . . more often than he could count.

"Alexander, how about a riddle?" Paul glanced over at him, and he winked back.

"A certain god creates a city and settles a people there. He gives them farms and a flowing river. But they forget about him and cease to worship him. He comes down to earth from the sky and appears to them as a giant. He demands worship and respect. They fear him and hide. He puts them in chains and forces them to worship him. Is this god great?"

"He is strong, but terrible." Alexander shuddered at this thought.

Paul went on.

"A certain deity was very wealthy but became cursed with a disease and was dying. He called out to a healing god, 'Save me and I will give you half of my wealth.' The healing god said, 'Give me all your wealth and I will restore you.' The deity agreed. The healing god gave him a magic seed to eat. When he swallowed it, the seed reversed the disease, but turned the deity into an ordinary mortal, an old man who was frail. Alexander, is this god great?"

"He is clever, but greedy. How many more stories do you have? They're terrible!"

"Just one more," Paul assured him.

"There was a certain village who worshipped a certain god. Let's call this god, 'Agape.' A rival being, Skotia, came to the village and told the people Agape was going to betray them. The people panicked, and Skotia offered them a deal. His protection and patronage if they pledged allegiance to him alone. They signed a pact to honor Skotia above all. But soon they realized they were duped and wanted out of this deal. Skotia said, "To break the pact, you must sacrifice one human to me." The people argued among themselves, "Who should be handed over?" No one wanted to die, so they all agreed they would pick the least important, the poorest person. There were several destitute villagers who, in their desperation, resorted to theft and murder to gain enough money to prove they were worthy. The village quickly devolved into violent chaos."

"Agape saw this commotion from heaven, had pity on the people, and executed a plan with a heavy heart. He had only one son, but his son could transform into another being, even a human. So, he sent his son, Soter, to the village as a poor slave, penniless in fact. He went to the town square and said, 'I will die.' And so they killed him to appease Skotia."

"Alexander," Paul asked, "is this god great?"

Alexander knew this third example was meant to be the correct answer, but he couldn't exactly explain why. "Paul, why would Agape do this for such an evil people?"

"Love," Paul said, matter-of-factly. There was a long silence.

"Where do you come up with such strange stories?" Alexander said, feeling a mixture of amusement, confusion, and a hint of wonder. "The gods are like emperors and princes. We serve them, they don't . . ." Alexander glanced over at Paul, but he wasn't there. Alexander had kept walking and talking, but clearly Paul had stopped. Alexander glanced back, Paul was about three meters behind him resting on his knees, arms raised to the sky.

"Oi," Alexander yelled, "what're you doing? Are you hurt?"

"I'm praying."

"Why?"

"Because God is great! His love is amazing!"

Alexander muttered to himself, "I like this guy." Then he yelled to Paul, "Get up, I smell street vendor grub. Buy me some food, and I'll listen to more of your odd stories."

"Deal. My next story involves a Jewish girl named Miriam. She was a nobody from nowhere in particular, but one day a heavenly messenger appeared to her with good news for her and for the world. . . ." As they continued walking, the great Artemis temple came into view, but Alexander didn't even notice—he was hanging on Paul's every word.

Worship and the Clash of Divinities

I am the first to admit that I am not a professional fiction writer. So, whether you found that little exercise in narrative valuable or not, I want to explain why I chose to begin in this way. My goal was to picture Paul as a worshipper in the midst of a Greco-Roman world of competing divinities and deities.

As I have already mentioned, we know Paul as apostle, writer, theologian (or artisan, prisoner, social agent, mentor, negotiator, etc.). But before he was any of these things, first and foremost he was a devotee, a worshipper. He was not a philosopher in the formal sense. The one thing that motivated the man we read in the New Testament who took responsibility for the Gentile churches was his reverence for and service to God for the sake of Jesus Christ.

Paul was a *Christianos*. We know this Greek term in translation as "Christian," and, to be honest, Paul himself didn't use this term (see Acts 11:26; 26:28; 1 Pet 4:16). After Paul's death, probably sometime towards the end of the first century CE, it came to describe a group of people, of which Paul was an important founder. What does *Christionos* mean?[6] It doesn't really identify an adherent to a religion called "Christianity." That's anachronistic. It is analogous to the terms "Herodian" (Matt 22:16) and "Nicolaitan" (Rev 2:6, 15)—someone devoted to a particular leader or deity, over and against other leaders and deities. Paul was a *Christos*-devotee.[7] As a slave of Christ, he gave himself fully to Christ. So, my story testifies to the way of Christ and the *Christianoi* over and against other cults.

Figure 7. Bartolomé Esteban Murillo, *La Conversión de San Pablo*.

6. For a robust academic analysis, see Horrell, "Label *Christianos*."
7. Caulley, "*Christianos* and Roman Imperial Cult."

We are accustomed to hearing that the Greco-Roman world was polytheistic. A typical Roman worshipped many gods, but Jews and Christians did not. This is true, but persons and communities disagreed about how those many gods should be worshipped and especially which deities should be prioritized or given higher honors.[8] Some historians use the term *megatheism* to represent the idea that there were different perspectives and formulations about which god is greatest.[9] Alexander, for example, probably thought Artemis was the greatest, or perhaps just under the highest Olympians. Paul gave this honor to his own god.

This kind of competitive theo-economics was commonplace in antiquity. Worship was not primarily understood as a set of practices such as singing songs and gathering in a temple for prayer and a message. These are forms of worship, but they are not the definition of worship. Worship was about paying a deserving god his due; serving and glorifying someone greater than yourself.[10] Worship was all about devotion—not *devotions*, like sitting at Starbucks with your copy of *Jesus Calling*—but giving allegiance to the king, taking instruction from a military commander, or doing as a father wills. Paul was hoping to convince Alexander that *his* god alone was worthy of his ultimate devotion and even his exclusive faith, just as a slave cannot have two masters (Matt 6:24).[11]

Paul was an innovator on many levels. That much is clear. He was a man of his time, of course, but he was also inspired to step outside of cultural conventions for the sake of a passion and a mission. Even his letters are innovations. Paul seems to have successfully fused the philosophical essay with the personal letter.[12] Most ancient personal letters were the length of a long paragraph or at most a page. Paul, by contrast, wrote sometimes thirty times that length. He had a lot to say. But what do all these words from the great apostle tell us about him? He taught "theology," of course. But often we miss the obvious thing staring us right in the eyes when we read his letters: his writings are first and foremost expressions of a worshipper, a devotee, a *Christianos*. Thus, his letters clearly serve as evidence of Paul's worship.[13]

---

8. See DesRosiers and Vuong, eds., *Religious Competition in the Greco-Roman World*, especially 1–10 and 11–14.

9. Bitner, "Acclaiming Artemis."

10. See Champion, *Peace of the Gods*, xi–xxv.

11. This is made explicit in Paul's letters in 1 Thessalonians 1:9–10, where he reminds the Thessalonians how they turned from (all) idols to serve one God. That this serves as a central conviction of the earliest Christians is explained and defended by Twelftree, *Gospel According to Paul*, 48–51.

12. Boring, *Introduction*, 196–97.

13. Heil, *Rituals of Worship*, 1–4.

Put another way, Paul not only talks about worship in his writings, he also *models* worship. There is so much that could be said about this, but I will limit my focus to two textual occurrences. First, we will look at his "spontaneous" liturgical and doxological moments—worship outbursts, as it were. Then we will also examine the three so-called "christological hymns" in his letters (Phil 2:6–11; Col 1:15–20; 1 Tim 3:16)—his most famous specimens of what we call "liturgy."

Spontaneous Liturgical and Doxological Moments in Paul's Letters

In at least a half dozen cases in Paul's letters, he seems to break from his argument to praise God (often capped off with a hearty "Amen!"). In the case of a text such as Romans 16:25–27, Paul offers an extended prayer that provides the context of his admiration of God. But otherwise, it appears largely extemporaneous. That is, in writing to his letter recipients, he becomes so filled with awe at the wonder of God and Christ that he cannot help but burst into exultation. You might call them "hiccups of hallelujah"!

If we had to break down those doxological moments into categories—I don't think Paul used these categories, but they might be helpful for heuristic reasons—we might create two groups. One such group involves Paul's wonder at the greatness of God's power and the grandeur of the divine plan. For example, in Romans 9:4–5, Paul recounts how God blessed Israel with the covenant and guidance in worship, and the patriarchs who led to the birth of the Messiah, "who is over all, God blessed forever. Amen." As Paul ponders how God has been at work all along to bring redemption, climactically through his Son the Messiah Jesus, he explodes with gratitude. This is an important part of Paul's most famous letter. In Romans 9–11, Paul has the difficult job of explaining how God's people, Israel, fit into the sovereign plan, as Gentiles are turning to the faith in large numbers. Paul makes it clear that God has not changed his mind. God has not given up on his people. He is making room for a larger family, grafting in Gentiles. But Israel has the special privilege of bringing forth the Messiah from *their* lineage. In the end, God's mercy and love will fall on Gentile and Jew alike, so God should be worshipped and blessed by all.[14]

In Philippians, Paul spends time at the end of the letter addressing the gift that this church sent to him during his imprisonment. Scholars sometimes refer to this as Paul's "thankless thanks,"[15] because he wants to express

---

14. See Grieb, "Paul's Theological Preoccupation in Romans 9–11."
15. Peterman, *Paul's Gift from Philippi*, 13–19.

gratitude to God but stops short of actually thanking him. However we resolve this conundrum, Paul does interpret this gift as their sacrifice of love to God, and as God's gift to Paul. In 4:19–20, Paul notes how "my God will fully satisfy every need of yours according to his riches in glory in Christ Jesus. To our God and Father be glory forever and ever. Amen!" Prisoner Paul, sitting in dark and dank confinement, remembers and recognizes the extravagant abundance of blessings that he himself knows in and through and because of Christ Jesus. What a generous God! The Philippians were wrestling with challenges including persecution (1:29–30), concerns about their friend Epaphroditus (2:26–28), as well as internal disunity (2:1–4; 4:2–3). Paul models for them hope in a God who comes through every time. Paul expresses confidence that God will "rescue" (*sōteria*) him (1:19), but that divine deliverance might not mean that he goes on living. His objective is to honor and magnify Christ, "whether by life or by death" (1:20). Paul, then, urges and exhorts the Philippians to "work out your own deliverance" (2:12, my translation), again not necessarily praying for and expecting a hand from heaven plucking them out of suffering. God has promised to attend to their needs, and they have but only to worship and to trust and to be on the lookout for amazing things.

Ephesians itself is probably the Pauline text that is closest to a formal liturgy from beginning to end, full of elevated prose that points to the grace of God. In the middle of the letter, Paul addresses the Ephesians' suffering. Much as he does with the Philippians, Paul reminds them of the riches of God's gifts and glory; here it is his gift of strength to endure and overcome in faith and perseverance (3:16–17). Paul prays for them to be filled with knowledge of the love of God and God's own fullness—such a deep experience of his empowering presence that they can see the work of God even in suffering. *God is at work, he is not dormant or absent*, Paul reminds them; *in fact, he will do even more than we ask for*, "to him be glory in the church and in Christ Jesus to all generations, forever and ever, Amen" (3:21). As Paul transitions to the next chapter, he reminds them of his imprisonment, his chains. With his hands clasped, chains rattling, he begs them to lead a life worthy of their calling, as one body, formed together by one Spirit, worshipping one Lord, with one faith and baptism (4:1–6).

One more example in this category. In 1 Timothy, towards the end, Paul records a kind of Christian virtue list for his disciple.[16] *Pursue godliness,*

---

16. There is ongoing scholarly debate about whether 1 Timothy was genuinely written by Paul. For my part, I assume some form of mediated authorship, perhaps through a friend or letter secretary. In any case, regarding the subject of this essay, the liturgical moments in 1 Timothy resonate with undisputed letters like Romans and Philippians. Therefore, I find it worthy of inclusion here; for a robust discussion of the authorship

fight the good fight, testify boldly, be found faithful until Lord Jesus Messiah returns (1 Tim 6:11–15). When will this happen? Only God knows, Paul says (6:15). But that elicits awe for Paul, as this God who is greater than our mind and plans is King of kings, Lord of lords, the immortal one who rests in the realm of holy light; he is too great for our eyes to see, let alone One who could explain to our finite minds his divine plan: "to him be honor and eternal dominion, Amen!" (6:16).

So, then, a first set of these outbursts of worship from Paul ("hiccups of Hallelujah") involve him contemplating the greatness of God in awe and wonder at his glory. Equally impactful for Paul the worshipper is the love and mercy of God. In Romans 11, Paul directs the churches in Rome to God's mission to show mercy to all (11:32). How does this work? Paul leaves it to the One whose judgments are unquestionable and whose ways are inscrutable (11:33). At the end of it all, we are all at the mercy of God. We have nothing to offer. "For from him and through him and to him are all things. To him be the glory forever. Amen" (11:36). Paul knew this divine mercy not just in theory, not merely from a distance as he observed others. Rather, he had experienced God's clemency firsthand in a powerful way, confiding to Timothy his own unworthiness. Allow me to paraphrase 1 Timothy 1:13–16:

> Jesus Christ met me as a Christian-killer, I was full of rage. But Jesus took pity on me, because I was stupid. Instead of punishing me, he dumped on me a sea of grace. Jesus came to save sinners, but it was like he was looking for the worst one, and that's me. Because if I can be saved, anyone can.
>
> Raise a toast, Timothy, to the Great King who hatched this incredible plan. Can any god or ruler compare?

To sum up, and to paint with the broadest of brushstrokes, there were two big notions that prompted Paul to seemingly spontaneous worship in his letters: the mind-blowing, imagination-expanding greatness of God—his glorious plan, his great power, his immortality, invisibility, and perfect wisdom—and also his unmatchable love demonstrated in mercy, humility, and self-giving. Of course, these things go together in Paul's mind. God's greatness is reflected in his mercy and love. His mercy and love make God all the greater.

---

question that makes room for Paul's apostolic authority and voice in 1 Timothy, see Johnson, *Constructing Paul*, 19–41.

The Pauline Odes to Jesus

I have addressed a small handful of the many interjections of doxological elation that may be found in Paul's correspondence. Here I want to talk about a few texts that played a more significant role in his letters: scholars often refer to these as Paul's *hymns*, which are poetic tributes or odes to Jesus.[17] There are three of these (Phil 2:6-11; Col 1:15-20; 1 Tim 3:16), and they give us insight into Paul's expression of worship, wonder, and awe.

Philippians 2:6–11: The Humble Son of God, Highest Lord Who Made Himself like a Slave

In the midst of Paul's instruction to the Philippians to reevaluate their understanding of power and status, he holds up Christ as the ultimate model of a proper mindset that puts God and others before self (2:5).

> Who once shined with the divine glory of God,
> But did not cling to his divine status with a tight fist,
> Instead he willingly made himself nothing
> As when one looks upon a common slave,
> So he took the humble form of a mortal.
> And just as he was found to be an ordinary human,
> Indeed he lowered himself,
> Becoming subject to the point of death—even death by shameful crucifixion.
> As a result of this obedience, God lifted him up on high,
> And bestowed upon him a superlative title,
> Such that when all hear the name Jesus,
> Every knee will bend in the heavens, on earth, and below,
> And every tongue will confess "Jesus Christ is Lord,"
> And all this will bring ultimate glory to God the Father.[18]

If one were to compare Paul's ode here to the psalms, this would be considered a type of narrative; Paul honors Christ by telling his story. Christ temporarily gave up his heavenly status and glory to obey the Father's plan to save mortals. He humbled himself and voluntarily became a victim at

---

17. Gordley, *New Testament Christological Hymns*, 3–37. I favor the concept of "ode" because in the Greco-Roman world these would reflect not only the honoring of someone, but also holding them up as an example of virtue, someone to imitate. This is clearly how Paul viewed the person of Christ. Christians could not imitate Christ perfectly, but they could aspire to "walk in his ways," that is, adopt his mindset and virtuous habits.

18. This is my own translation (Gupta, *Reading Philippians*, 50).

the hands of the humans he helped to create. The Father did not recognize Christ merely for his glorified status, but now all the more for his self-sacrificial generosity and his cruciform obedience. So Jesus Christ is given *even more* reason to be honored and worshipped. Rather than scratch and claw his way to the top of social power, like the mass of humans are wont to do, he climbed *down* the ladder of success to raise *us* up.[19] We wonder at athletic champions and the lifestyles of the rich and famous; Paul marveled at the humble grace of God.

Colossians 1:15–20: The Mystery of the Incarnation

> The Son is the image of the invisible God,
> The firstborn over all creation.
> For in him all things were created: things in heaven and on earth, visible and invisible,
> Whether thrones or powers or rulers or authorities;
> All things have been created through him and for him.
> He is before all things, and in him all things hold together.
> And he is the head of the body, the church;
> he is the beginning and the firstborn from among the dead,
> So that in everything he might have the supremacy.
> For God was pleased to have all his fullness dwell in him,
> And through him to reconcile to himself all things, whether things on earth or things in heaven,
> By making peace through his blood, shed on the cross.

In many ways the Colossian "Christ Hymn" resembles the one in Philippians. Christ is supreme, creator, preeminent one, head of church, leader of the resurrection. All this would not be hard to believe when attributed to someone called Son of God. What is unbelievable is that the *fullness* of God could dwell in a human (1:19) and that God's plan to redeem the world involved the shedding of his blood and death on a shameful cross. True peace, Paul came to understand, does not happen when one powerful group sheds the blood of the weaker group. Violence begets violence. Christ gave *himself* up. He endured the cross to make peace. Paul goes on in his letter to the Colossians to talk about how Christ's humble sufferings and afflictions teach us how to absorb suffering as part of the gospel mission (1:24). So why does Paul honor and worship Christ? Because he is great? Yes, of course. But

---

19. Hellerman, *Reconstructing Honor*, 129–56.

all the more because he proves his greatness by his willingness to suffer for us, in his sacrifice.[20]

1 Timothy 3:16: The Incarnate Son of God, Redeeming Our Flesh

In Paul's first letter to his associate Timothy, he offers a short liturgical reflection:

> who [Christ] was manifested in the flesh
> Vindicated in the Spirit
> Seen by angels
> Preached in the nations
> Believed in the world
> Lifted up in glory.[21]

The context here is Paul's exhortation for Timothy to prevent false teachers from spreading their toxic doctrines in the Ephesian church. Paul offers this short—one verse—worshipful word as a concise précis of the gospel. Like other Pauline poems, it is focused squarely on Jesus Christ, the "he" of the hymn. But unlike Philippians and Colossians, the focus of the poem is not on the death or crucifixion of Christ but the real humanity of the Savior, the Son of God who became human. Paul's point is that we should be in quiet awe, with rapt attention, witnessing the retelling of the great *humanification* of God's divine Messiah. "Manifest in body," *who could believe it?* But Christ was validated by the Spirit. The heavenly angels are witnesses of the incarnate Son of God. This testimony spread throughout the whole world—and finally he was taken up in glory. Paul's liturgy is wonder-inspiring for what it says, but I think even more so for what it does *not* say. Ancient Greco-Roman accounts of earthly visitations and divine transformations into human form begin in a similar way, but usually end with something like, *then the god Hermes transformed back into his nonhuman body.*[22] Paul says no such thing. Into the flesh he came, and in some mysterious way, a bodily being he remains, even after his ascension and reglorification. This might be the heart of the so-called "mystery of piety" that Paul talks about at the opening of this passage. We revere, we honor,

---

20. For an extended discussion of the Colossian hymn, see Gupta, *Colossians*, 51–60. More generally, on the honorable self-sacrifice of Jesus, see Gorman, *Cruciformity*, esp. 9–18.

21. This is my own translation.

22. Most famously, we have such accounts narrated in Ovid's *Metamorphoses* (e.g., Zeus and Hermes disguised as wayfarers) (see Buxton, "Metamorphoses of Gods into Animals and Humans").

we worship a divine Christ who became one of us and fundamentally transformed the human category in his unique humanity. He became like us, so that we could become like him (so Irenaeus famously put it). That doesn't make us divine, but it does secure hope that God will see mortals through to redemption for the sake of his Son Jesus Christ.[23]

Conclusion

Christians have historically looked to Paul as the great doctor of our faith. And he is, but there is much to see when we look at Paul through the lens of worshipper, a model of praise, awe, homage, and wonder. When we search his writings for key moments of worship, we find many: some lengthy and formal, and others as doxological interjections.

Like his peers throughout the Greco-Roman world, Paul wondered at the grandeur and supremacy of the divine, the realm above and beyond our often myopic minds and eyes. But I think what *really* brought Paul to his knees—what produced tears in his eyes, what put a song in his heart and pen—is the compassion, humility, and self-sacrifice of Jesus Christ: who emptied himself and became like a slave; who shed his own precious blood for us, who crossed over into our realm of body and flesh—an unprecedented and unfathomable act in Paul's world.

Paul seems to have stopped almost every time his mind and heart pondered the goodness and generosity of God, and this happened a lot. There is something we can learn here from Paul. He witnessed constantly to a God worthy of praise. When we read his letters, may we be inspired by a pensive apostle, by a thankful apostle, by a testifying apostle, and yes, by a doxological apostle.

---

23. My friend, the theologian Javier Garcia, reminded me recently of this poignant affirmation by Dietrich Bonhoeffer: "God changes God's form into human form in order that human beings can become, not God, but human before God" (*Ethics*, 96).

10

The Wonder of Cinema in Dorothy L. Sayers and Spike Lee

CRYSTAL L. DOWNING

> The function of imagination is not to make strange things settled, so much as to make settled things strange; not so much to make wonders facts as to make facts wonders.
>
> —G. K. CHESTERTON, *THE DEFENDANT*

At the beginning of the Word we read "In the beginning God," and proceed to discover that God spoke creation into existence: the word is creative. Furthermore, rather than declaring or pronouncing creation to be "good," God sees that it is already good: forms of the phrase "God saw that it was good" are repeated seven times in the first chapter of Genesis. It would seem that the Creator of the Universe reveled in the wonder of creation. The culmination of God's creative wonder appears in verse 27: "So God created humankind in his image, in the image of God he created them, male and female he created them."[1] Inspired by this celebration of the *imago Dei*—Latin for *the image of God*—I wish to explore how the goodness of creation applies to one of the most influential modes of creation in our era, cinema, which relies

---

1. Scripture quotations are from the NRSV.

upon seeing. Laying the theoretical groundwork for my discussion will be a person C. S. Lewis identified as one of the four most important influences on his spiritual life, Dorothy L. Sayers, whose theology of creativity I will illustrate with the cinematic wonders of Spike Lee. As one of the preeminent African American filmmakers living today, Lee powerfully illustrates that Black lives matter because creation matters.

Spike Lee's birth in 1957 preceded the death of Dorothy L. Sayers by a mere nine months. Herself born to an Anglican clergyman in 1893, Sayers graduated with honors from Oxford University, where, though never renouncing her Christian faith, she tended to compartmentalize it. Establishing her reputation in the 1920s as the creator of best-selling detective fiction, Sayers made her amateur sleuth Lord Peter Wimsey decidedly *not* Christian, having him value the artistic wonder of church architecture and music rather than its content. Her fame intensified in 1930 when she became one of the founding members of London's prestigious Detection Club, along with G. K. Chesterton and Agatha Christie.

Then, in 1936, Sayers's spiritual life started to change. Invited to follow in the footsteps of T. S. Eliot by writing a play for performance in Canterbury Cathedral, she found herself questioning how she could integrate her vocation as a best-selling author with Christianity. Her Wimsey-like wonder over the cathedral's majestic beauty, constructed in celebration of the Creator, caused her to contemplate the relationship between theology and the arts. The end result, a 1937 play called *The Zeal of Thy House*, helped ignite a book several years later called *The Mind of the Maker*: an exploration of the wonder of creation that C. S. Lewis considered "indispensable."[2]

Aiding her "Christian aesthetic," as Sayers came to call it, was Scripture.[3] Because the opening chapter of the Bible describes God as a Creator, Sayers argues that humans most fully reflect God's image, the *imago Dei* announced in Genesis 1:27, through their own creativity. After all, God in that chapter is not presented as a judge, not as a lawgiver, not as a redeemer: the God in whose image we are made is a maker. Those attuned to Scripture must therefore pay attention to the fact that God pronounces as "good" creations that are other to God's own self—from the sun and seas to plants and people. The fall, in fact, occurs when Adam and Eve choose to put self above the God-commanded otherness of "the tree that is in the middle of the garden" (Gen 3:3). Significantly, the serpent's temptation, "you will be like God," warps God's actual word, wherein male and female are created

---

2. Lewis, *Miracles*, 101.
3. Sayers, "Towards a Christian Aesthetic."

"in the image of God," not divinely "like God." Elevating self to the status of God, Adam and Eve got what they asked for: to fend for themselves.

But God so loved the world that he gave his only begotten Son to bring us back to the garden (John 3:16). Not coincidentally, John begins his Gospel by echoing the beginnings of Genesis: "In the beginning was the Word, and the Word was with God, and the Word was God. He was in the beginning with God. All things came into being through him, and without him not one thing came into being." The wonder of creation, in other words, is at the beginning of Christian belief, inseparable from the light of the world. Indeed, John mirrors the beginning of Genesis, "'Let there be light,' and there was light" (1:3), when he says of Christ, "in him was life, and the life was the light of all people" (1:4). John's words, of course, influenced the centuries-long development of trinitarian doctrine, which establishes that otherness is inherent to God's very nature, for God is three persons in one substance.

Overwhelmed with the wondrous profundity of trinitarian doctrine, Sayers argues that because the Maker of the universe is triune, human making is triadic as well. Mirroring the Creator God—Father, Son, and Holy Spirit—the *imago Dei* is fulfilled through an interdependence among what Sayers calls Creative Idea, Creative Energy, and Creative Power. To illustrate this construct she gives the example of writing a book. Creative Idea correlates to a book as it is first conceptualized; Creative Energy aligns with the process of writing the book, of incarnating the Idea with the *word* on the page. Creative Power, then, is the book's effect on the reader, the first of which is the author herself.[4] As all earnest writers know, essential to effective composition is reading back what one has already written in order to assess its power. Through the Energy of revising, the author's original Idea continues its incarnation, moving from a Bethlehem of thought to a triumphal entry of expression that generates Power. The three are one in the act of creation. Once the book is published, the Power spreads to more and more people, much as the Holy Spirit touched people with tongues of fire after Christ's ascension: tongues, of course, associated with the wonder of new words.

Though Sayers exemplifies "trinitarian" creativity using her own experience as an author, she makes clear that the *imago Dei* applies to all the arts. I have viewed with wonder, for example, the creative process of Christian painter Catherine Prescott, whose award-winning portraits have been selected for exhibition by the Smithsonian's National Portrait Gallery

---

4. Sayers, *Mind of the Maker*, 38–41.

in Washington, DC.[5] Whenever I visited her studio in central Pennsylvania, where she and I were colleagues at Messiah College, she would tell me how she got the Idea for her current portrait, showing me the photographs she took to energize her Idea as she incarnated it on canvas. While explaining her work, she would often extend a finger to the painting in order to point out something she decided to change, her Idea taking new form due to the Power of her viewing eye. It reminds me of Michelangelo's depiction of the Creation on the ceiling of the Sistine Chapel: God's finger reaches out to the extended hand of the reclining Adam, whose body, though created, looks limp, as though needing Energy. And framing God like a halo is an audience of angels, viewing the Power—we might call it the *wonder*—of God's creative act.

In Sayers's terms, Michelangelo thus reflects his own understanding of the creative process: his Idea for the image, his Energy painting it, and his own viewing of its Power as he paints it. The Creative Power of Michelangelo's work then spreads through the world as millions of viewers crook their necks back to stare in wonder at the Sistine ceiling. The Power they feel reflects, if even in a glass darkly, the power felt in the upper room at Pentecost when the Spirit came as a mighty wind. But first, the Power was felt by the creator Michelangelo, viewing and shaping his painting until he "*saw*" that it was "good."

Making painters key to several of her novels, Sayers asserts that the "idea of art as creation"—in fulfillment of the *imago Dei*—is "the one important contribution that Christianity has made to aesthetics."[6] Unfortunately, it is a contribution that Protestants have tended to marginalize. Believing that faith should be guided solely by truths communicated in the Bible, many early Protestants repudiated the wonders of human creation, as when troops representing Henry VIII rode their horses into centuries-old monasteries and destroyed works of beauty. Granted, the destruction was politically motivated, Henry VIII wanting to remove signs of Roman Catholicism from England after the pope denied his divorce from Katherine of Aragon. And, granted, many pre-Reformation Catholics did indeed seem to worship human creations more than the Creator of the universe. Nevertheless, British Puritans a century later went even further than Henry in their destruction of human creations. They not only shut down theaters, including Shakespeare productions, but also destroyed church beauty, painting over Bible-inspired frescoes with whitewash. To this day, you can visit tiny churches along the

---

5. See www.prescottpaintings.com.
6. Sayers, "Towards a Christian Aesthetic," 61.

Welsh-English border and see where brilliant colors are slowly reappearing as the Puritan whitewashing gradually erodes.

The Puritans who ruled England from 1649 to 1660 outlawed creative celebrations of Christmas, prohibiting Christmas caroling as well as wreaths placed on doors. Seeking to set an example for all Protestants, Puritan leaders during the interregnum even held Parliament on December 25.[7] Ironically, then, one of the most famous fictional creations in the English language, Charles Dickens's Scrooge, was not that unusual in his demand that Bob Cratchit work on Christmas Day; Scrooge was merely maintaining a practice that had been instituted by earnest Christians seeking to purify the faith centuries earlier. It's no wonder that an essay about Dickens published in 1903 was titled "The Man Who 'Invented' Christmas," by which the author meant a celebration freed from Puritan restrictions: a celebration of family and creativity.[8]

That same year, Edwin S. Porter created the first narrative film to be produced in America: *The Great Train Robbery* (1903). And Protestants have tended to ignore the artistry of cinema ever since. Reducing film to a "content delivery system," theologians write books emphasizing Christian concepts that can be extracted from movies while marginalizing the wonders of camera work and film editing.[9] In Sayers's terms, such approaches disregard the incarnational Energy of creation, since, as she puts it, "the *visible* structure of the work belongs to the son [sic]."[10] Perhaps not coincidentally, Sayers tried her hand at screenwriting before establishing her reputation as the creator of Lord Peter Wimsey, and she socialized with people in the film industry while she was conceptualizing *The Mind of the Maker*. She clearly recognized that creativity on the screen synthesizes Idea (as conceived by screenwriters and directors) with Energy (as incarnated through filming and editing), the finished work generating the Power of creative reflection in receptive viewers. The initial viewers, of course, are the writers, producers, director, and actors who watch the "rushes" or "dailies"—the unedited product shot each day—in order to make changes in their work: Idea, Energy, and Power all engaged in the wonder of creation. Whether the filmmakers are Christians or not is beside the point. Sayers asserts that even atheists who are committed to what she calls "the integrity of the work" have experienced the threefold nature of creativity.[11] In other

---

7. Parker, *Christmas and Charles Dickens*, 46.
8. Parker, *Christmas and Charles Dickens*, 14–16.
9. Downing, *Salvation from Cinema*, 24.
10. Sayers, *Mind of the Maker*, 162 (emphasis mine).
11. Sayers, *Mind of the Maker*, 223, 224, 225.

words, their experience of creation endorses the wonder of Christian truth even if filmmakers don't, their work illustrating that *all* humans are created in the image of a triune Creator.

Of course, many created works, especially in the realm of cinema, do not fulfill the *imago Dei*. This is due to what Sayers calls "Scalene Trinities," by which she means an imbalance wherein one of the three components—Idea, Energy, or Power—is either overemphasized or overlooked.[12] She compares such imbalances to heresies that have marred Christianity for millennia. The Arian heresy, for example, developed among earnest Christians who used Scripture to argue that Jesus was not co-eternal with God the Father. After all, the apostle Paul told the Colossians that Jesus was "the first *born* of all creation" (Col 1:15), not a participant in the *making* of creation. Because Arians overemphasized the humanity of Jesus, Sayers coined the term "artistic Arianism" to describe a creative work that is all Energy with no recognizable Idea: "all technique and no vision," as she puts it.[13] Cinematic examples are legion, apparent in movies that offer little more than spectacularly impressive CGI, jaw-dropping special effects, breathtaking settings, and/or stunning costuming while providing nary an original thought about human nature. In such Arian movies, truths about existence are limited to artificial notions of right versus wrong, *right* usually aligned with protagonists' choices, *wrong* with those of their antagonists.

The opposite extreme, according to Sayers, is all Idea with little attention to artistic excellence, which she aligns with "propaganda novelists and dramatists."[14] In an essay written while *The Mind of the Maker* was going to press, in fact, Sayers gives the example of movies made by puritanical Christians who seem to assume that an evangelistic message is all that matters. Arguing that "God is not served by technical incompetence," Sayers states,

> The worst religious films I ever saw were produced by a company which chose its staff exclusively for their piety. Bad photography, bad acting, and bad dialogue produced a result so grotesquely irreverent that the pictures could not have been shown in churches without bringing Christianity into contempt.[15]

Sayers aligns such Christian disregard for the Energy of creation with Manichaeism, a heresy that attracted Augustine for many years. Inspired by a third-century Persian prophet named Mani (or Manes), Manichees

---

12. Sayers, *Mind of the Maker*, ch. 10.
13. Sayers, *Mind of the Maker*, 173.
14. Sayers, *Mind of the Maker*, 173.
15. Sayers, "Why Work?" 80.

(as Sayers spells it) believed in a cosmic battle between darkness and light, aligning matter with darkness and spirit with the light. Augustine admits his attraction to Manichaeism in his *Confessions*, telling God,

> there are certain people who don't like your works, and they say that you made many of them, such as the framework of the sky and the arrangements of the stars, under the force of necessity; . . . They say that there are other things you didn't make or even assemble, such as all animate creatures, including the tiniest living things and whatever clings to the earth with its roots. Rather, they say, a consciousness at war with you, an alien essence not created by you, but opposed to you, gives birth to and shapes these things in the lower regions of the world.[16]

Since, for Manichees, matter was created by an essence at war with God, the concept that God would enter the world through the medium of flesh was outrageous.

Sayers, in contrast, emphatically argues that matter matters for Christians. As she explained in a radio broadcast that aired several weeks after *The Mind of the Maker* was published,

> The Church does *not* say that matter is evil, nor that the body is evil. For her very life, she dare not. For her whole life is bound up in the doctrine that God Himself took human nature upon Him and went about this material world as a living man, with a human body and a human brain, and that he was perfect and sinless in the body as out of the body, in time as in eternity, in earth as in heaven. That is her creed; that is her dogma; that is the opinion to which she stands committed.[17]

Those who ignore, if not deny, this creed often end up reinforcing Manichaean dualism.

There is another, perhaps even more disturbing, Manichaean battle between light and darkness that has warped Christianity over the centuries. In *The Civil War as a Theological Crisis*, Mark Noll exposes how nineteenth-century Christians, in both the North and the South, argued that the intellectual "elites" who supported the abolition of slavery were "unbiblical."[18] Seeming to align goodness with light skin and evil with darkness, defenders of slavery treated racialized Black persons as not fully human, as though their matter did not matter.

---

16 Augustine, *Confessions*, 474–75.
17. Sayers, "Sacrament of Matter," 40.
18. Noll, *Civil War*, 49, 115.

Lest this sound far-fetched let me share an experience from well over a century later. In the 1980s, my husband and I visited a college friend, fresh out of seminary, who had accepted his first pastorate in a southern state. He told us how the church welcomed him with open arms, making him meals and bringing him gifts. Though joyfully decorating their church for the Christmas holidays, his congregants balked when he, their blonde-haired, blue-eyed pastor, suggested they should invite local African Americans to their services. Telling him such actions were "unbiblical," they proceeded to quote from the first chapter of Genesis: "And God separated the light from the darkness" (v. 4)—a Manichaean justification of segregation if there ever was one.

Sayers, in contrast, repeatedly denounces the Manichaean heresy in her writings, believing that all of God's creation matters. In 1953 she actually wrote an essay asserting that different races and ethnicities display "a variety in the human race that ought to be pleasing and interesting," going so far as to denounce the "fear and disgust" many people have toward "difference" as "evil." Having lived during the Nazi Holocaust, she felt especially sensitive about this issue, arguing that "the minute we begin to despise and dislike another man, who has offered us no injury, simply and solely because he is 'foreign'—if we start off with a prejudice against him because he is a Jew or a Turk or a South Sea Islander . . .—then we are letting difference become division," which, she suggests, is Satan's primary goal.[19]

Surely adding to Sayers's distress was the way that those demonized by Manichaean readings of the Bible were also denied support for their creativity, thus eliminating them from participation in the *imago Dei*. Once again, examples are legion. In 1938 a firm wanting to produce the first German translation of *The Hobbit* wrote Tolkien asking if he was Aryan, implying that his creative matter did not matter if he was tainted by Jewish blood. Incensed, Tolkien replied, "If I am to understand that you are enquiring whether I am of Jewish origin, I can only reply that I regret that I appear to have no ancestors of that gifted people." And he proceeds to tell his agent to "let a German translation go hang," explaining, "I have many Jewish friends, and should regret giving any colour to the notion that I subscribed to the wholly pernicious and unscientific race-doctrine."[20] Not coincidentally, Tolkien's idea of art as "sub-creation" parallels Sayers's sense of the *imago Dei*.[21] As far as both were concerned, all humans should be encouraged to exercise their creativity, because all humans are created in God's image. Human creation, in both senses, matters to God.

---

19. Sayers, "Is there a Definite Evil Power?," 49, 51.
20. Carpenter, ed., *Letters of J. R. R. Tolkien*, 37–38.
21. Tolkien, "On Fairy-Stories," 67.

Americans, of course, reflected Manichaean attitudes about race and creativity long before the Nazis did. In 1903, the same year that Dickens was celebrated as "the man that invented Christmas" and Porter was celebrated as the inventor of narrative cinema in America, Crayola developed a box of forty crayons in which a pinky beige color carried the name "flesh" on its paper wrapper. Dark skin, the crayon implied, is not really *human* flesh—an implication that lasted until Crayola changed the color's name to peach in 1963, six years after Sayers died. Fortunately, despite constant reiteration that their matter does not matter, African Americans continued to revel in the wonder of creativity, fulfilling the *imago Dei* despite attempts to suppress it. There are, of course, many breathtaking examples of Black creativity and of the racism it had to surmount, but I'll give one lesser known creation before moving on to the wonders of Spike Lee. In 1947, the same year Sayers published her lecture titled "Towards a Christian Aesthetic," the first African American comic book was "created," to use a reviewer's apt word, "by an all-Black staff." Though their work was a "ground-breaking success," the Black comic-book creators were unable to produce a second issue because "white paper mill owners refused to sell [them] the pulp needed to print the comics."[22] Their creation, it seems, did not matter.

Examples like these heighten the integrity of artists such as Spike Lee. I say this because the understandable temptation of unjustly marginalized people is to perpetuate Manichaean binaries by inverting them, such that darkness repudiates the light. I first thought about this when I encountered the work of postcolonial theorist and Harvard professor Homi Bhabha, a Parsi born in India, who grapples with the racism that has wracked both India and the Americas. But rather than denounce colonial oppressors, he writes, "Must we always polarize in order to polemicize? . . . Can the aim of freedom of knowledge be the simple inversion of the relation of oppressor and oppressed, centre and periphery, negative image and positive image?"[23]

These seem to be the same questions asked by Spike Lee, whom I consider to be a Shakespeare of the silver screen. Recognizing that not all of Shakespeare's plays are great works of art, I would say the same about Lee's films. Nevertheless, both dramatists, at their best, refuse to endorse Manichaean dualism. In *The Merchant of Venice*, Shakespeare subtly challenges the anti-Semitic assumptions of his day about a villainously greedy Jew when he has Shylock deliver that heartrending speech, "Hath not a Jew eyes, / Hath not a Jew hands, organs, dimensions, senses, affections, passions?" (Act 3 Sc 1). In other words, Shylock's created matter matters.

22. Stapinski, "Superheroes."
23. Bhabha, "Commitment," 2353.

Shakespeare's Hamlet, one of the most famous creations in the history of literature, explicitly questions clear-cut Manichaean distinctions between good and evil. Unlike the despicably self-serving politician in *Richard III* to whom Shakespeare gives the line "Conscience is but a word that cowards use" (Act 5 Sc 3), Hamlet delivers the more sensitive line, "Conscience doth make cowards of us all" (Act 3 Sc 1). In other words, doing the right thing is not always self-evident and clear cut.

Significantly, *Do the Right Thing* (1989) is the title of the movie that many consider to be Spike Lee's first work of cinematic wonder. The film refuses a simplistic polarizing inversion of white racism. Instead, it establishes pluralism within an African American neighborhood in Brooklyn, showing strengths and weaknesses in both traditionalists and rioters, community protectors and self-promoters, women demanding attention and men seeking to escape them, the friendly white owner of a pizzeria and his obnoxiously racist son. Furthermore, Lee has African Americans themselves make racially insensitive comments about Italians, Koreans, and Jews.

Rather than making a Manichaean propaganda film, Lee reflects the wonder of Sayers's trinitarian aesthetic. As recounted in his production journal, his original concept involved a Black neighborhood responding to oppressive summer heat, but the plan started to change in the process of composition: "It's funny how the script is evolving into a film about race relations."[24] In Sayers's terms, his Idea was enhanced by the Energy of composition. Of course, Lee's race affected the way he saw reality, just as C. S. Lewis's faith affected the way he presented truth. Lewis didn't start out writing *The Lion, the Witch and the Wardrobe* in order to evangelize others; instead the Idea of "a Faun carrying an umbrella and parcels in a snowy wood" ignited his creativity.[25] But because Lewis was Christian, his narrative evolved into a story about a Christlike lion. Both Lewis and Lee illustrate Sayers's assertion that "the creator's love for his work is not a greedy possessiveness; he never desires to subdue his work to himself but always to subdue himself to his work. The more genuinely creative he is, the more he will want his work to develop in accordance with its own nature, and to stand independent of himself."[26]

Spike Lee implies the independence of *Do the Right Thing* from his own "greedy possessiveness" through the less than admirable character he plays in the film: Mooky, a pizza deliveryman motivated by self-interest. We see one of Mooky's flaws as he insouciantly walks over a little girl's chalk

---

24. Quoted in Bordwell et al., *Film Art*, 410.
25. Lewis, "It All Began with a Picture," 42.
26. Sayers, *Mind of the Maker*, 130.

drawing in the street: a visual symbol of how little he cares for the toddler son he has sired. His main concerns seem to be receiving sexual gratification from Tina, the toddler's mother, and getting his paycheck from Sal, the pizzeria owner. When Sal uses a racial slur during an argument with Black customers, Mooky takes action by throwing a garbage can through the window of the pizzeria, which instigates a riot that sets fire to Sal's twenty-five-year-old establishment, a restaurant beloved by both whites and Blacks. Significantly, Lee splices together two takes of the can-throwing shot, as though to highlight two ways viewers might see the action: either as a necessary revolt from the evils of racism, or as a futile act of violence that exacerbates racial tensions. The visual matter of the film matters.

Do the Right Thing thus embodies words Homi Bhabha published the exact same year (1989): "the agents of political change [are] discontinuous, divided subjects caught in conflicting interests and identities."[27] To throw or not to throw, that is the question. Reinforcing the dilemma is a character in the movie who wanders through the neighborhood attempting to sell two different pictures of Black leaders: one of Martin Luther King Jr., a promoter of peaceful protest, the other of Malcolm X, an advocate of revolutionary violence. Both agents of change, they represent the conflicting interests and identities of Mooky, who, like Shakespeare's Hamlet, wonders

> Whether 'tis nobler in the mind to suffer
> The slings and arrows of outrageous fortune,
> Or to take arms against a sea of troubles,
> And by opposing end them? (Act 3 Sc 1)

Which choice is the "right thing"?

Significantly, Spike Lee ends *Do the Right Thing* by scrolling quotations from Malcolm X and Dr. King that argue opposite positions. The film then ends *not* with separate photographs of each, but with a picture of Malcolm X and Dr. King together shaking hands. As the authors of *Film Art* summarize, "the implication is that each position is viable under certain circumstances."[28] Like the truths of Christianity, the answer is both/and, much as Jesus often models the both/and of truth. He tells the rich young man that the only way to eternal life is through selling all his possessions and following him (Matt 19:16–21), but he tells Nicodemus that salvation is only a matter of belief (John 3:1–21). And Christ's apostles similarly reinforce the both/and of truth. Paul tells the Ephesians that salvation is a gift, "not the result of works, so that no one may boast" (2:9), but James makes

---

27. Bhabha, "Commitment," 2363.
28. Bordwell et al., *Film Art*, 411.

clear that "faith by itself, if it has no works, is dead" (2:17). It is both/and, like our Savior, who is both fully human and fully divine. Most heresies, in fact, reflect either/or thought, like that of Manichaean and Arian Christians.

Spike Lee thus illustrates what Sayers argues in *The Mind of the Maker*: "material creation expresses the nature of the Divine Imagination."[29] Significantly, Lee answered the question "Do you believe in God?" with "Yes. I have faith that there is a higher being. All this cannot be an accident."[30] Notice how he affirms the idea of a transcendent Creator due to the wonder of creation. As Sayers explains in *The Mind of the Maker*, "This experience of the creative imagination . . . in the artist is the only thing we have to go upon in entertaining and formulating the concept of creation."[31] Indeed, Lee sees all genuine creation as good and not just in cinema that exposes the evils of racism, as many of his films do. When he lists his favorite movies, he includes great works from Old Hollywood, including multiple films by Elia Kazan: *A Streetcar Named Desire* (1951), *On the Waterfront* (1954), and *A Face in the Crowd* (1957). Though Kazan's testimony at the McCarthy hearings ended the careers of some Hollywood creators, whom Kazan accused of Communist sympathies, Spike Lee recognizes, like Sayers, that "the integrity of the work" speaks louder than the worker. When confronted in an interview about his love for the work of Kazan, Lee responded, "Maybe what he did was wrong, but I can make that separation between the man and his work."[32] Sayers did something similar in the play that changed her life.

In *The Zeal of Thy House*, Sayers develops a story around the character of an actual historical figure: the architect who rebuilt part of Canterbury Cathedral after it was destroyed by fire in the twelfth century. Named William of Sens, Sayers's character starts taking his own creativity too seriously, making himself equal with his Creator by saying, "This church is mine / And none but I, not even God, can build it."[33] As with Adam and Eve in the garden of Eden, William considers himself "like God" rather than "in the image of God." And Sayers symbolizes his fall with a literal fall from scaffolding as he places the keystone into an arch. Only after being crippled by his fall does William recognize and confess his sin of pride, saying something that anticipates Spike Lee's comment about separating Elia Kazan from his work. William states, "let my work, all that was good in me, / All that was God, stand up and live and grow. / The work is sound, Lord God, no rottenness

---

29. Sayers, *Mind of the Maker*, 42.
30. Papamichael, "Getting Direct," sixth question.
31. Sayers, *Mind of the Maker*, 42.
32. Papamichael, "Getting Direct," eighth question.
33. Sayers, *Zeal*, 68.

there—/ Only in me." Sayers even has a godly prior confirm this view, saying "all the truth of the craftsman is in his craft. / Where there is truth, there is God; and where there is glory, / There is God's glory too."[34] The wonder of art cannot be judged by the sins of the artists, "since all have sinned and fall short of the glory of God" (Rom 3:23).

Separating, like Sayers, the sins of the maker from the wonders of the made, Spike Lee has been criticized for his support of white artists accused of sins far more egregious than those of Kazan. In June of 2020 he said of filmmaker Woody Allen, accused of child abuse, "Allen is a great, great filmmaker and this cancel thing is not just Woody.... I don't know that you can just erase somebody like they never existed. Woody's a friend of mine. I know he's going through it right now."[35] Because he refuses to endorse Manichaean cancel culture, wherein one side is in the right and the other must be destroyed, Lee has been excoriated on social media. Significantly, something similar happened to the philosopher who most influenced Homi Bhabha: Jacques Derrida. Even though Derrida was expelled from school in 1942 because he was a Jew, he later defended his friendship with a literary critic who had "once written anti-Semitic articles for the Nazi-controlled press in Belgium."[36] Not coincidentally, Derrida is most famous for his work on deconstruction, which advocates both/and thinking rather than either/or views of truth. In fact, Derrida defined deconstruction as "openness toward the other,"[37] an openness we see modeled by our triune Creator.

Lee communicates openness to the other by including clips from and/or allusions to the history of cinema into his own films. Perhaps the most stunning example appears in *BlacKkKlansman* (2018), which dramatizes historical Ku Klux Klan activities in Colorado Springs during the 1970s. Interspersed throughout the movie are clips from D. W. Griffith's film about the American Civil War, *The Birth of a Nation* (1915), which is considered not only one of the most artistically advanced films since Porter's *The Great Train Robbery* (1903), but also one of the most racist; its sympathy with the Confederate cause reignited KKK activities in America. By including clips from the controversial film, Spike Lee suggests that cinema itself can be both/and, reflecting the wonder of creation and the sins of humanity. *The Birth of a Nation* is thus part of Lee's identity, for he has been shaped not only by the great cinematic art that preceded him, but also by the racism that it perpetuated. The "other" defines him in more ways than one.

34. Sayers, *Zeal*, 99, 59.
35. Quoted in Aquilina, "Spike Lee defends Woody Allen," para. 2.
36. Derrida defends his friendship with Paul de Man in "Like the Sound," 590–652.
37. Quoted in Kearney, ed., "Dialogue with Jacques Derrida," 124.

Spike Lee, in fact, explores the "other" in one of his most respected films: *Da 5 Bloods* (2020). While exposing the racism encountered by African Americans who fought in Viet Nam, the film also alludes to war movies that shaped Lee's sensibilities as a filmmaker, as though agreeing with a statement Sayers makes in *The Mind of the Maker*: "each new work should be a fresh focus of power through which former streams of beauty, emotion, and reflection are directed."[38] For example, Lee readily admits the influence of Francis Ford Coppola's *Apocalypse Now* (1979): a famous movie about the Viet Nam War that itself was a "fresh focus of power" through which flow streams generated by Joseph Conrad's controversial novel *The Heart of Darkness* (1899). *Da 5 Bloods* also intentionally echoes shots and/or scenes from *The Treasure of the Sierra Madre* (1948), John Huston's classic film, as well as David Lean's Oscar-winning movie about World War II, *The Bridge on the River Kwai*, released the year Spike Lee was born and Sayers died.

Significantly, like *The Bridge on the River Kwai*, which shows enemies collaborating to build a bridge, *Da 5 Bloods* defies a simplistic Manichaean binary of good versus evil. In the film, four Black veterans return to Viet Nam forty years after their service. Their plan is not only to retrieve the corpse of their platoon leader, the fifth of the "bloods" as they call themselves, but also to find treasure that they had buried: gold bars the CIA intended to give the Lahu people as payment for their help fighting the Viet Cong. There are thus several kinds of burial in the film: unearthing not only a buried treasure along with a beloved commander's corpse, but also the protagonists' awareness of their own complicity with racism. By appropriating payment that was promised to another race, the Black veterans ironically echo the unfulfilled promise given to freed slaves after the Civil War: a promise of forty acres and a mule.[39] Though naming his independent film company "Forty Acres and a Mule" in acknowledgement of the racism that still mars America, Spike Lee displays both/and complexity through the Energy of his visual structure. For example, the four veterans who return to Viet Nam to find their blood brother are played by the same actors both in the present and in flashback scenes. Unlike most movies with flashbacks, however, Lee uses no makeup or CGI to make the sixty-something actors look forty years younger. As a result we are constantly aware of the characters' both/and nature: we see each as both young and old, both callow and mature, both victim and victimizer.

I borrow the words *victim* and *victimizer* from another artistic production about war: a play called *The Just Vengeance* (1946) by Dorothy L.

---

38. Sayers, *Mind of the Maker*, 121.
39. See Gates, "Truth Behind '40 Acres and a Mule.'"

Sayers. Written not long after the end of World War II, a war that seems to warrant clear-cut distinctions between good and evil more than any other in modern history, Sayers refuses to reduce human behavior to Manichaean binaries. Instead, her script focuses on an airman who, after being killed by the Nazis, finds himself in a type of limbo, where he agonizes over his complicity with the death of innocent people:

> We drop a bomb
> And condemn a thousand people to sudden death,
> The guiltless along with the guilty. Or we refuse
> To drop a bomb, and condemn a thousand people
> To a lingering death in a concentration camp.[40]

To drop the bomb or not to drop the bomb: that is the question. Sayers proceeds to call this wartime dilemma "the injustice of justice,"[41] and she situates this paradox in the truth of Scripture, having a company of the dead perform a play for the airman that leads him through Scripture to the paradox of Christ's both/and nature. Fully human and fully God, Jesus was unjustly crucified, yet justified all sinners through the resurrection. And Sayers suggests that all of us, created in God's image, are both/and as well, if even in a different way. As a character in *The Just Vengeance* puts it,

> Do not you all
> Suffer with Abel and destroy with Cain,
> Each one at once the victim and the avenger
> Till Cain is Abel, being condemned for Abel,
> And Abel Cain, in the condemning of Cain?[42]

Those same words could apply to the double nature of the characters in *Da 5 Bloods*: each is both just and unjust, both old and young, both Cain and Abel.

How then do we live with this paradox? Sayers provides an answer through her play within the play when the performer playing Jesus proclaims before his death, "there is no justice in the Gospel, / There's only love," and, after his resurrection, "Instead of your justice, you shall have charity."[43] Spike Lee makes a similar point, not only showing the veterans praying over the remains of their beloved leader in Viet Nam, but also including Marvin Gaye's "God Is Love" in the musical score. More importantly, he ends *Da 5 Bloods* with acts of love and charity. In a montage of shots that closes the film, we see the veterans back in their hometowns, giving away treasure they

---

40. Sayers, *Just Vengeance*, 288.
41. Sayers, *Just Vengeance*, 340.
42. Sayers, *Just Vengeance*, 314.
43. Sayers, *Just Vengeance*, 327, 350.

stole in Viet Nam to people and programs in need. Though their appropriation of gold meant for the Lahu people was unjust, they make it the source of charity; like us all, they are both Cain and Abel.

Though I cannot say whether Spike Lee is a Christian, I do know that he fulfills Sayers's sense of the *imago Dei*. Committed to art that not only fills us with wonder but also captures the paradoxes of existence, he illustrates Sayers's subversive definition of Christian work: "the only Christian work is good work well done."[44]

---

44. Sayers, "Why Work?," 78.

PART IV

Wonder and the Church

Fourth canto | Karen An-hwei Lee

Eternity under the olives, Hebrews 2:4

And God confirmed the message
by giving signs and wonders
and various miracles

and gifts of the Holy Spirit.
In the soft milk light
of dawn, the little children

run to see our Messiah
strolling on the side of a hill
under the olive trees—

soon rose-colored on a cross
taking on the sins of the world,
the bread of life flayed, torn,

buried, then rising to glory. Of all
the signs and wonders, your gift
of salvation is most miraculous.

"Four Cantos on Wonder." Performed by the New Arts Trio to music composed by Misook Kim for the Wheaton Theology Conference (April 2021). Italicized verses: New Living Translation of the Bible (2015) by Tyndale House.

11

Disciplining Wonder in the Orthodox Christian Tradition

MARCUS PLESTED

The Orthodox Christian Tradition is distinguished by a marked emphasis on themes of wonder and amazement at the many-splendored mystery of salvation. This essay will draw on the resources of the Orthodox Christian tradition (patristic, ascetic, liturgical, and iconographic) to explore and inculcate a distinctly Orthodox take on the theme of wonder. From the glories of the creation hymned in Basil's *Hexameron* to the raptures of the mystics and the amazement of the Russians on first experiencing the Divine Liturgy, the Orthodox tradition is a treasury of wonder-full material both old and new. This emphasis on wonder stands in some contrast to a tendency within much of the Western Christian tradition to insist on rational cognizance wherever possible and to favor a pared-down liturgy free from extraneous sensory distraction. But it would be wrong to suppose that this is simply a case of a mystical and exuberant East *versus* a rationalistic and sober West. On the contrary, the Orthodox tradition consistently inculcates a *disciplining* or even a discipling of wonder that serves not so much as a rational check and balance but rather as a means of channeling and directing the human person—mind, soul, and body—to deifying union with the unoriginate Creator.

Through the Wardrobe

When one enters an Orthodox church for the first time, the impression can be quite overwhelming: hosts of images—of our Lord, the Mother of God, the saints and angels—clouds of incense, lamps and lights all over the place, chanting in a language one may or may not understand, priests and deacons in splendid vestments, people standing or moving around—lighting candles, making the sign of the cross, bowing before and kissing icons, telling their prayer ropes.[1] One has the sense of entering a new world. As one young visitor put it to me on entering an Orthodox church for first time: "it's like Narnia." I have always found this reference tremendously apt, not least because it chimes with C. S. Lewis's own expressed preference for the Orthodox liturgy over any other.[2]

One reason children, in particular, often do quite well in an Orthodox church is that there is so much happening on a multisensory level. Certainly, the experience of worship in an Orthodox Church setting offers a sharp contrast to the rather more pared-down sensorium of most Western churches, both Protestant and Catholic. Orthodox worship is also markedly less exclusively focused on rational comprehension than on the dizzying experience of encounter with the divine other. And while the reading of Scripture is absolutely at the heart of the liturgy, and the texts of the liturgy themselves profoundly biblical, the sermon is something of an optional extra and never the high point of the ecclesial synaxis.

I am the last person to want to set up a dichotomy between a sober and rationalistic West (bad) and an exuberant and mystical East (good). We have our downsides too in the Orthodox Church—from controversies over the *filioque* or the church calendar to jurisdictional infighting and ethnic particularism. Equally, it is of course perfectly possible to be rapt into the third heaven in the midst of an Anglican Evensong or a low-church revivalist meeting: "The Spirit bloweth where it listeth" (John 3:8). But there does seem to me to be something distinctive about the nature of Orthodox worship, something that closely adheres to St. Cyril of Jerusalem's maxim: "Our purpose is not to explain God, but to glorify him."[3] Even the very

---

1. Cf. C. S. Lewis's own account of a visit to an Orthodox church: "What pleased me most about a Greek Orthodox Mass I once attended was that there seemed to be no prescribed behavior for the congregation. Some stood, some knelt, some sat, some walked; one crawled about the floor like a caterpillar" (*Letters to Malcom*, 10).

2. Reflecting on a trip to Greece in 1960 and his participation at the Easter service on Rhodes, Lewis remarked to his biographer George Sayer that "he preferred the Orthodox liturgy to either the Catholic or Protestant liturgies" (Sayer, *Jack*, 231).

3. Cyril, *Catechetical Discourses*, 6.5, in Yarnold, *Cyril*, 74.

term ORTHODOXY is sometimes explicated in terms of not only "correct" or "right belief" ("right thinking"), but also "right worship" or "right glory." This double sense, which perhaps works slightly better in Church Slavonic than in Greek, is a false etymology with no patristic precedent but does nonetheless adventitiously express a certain truth: in orthodoxy, theology is inherently liturgical and inherently doxological.

Holy Wisdom

Something of the liturgical and doxological matrix of Orthodox theology can be further gleaned from the colorful and doubtless rather embellished account given in the *Russian Primary Chronicle* for 987 AD. In this account, the Grand Prince Vladimir of Kiev, then a pagan, received emissaries from Latin, Muslim, and Jewish powers—all seeking to convert the powerful potentate and his rich realm to their own faith. None made much of an impression but the Greeks from Constantinople, by contrast, were "wondrous (чюдно) to hear," speaking with great art of the whole history of the world and of the promise of the world to come.[4] His interest piqued, Vladimir sent out envoys to explore these different faiths further. The envoys found little of worth among the Muslim Bulgars: "When we journeyed among the Bulgars, we beheld how they worship in their temple, called a mosque, while they stand ungirt . . . there is no happiness among them, but instead only sorrow . . . Their religion is not good." The Germans—the Franks, that is—come out little better: "Then we went among the Germans, and saw them performing many ceremonies in their temples; but we beheld nothing wondrous or beautiful there."[5] "Nothing wondrous or beautiful"—no wonder, no beauty. Such was their impression of Latin worship. The envoys went on to the Roman Empire centered on Constantinople—the city they called Tsargrad, city of the emperors.

> Then we went on to Greece, and the Greeks led us to the edifices where they worship their God, and we knew not whether we were in heaven or on earth. For on earth there is no such splendour or no such beauty, and we are at a loss how to describe it. We know only that God dwells there among men, and their service is fairer than the ceremonies of other nations. For we cannot forget that beauty.

---

4. *Russian Primary Chronicle*, 110–11.
5. творяща а красоты не видѣхомъ никоеяже. *Russian Primary Chronicle*, 110–11.

Note the emphasis on themes of amazed wonder and overwhelming beauty. While the words and persuasion of the Greeks were of vital importance in the process of conversion, it was the *experience* of worship that proved the decisive factor in persuading the Rus' to embrace Christianity in its Orthodox form. The rest, as they say, is history.

Such experiences have proved remarkably consistent in accounts of Orthodox liturgical experience. Writing from exile in 1936, Wassily Kandinsky spoke of his yearning for the "wonderful beauty" of the Orthodox Easter services of the ancient churches of Moscow.[6] Another exile, the great theologian Fr. Sergius Bulgakov, fresh from his expulsion from Soviet Russia in 1922, wrote eloquently of his feelings on entering for the first time the Great Church of the Holy Wisdom, Hagia Sophia, in Constantinople—the same church visited almost a thousand years before by his distant forebears. In his journal, Bulgakov records his gratitude for being vouchsafed an experience of this extraordinary building:

> Of all the wonderful churches I have seen, this is the most absolute, the universal Church. The words of the Easter anthem ring in my mind: "Lift up thine eyes, O Zion, and behold: thy children have come to thee from the west and the north and the south and the east shining with the divine light." [. . .] Human tongue cannot express the lightness, the clarity, the simplicity, the wonderful harmony which dispels all sense of heaviness—the heaviness of the cupola and the walls. An ocean of light pours from above and dominates all this space, enclosed and yet free. The grace of the columns and the beauty of their marble lace, the royal dignity—not luxury, but regality—of the golden walls and the marvellous ornamentation: it captivates and melts the heart, subdues and convinces. It creates a sense of inner transparency; the weightiness and limitations of the small and suffering self is gone, the soul is healed of it, losing itself in these arches and merging into them. It becomes the world: I am in the world, and the world is in me. And this sense of the weight on one's heart melting away, of liberation from the pull of gravity, of being like a bird in the blue of the sky, gives one not happiness, not even joy, but bliss. It is the bliss of some final knowledge of the all in all and of all in oneself, of infinite fullness in multiplicity, of the world in unity.[7]

---

6. Kandinsky, *Kandinsky und Ich*, 233.

7. Bulgakov, *Bulgakov Anthology*, 13. Bulgakov knew the church as a mosque, as it was from 1453–1934 and is now, alas, once again.

Note that for Bulgakov this bliss-full experience is understood as an experience of the divine coinherence, of presence of God in the world and the world in God. This, for Bulgakov, is wisdom or Sophia—"the real unity of the world in the Logos." While there are some problems with Bulgakov's theology of the divine wisdom (or sophiology), there is no doubt about his conviction that all mystical experience—of wonder, beauty, truth, and glory—coheres in the one who is Wisdom, our Lord and God and Savior Jesus Christ—"the wisdom and power of God" (1 Cor 1:24).

I make this point not to detract from anything I am saying about the wonder of Orthodoxy but on the contrary to emphasize that its wondrousness always has a disciplined focus—and that focus is Christ as both created and uncreated wisdom. "The beginning of philosophy," says Plato, "is a sense of wonder."[8] For Christians, Christ is the highest and only true wisdom whom we seek and love (*philo-sophia*). The wonder of Orthodox worship is not a synaesthetic free-for-all or mystical muddle but operates according to strict theological criteria. To repeat, even Vladimir's emissaries were packed off to Constantinople only after hearing a learned disquisition on salvation history. "Right worship," in short, demands "right belief" and *vice versa*. The wisdom of right belief and the wonder of right worship are mutually reinforcing and ultimately inseparable categories.

I shall in the remainder of this essay attempt to flesh out further the theme of wonder in the Orthodox Christian tradition drawing on various patristic, ascetic, liturgical, and iconographic sources. I shall pay particular attention to the "disciplining" of wonder in accordance with theological and ascetical wisdom. While many of the sources I shall deal with belong to or may in principle be drawn on by all Christians, and while the Orthodox tradition is perfectly capable of finding grounds for wonder outside her historical bounds, I hope to explore and inculcate a distinctly Orthodox take on the theme of wonder and the disciplining of wonder in wisdom.

Sacraments

In keeping with the liturgical and ecclesial focus of my opening sections, I shall begin with some observations regarding the sacramental practices of Orthodoxy. The sacraments, or "mysteries" as they are more properly called, are routinely described as "spine-chilling" or "awe-inspiring."[9] With elements of drama drawn straight from the Hellenic mystery religions,

---

8. Plato, *Theaetetus*, in *Platonis Opera* I, 155d. This experience is also spoken of as "dizziness" (155c).

9. From the Greek φρικτός; cf. Yarnold, *Awe-inspiring Rites*, ix.

the passage from darkness into light, from ignorance to knowledge, is constantly reenacted in the liturgy of the hours and perhaps most obviously in the Easter vigil as the church plunged into darkness bursts into the fire of the paschal "light without evening." Circular movements—always anti-clockwise—express the simultaneously cyclical and linear character of liturgical time. Constant repetition is a given. As the deacon periodically intones: "again and again, let us pray unto the Lord"—and again, and again, and again. In the liturgy it is always "now"—not the *chronos* of the world but the *kairos*, the eternal now, of the kingdom: "*Today* is the beginning of our salvation."[10]

The Orthodox liturgy is strictly disciplined. Fasting is a prerequisite for communion while bodily actions (kneeling and prostration) form an integral part of many services, especially in Great Lent. The liturgical texts are permeated with Scripture and packed full of dogmatic theology. There is, moreover, virtually no room for liturgical innovation. The form and structure of the services is based on a complex set of interlocking cycles that repeat themselves only once a century. Here we have splendid variety with no need to worry even about hymn selection.

Orthodox churches maintain like no others the ancient *disciplina arcani* or discipline of secrecy. Harking back to the days of Roman persecution, one still hears in the Divine Liturgy immediately before the recitation of the creed the injunction "The doors, the doors!," signifying the need to quite literally close the doors to avoid possible profanation of the mysteries by hostile intruders. This injunction tragically became once again a grim reality in recent communist persecutions with priests rapidly consuming the gifts routinely, as police or soldiers broke in. The elaborate opening and closing of the doors in the iconostasis together with the veiling of the sanctuary by a curtain serve to underpin the hallowedness of the mystery being enacted.

And then there is the singing. No words are simply said in the Divine Liturgy but rather chanted or sung. Whether this is the powerful boisterousness of Byzantine chant or the more complex and ethereal harmonies of Russian polyphony, unaccompanied music is an inescapable feature of Orthodox worship. There are no said services or low masses—no services without incense even. Orthodox worship is always full-on and wonder-full.

The sheer physicality of Orthodox worship is another notable feature: from the use of real bread and real wine communicated via a liturgical spoon to baptism by full immersion of slippery children lathered in olive oil. From the flowers strewn over the representation of the tomb at Good Friday to the

---

10. Hymn for the Annunciation in *Festal Menaion*, 445. Orthodox festal hymns routinely begin in this way with the eternal "now."

dousing of the whole congregation with holy water at Theophany. This is a Church in which matter *matters*.

Icons

"Matter matters" is also, incidentally one of the best ways of summing up the theology of the icon. As St. John of Damascus forcibly argued in the eighth century, at a time when the Christian Roman emperors were smashing and destroying religious images,

> In former times God, who is without form or body, could never be depicted. But now when God is seen in the flesh conversing with men (Baruch 3:38), I make an image of the God whom I see. I do not worship matter; I worship the Creator of matter who became matter for my sake, who willed to take his abode in matter; who worked out my salvation through matter. Never will I cease honouring the matter which wrought my salvation! ... Through it my salvation has come to me. Was not the thrice-happy and thrice-blessed wood of the cross matter? Was not the holy and exalted mountain of Calvary matter? What of the life-bearing rock, the holy and life-giving tomb, the fountain of our resurrection, was it not matter? Is not the ink in the most holy Gospel-book matter? Is not the life-giving altar made of matter? From it we receive the bread of life! ... Do not despise matter, for it is not despicable. God has made nothing despicable.[11]

It is because matter *matters* that sacred art is even conceivable. And it is because the whole question of the propriety of sacred art was thrown into vociferous debate within the period of Byzantine iconoclasm that the Orthodox remain especially devoted to the art of the icon. As John goes on to argue, the production of the icon involves all the senses: "We use all our senses to produce worthy images of him, and we sanctify the noblest of the senses, which is that of sight." Through such images, we are led to worship God, "the worker of wonders."[12] The dazzling array of icons that one encounters in each and every Orthodox church serves as eloquent testimony to the principle that "matter matters" and that the material creation can, through sacred art, bring us into the very presence of the one who became matter for our salvation.

---

11. John of Damascus, *Divine Images*, 16.
12. John of Damascus, *Divine Images*, 17.

Figure 8. *Christ Pantocrator*, **Saint Catherine's Monastery, Mount Sinai, Egypt.**

Orthodox iconography is an inherently disciplined endeavor—always careful to distinguish between the absolute adoration and worship owed only to God and the relative veneration paid to his image, and to the images of the Mother of God, the saints, and the angels. The christological parameters of the icon are particularly exact: in the icon we depict neither the humanity nor the divinity in isolation but strictly the single *hypostasis* or person of God the Word incarnate—the visible and human face of the invisible God.

The disciplining of wonder within iconography is further maintained through the rather strict set of criteria that inform the painting of an icon. First and foremost, iconography is itself an ascetic discipline requiring intense practical commitment on the part of the iconographer—set prayers, participation in the sacraments of the Church, and obedience to the tradition. The Orthodox icon works within certain set parameters, including defined physical characteristics, colors, architecture, scenery, composition, and so forth. Thus there is no need for Peter, for example, to have a set of keys for us to know it is Peter—Peter is Peter because he looks like Peter (close cropped white beard and hair, *et cetera*). That said, there is room for a tremendous amount of artistic creativity and variety within those defined parameters. This disciplining of wonder only serves to liberate true sacred art from the artistic ego or from the relentless pursuit of mere novelty. It also unleashes in a superlative way the proper potentialities of the created order when rightly directed.

Cosmology

"O Lord, how manifold are thy works! in wisdom hast thou made them all: the earth is full of thy riches" (Ps 103/4:24). The wondrous nature of the creation is a prominent feature of Orthodox cosmology. St. Basil the Great's *Hexaemeron* expresses this particularly well, hymning with awe and amazement the extraordinary wisdom embedded in the creation, from the tiniest drop of water to the riches and complexity of the animal creation. All of creation directs us to the supreme beauty, goodness, and truth of the Creator who is himself Wisdom:

> It is he, beneficent nature, goodness without measure, a worthy object of love for all beings endowed with reason, the beauty the most to be desired, the origin of all that exists, the source of life, intellectual light, impenetrable wisdom, it is he who in the beginning created heaven and earth. (*Hexameron* 1.2)

The wisdom of the Creator is seen in every living thing: scorpions and stingrays, elephants and mice, geese and swans, bees and wasps, birds and butterflies. Towards the end of the treatise, Basil regrets that he cannot adequately describe every single facet of the creation and begs his listener to live always with a sense of wonder:

> Studious listener, think of all these creations which God has drawn out of nothing, think of all those which my speech has left out, to avoid tediousness, and not to exceed my limits; recognise everywhere the wisdom of God; never cease to wonder, and, through every creature, to glorify the Creator. (*Hexaemeron* 8.7)

Note again the connection between wisdom and wonder: wonder must have a direction and that direction, that orientation, is God—the supreme Wisdom.

"Wondrous is God in his saints"[13]

Basil's sense of the wondrousness of the created order is of course no isolated phenomenon. Again and again in the ascetic tradition, we see an essentially analogous sense of wonder at the glories of creation. St. Isaac of Nineveh (*vel* the Syrian) is a particular good example. For Isaac, writing in the seventh century in what is now Iraq, pure prayer entails prayer for the whole created order:

> The heart that is enflamed [with love] embraces the entire creation—man, birds, animals, and even demons. At the recollection of them, and at the sight of them, such a man's eyes fill with tears that arise from the great compassion that presses on his heart. The heart grows tender and cannot endure to hear of or look upon any injury or even the smallest suffering inflicted upon anything in creation. For this reason such a man prays incessantly with tears even for irrational animals and for the enemies of truth and for all who harm it, that they may be guarded and forgiven; even on behalf of the various reptiles, on account of his great compassion which is poured out in his heart without measure, after the example of God.[14]

An exactly similar sense of the cosmic compassion is found in Dostoevsky's Staretz (or Elder) Zossima who is himself an amalgam of preexisting ascetic teachings:

> Love all God's creation, both the whole and every grain of sand. Love every leaf, every ray of light. Love the animals, love the

---

13. θαυμαστὸς ὁ θεὸς ἐν τοῖς ἁγίοις αὐτοῦ (Ps 67:36 LXX). This verse is routinely used in the Orthodox liturgical tradition to speak of the saints as opposed to the "holy places" (KJV) or "sanctuary" (RSV) more commonly referenced in English translations of this verse (Ps 68:35).

14. Isaac of Nineveh, *Ascetic Homilies* I.74, in *Syriac Fathers*, 251.

plants, love each separate thing. If thou love each thing thou wilt perceive the mystery of God in all; and when once thou perceive this, thou wilt thenceforward grow every day to a fuller understanding of it: until thou come at last to love the whole world with a love that will then be all-embracing and universal.[15]

Such sentiments are found throughout the Orthodox tradition. Another Russian, St. Silouan the Athonite, whom Thomas Merton called the most authentic monk of the twentieth century, observed: "The Lord bestows such rich grace on his chosen that they embrace the whole earth, the whole world, with that love."[16] Silouan's disciple, St. Sophrony of Essex (*vel* the Athonite) recalls a walk with his spiritual father on one of the many paths of Mount Athos. Casually swiping out with his stick at a clump of overhanging grass, Sophrony found that this thoughtless action grieved his companion, for which he felt ashamed. As he goes on to write: "The Staretz [Silouan] used to say that the Divine Spirit teaches one to spare every living thing, and so not needlessly harm leaf or tree. "That green leaf on the tree that you needlessly plucked—it was not wrong, only rather a pity for the little leaf. The heart that has learned to love is sorry for all created things."[17]

St. Silouan's acute sense of the preciousness of all creation speaks of the thinness of the veil between the material and the spiritual. Properly attuned, the soul passes directly from matter to spirit in wondrous awe:

> On earth the soul has only to touch upon the love of God for the sweetness of the Holy Spirit to transport her with wonder at her beloved God and Heavenly Father. O how the Lord loves His creation![18]

Another contemporary saint, St. Nektarios of Aegina, was reportedly able to open up to others the capacity to see and hear the wondrous glory and unceasing doxology of the creation. One of his spiritual children, a nun at the monastery he had founded, came to him in some confusion over the numerous biblical references to the praise and glorification offered by the creation, most notably in the Psalms. Passages such as: "Let the heaven and earth praise him, the seas, and every thing that moveth therein" (Ps 69:34); "Mountains and all trees, fruit trees and cedars, Beasts and all cattle, creeping things and flying birds ... Let them praise the name of Lord" (Ps 148:9–13).

---

15. Dostoevsky, *Brothers Karamazov*, 395.
16. Sakharov, *Saint Silouan*, 367.
17. Sakharov, *Saint Silouan*, 94, 376.
18. Sakharov, *Saint Silouan*, 366.

"I just can't hear it, father," she said, "I just can't hear their praise."[19] And just for a moment, through divine intercession, she was given to hear that praise, to hear that unending ontological hymn of wonder, and to glimpse the eternal wisdom in which all things are made.

Spiritual Senses

Some of the language of seeing and hearing that I have been using needs explanation. Another aspect of the Orthodox disciplining of wonder is the long tradition of reflection in the spiritual senses—the idea that there are within the human being faculties corresponding in some manner with the five physical senses, yet capable of direct apprehension of divine reality.[20] One of the most vivid articulations of the doctrine of the spiritual senses is to be found in the anonymous collection of fourth-century texts ascribed to Macarius of Egypt, often called the Macarian Homilies. The author, whom I habitually refer to simply as "Macarius," the blessed one can even define the very essence of Christianity in terms of the spiritual senses: "The reality of Christianity is this: the taste of truth, the eating and drinking of truth" (I 18.7.1–3). We might note here that it is the faculty of taste that is privileged, taste being perhaps the most immediate of the senses. This experience is also frequently evoked in terms of the vision of God as light—something that becomes an absolute hallmark of the Orthodox tradition in later figures such as St. Gregory Palamas and St. Seraphim of Sarov. For Macarius, this prospect of seeing God as light is founded on the mystery of the transfiguration on Thabor—a mystery all Christians are called to share in. For Macarius, this mystery is at the heart of St. Paul's teaching:

> The blessed Apostle Paul, the architect of the Church, forever anxious for the truth and not wishing that those who hear the word should be impeded by ignorance, indicated with great exactitude and clarity the goal of the truth and made known the perfect mystery of Christianity in every believing soul, this being to receive through a divine operation the experience of the effulgence of the heavenly light in holy souls in the revelation and power of the Spirit. (I 58.1.1)

Duly opened by the grace of the Spirit, the spiritual "doors of perception" allow humans to hear what cannot be heard and see what cannot be seen. The great Byzantine mystic St. Symeon the New Theologian (eleventh century)

---

19. Oral testimony reported by Dr. Philip Sherrard to the author in 1993.
20. See further Plested, "Spiritual Senses."

ruminates further on the nature of Paul's mystical experience and the "ineffable speech" he heard as he was rapt into the third heaven (and note that for the Orthodox Paul has always been primarily a mystical theologian—a theologian of direct mystical experience). According to Symeon, this "speech" was nothing other than

> the mystical and truly inexpressible contemplations, the transcendently splendid and unknowable knowledge given by the illumination of the Holy Spirit, by which we mean the invisible visions of the glory and divinity, beyond light and transcending knowledge, of the Son and Word of God. These contemplations, revealed the more manifestly and clearly to those who are worthy of them, show themselves as the inaudible auditions of unutterable speech, the comprehension through incomprehension of things incomprehensible.[21]

For Symeon as for Macarius the true eternal wonder of the universe, wonder in its deepest theological sense, can be apprehended only by the opening and transformation of the spiritual senses. Without such faculties, it is all too possible to become entrapped in merely earthly beauty, earthly wonder and fail to penetrate beyond the veil of materiality.

Images and Imaginal

It is perhaps no coincidence that the spiritual teaching of both Macarius and Symeon is full of vivid images drawn from the material creation. This visual dimension gives their teaching an immediacy and impact that would otherwise be difficult to achieve. In many ways, such visual teaching is an inescapable feature of the human attempt to grapple with divine reality, so long as one never forgets the ontological and epistemological gap between creature and Creator. As Macarius puts it: "All these [spiritual realities] I have described with the use of visible things, through birds and beasts and all things which are seen, since it is impossible to express or to explain spiritual things otherwise."[22]

Macarius and Symeon are distinguished by the candor and vividness with which they evoke the experience of *theosis*—a process beginning even in this life.

---

21. Symeon, *Third Ethical Discourse*, in Symeon, *St. Symeon the New Theologian*, 1.121.

22. Homily III 16.3.1 in Macarius, *Pseudo-Macaire: Oeuvres spirituelles* I.

> Writing to the Corinthians, the blessed Paul declares: "We all with unveiled face contemplate the glory of God—that is to say the intelligible light—and are formed anew according to the same image, from glory to glory" (cf. II Cor. 3:18). Picture someone looking at the royal robes, purple, diadems, and the many other garments. He marvels at their variety, their elegance, their delightfulness, the beauty of the precious stones, and is never tired of the sight of their gladdening beauty. Or someone who looks at the sun and sees the dazzling brightness of its rays forming a living spectacle of variety in which each ray is greater than the next. Or someone who catches the dappled reflection of the sun in the water, leaping about and shifting in many varied ways. So it is with those who carry in themselves the heavenly image of Christ, who have the ineffable light within them and are clad in the purple of the heavenly king (that is to say the heavenly joy of the Spirit). When they perceive the beauty of the ineffable light within themselves, then they see with the "unveiled face" of the soul the incorruptible glory of the ineffable variety, how it is transformed "from glory to glory" in the richly varying beauty of the godhead, of which fleshly tongue cannot speak. For that which God does in his saints out of his immense bounty even while they are in this world is entirely beyond our ability either to conceive or to express.[23]

Macarius will even dare to imagine the heavenly glory of the saints:

> For the Lord is their home and tabernacle and city. They are clothed with a heavenly habitation not made by human hands, the glory of the divine light, having become children of the light. They do not look at one another with an evil eye, for evil has been cast out. There is neither "male nor female, bond nor free" (cf. Gal. 3:28) but all have been changed into a divine nature having become christs, gods, and children of God. Without indecency, brother may speak peace to sister for all are one in Christ. Reposing in the same light, one will look at the other and in that regard they will shine out again and anew in the truth, in the true vision of the ineffable light. Thus in many different forms and in many varying divine glories they look upon one another and each is amazed and rejoices with unspeakable joy seeing the glory of the other. (Collection II.34.2–3)

Symeon, for his part, joins Macarius in imagining the next life:

---

23. Logos I.10.3.1–2 in Macarius, *Makarios/Symeon*.

All creation, too, once made new, will become spiritual, and together with paradise will be transformed into an immaterial, unchanging, eternal, and intelligible dwelling place. The sky on the one hand will be incomparably brighter, in a manner indeed quite new, other and brighter than our visible sky, while the earth on the other hand will take on a new and inexpressible beauty, an unfading verdure, ornamented by shining flowers, varied and spiritual. The sun of righteousness will shine seven times more brightly, and the moon will gleam twice as bright as the sun which illumines it now. The stars will be like our sun—if, indeed, these are the same stars as are spoken of in the sublime thoughts of the wise. All things there are beyond speech, transcend thought, save only that they are spiritual and divine, joined to the intelligible world, and comprise another intellectual paradise and heavenly Jerusalem, made like and united to the angelic world, the inviolable inheritance of the sons of God.[24]

But while Symeon and Macarius are among the rare figures (along with C. S. Lewis in *The Great Divorce*) who dare to imagine life in the kingdom, both do so on the basis of profound ascetic experience and obedience to the truths contained in the Scripture and Tradition. While we can certainly speak of a rich imaginal faculty in such saints—and of course in many others, think of Ephrem or Isaac the Syrian—such rich imaginal faculties are invariably tempered by warnings as to the dangers of the unaided and undisciplined imagination—what the ascetic fathers tend to call "phantasia" or fantasy. There are countless warnings against *phantasia* in monastic texts. Evagrius of Pontus is particularly adamant on this point, counseling:

> Do not give any shape to the divine in yourself when you are praying, nor allow some form to stamp an impression on your intellect, but approach the immaterial immaterially and you will understand.[25]
>
> Do not in any way seek to receive some form, or shape, or colour at the time of prayer.[26]

For Evagrius, pure prayer demands the shedding of images. The intellect is to be stripped or "naked" of images as it ascends into union with unoriginated intellect. There is no place for any sort of imagination in the Evagrian schema—even no place, one might argue, for wonder. Figures such as

---

24. Symeon, *First Ethical Discourse*, in Symeon, *St. Symeon the New Theologian*, 1.41.

25. Evagrius, *Chapitres sur la prière*, 67.

26. Evagrius, *Chapitres sur la prière*, 114.

Macarius and Symeon adopt a more nuanced approach, allowing for the wonder-full operation of the imaginal faculty even in the highest reaches of mystical contemplation but always insisting on the need for strict ascetic and theological wisdom.

Conclusion

There is of course much more to be said about the theme of wonder within the Orthodox Christian tradition: from St. Gregory the Theologian's wonder at the simultaneous oneness and threeness of the triune God, to St. Isaac the Syrian's conviction of a "wondrous outcome" stored up by God in the matter of Gehenna, or the amazed wonder with which a disciple experienced a vision of divine light through the intercessions of St. Seraphim of Sarov. But the sketch given in this essay should suffice, at least, to delineate something of the "wonder of Orthodoxy" and something of the distinctive character of the theme of wonder within the Orthodox Christian tradition—in its liturgy and worship, in its saints and icons, in its teaching on spiritual senses and mystical experience, and its consistent sense of ascetic and theological disciplining. Wonder must, in short, always be tempered by and in wisdom if it is to lead us where we want to go—to Christ and his kingdom.

12

Songs and Symbols for an Overcoming Church

CHERYL J. SANDERS

The New Testament book of Revelation offers rich resources for reimagining and reconfiguring the liturgical practices and public witness of contemporary Christian congregations. In this essay, I offer a fresh reading of the letters to the seven churches in chapters 2–3 and brief surveys of select samples of the rich hymnody and imagery of Revelation toward the end of presenting an enhanced view of the Bible's prophetic template for empowering the church to overcome injustice on earth. In particular, I am concerned to show how words and images from the book of Revelation can illumine our modern understanding of the problem of race, the practice of reconciliation, and the possibility of radical inclusion. Starting from a faith-based vantage point of commitment to social justice, my task is to bring theological, ethical, and aesthetic sensibilities to bear upon insights from Revelation in order to imagine new ways to heighten awareness of three vital areas of Christian ministry and social engagement: justice-seeking struggle, spiritual formation for worship, and the celebration of inclusive community. The key question that guides my inquiry is how the depictions of justice, worship, and community that we find in Revelation illumine our vocation on earth and shape our orientation to heaven as our eternal destiny.

My intention here is not to provide a comprehensive exegetical commentary on the book of Revelation. My approach to Revelation is guided by the conviction that the Bible invites us to imagine God and God's work in the world, following the thought of Judy Fentress Williams. I draw great inspiration from her celebration of the "sanctified imagination" of African American preachers who "encouraged their communities to imagine aspects of God into their current circumstances."[1] Rather, I am seeking to highlight some of the social and ethical messages that modern Christians can receive and embrace from its stories, songs, and symbols, especially in view of our current dilemma of confronting the complicity of churches with racial injustice while at the same time seeking meaningful approaches to fostering reconciliation and inclusive community. I begin with an overview of scenes from the letters to seven churches whose stories represent variants of ecclesial responses to empire. What follows next is an analysis of Revelation hymnody, with attention to how lyrics and performance in worship respond to the violence and idolatry of empire. I conclude with an examination of a few key symbols in light of what they might signify to a church concerned for justice, worship, and community.

Scenes from Seven Letters to Seven Churches

My reading of the seven letters addressed to the angels of the seven churches is not focused on the faults and shortcomings of these churches, nor on the victory promised to them. Rather, I see these churches as emblematic of the struggles faced by faith communities whose commitment to Christian witness puts them in opposition to their standing as citizens of the Roman Empire and as consumers of the imperial economy.[2] The distinctive personality of each church is addressed in the letter, which also includes an assessment of each church's collective quality of character, including flaws and failures as well as traits worthy of admiration and emulation. Each letter issues a warning to repent or an exhortation to hold on; each concludes with a promise of victory and reward. Instead of viewing Revelation 2–3 as an indictment of the failures of churches, I regard these letters as a mirror or template for evaluating the variety of personalities that individuals bring to faith-based leadership. Further, the seven "stances" provide clear prescriptions for correction and spiritual transformation. Each letter is addressed to a church who is experiencing and responding to the adverse circumstances of imperial persecution and oppression. The promised outcome of victory is contingent upon truthful testimony, perseverance, and, in most cases, repentance.

1. Williams, *Holy Imagination*, xii.
2. Blount, "Revelation."

Figure 9. Albrecht Dürer, *The Revelation of St John: 2. St John's Vision of Christ and the Seven Candlesticks.*

The church in Ephesus is the puritanical church. They need more love and are called to repentance and a restored commitment to good works.

> I know your works, your toil and your patient endurance. I know that you cannot tolerate evildoers; you have tested those who claim to be apostles but are not, and have found them to be false.

> I also know that you are enduring patiently and bearing up for the sake of my name, and that you have not grown weary. But I have this against you, that you have abandoned the love you had at first. Remember then from what you have fallen; repent, and do the works you did at first. If not, I will come to you and remove your lampstand from its place, unless you repent. (Rev 2:2–5)[3]

The puritanical church is commended for maintaining its high moral standards, but exhorted to reflect on the failure to uphold the imperative to love—and repent. Repentance is not just a matter of words; it requires a change of mind, heart, and behavior. There is no reward for the unrepentant. Those who do repent will be rewarded with victory and a right to the tree of life in God's paradise.

The church in Smyrna is the persecuted church. They need encouragement to hold on.

> I know your affliction and your poverty, even though you are rich. I know the slander on the part of those who say that they are Jews and are not, but are a synagogue of Satan. Do not fear what you are about to suffer. Beware, the devil is about to throw some of you into prison so that you may be tested, and for ten days you will have affliction. Be faithful until death, and I will give you the crown of life. (2:9–10)

This letter reveals three ways the church suffers persecution in the world: troubling contradictions, fierce opposition, and threats of tribulation. This church lives in the paradox of remaining impoverished victims of economic injustice on the one hand, and blessed beneficiaries of spiritual prosperity on the other. The church is warned not to fear opposition; the most effective defense against the enemy is courage. The threat of tribulation is based on reliable predictions and not conspiracy theories. Faithfulness until death is the triumph of the persecuted church.

The church in Pergamum is the persevering church. Because some of them lack moral and doctrinal discernment, they are called to repentance.

> I know where you are living, where Satan's throne is. Yet you are holding fast to my name, and you did not deny your faith in me even in the days of Antipas my witness, my faithful one, who was killed among you, where Satan lives. But I have a few things against you: you have some there who hold to the teaching of Balaam, who taught Balak to put a stumbling block before the people of Israel, so that they would eat food sacrificed to idols

---

3. All references to the Bible are from the NRSV unless otherwise noted.

and practice fornication. So you also have some who hold to the
teaching of the Nicolaitans. Repent then. (2:13–16a)

Pergamum was a city of emperor worship. A member of the church was killed as a consequence of his faithful allegiance to Christ. What is the church supposed to do when there's no justice for the martyr? First and foremost, remain true to God's name, do not renounce faith in God, and resist idolatry, immorality, and the other practices of the dominant culture that God hates. There is no detailed description of who the Nicolaitans are or what they taught, but the Ephesian church is commended for their hatred of the works of the Nicolaitans, which the Lord also hates (2:6).

The church in Thyatira is the productive church. Those who make compromises are called to repentance; others, who have not accepted false teaching, are encouraged to hold on.

> I know your works—your love, faith, service, and patient endurance. I know that your last works are greater than the first. But I have this against you: you tolerate that woman Jezebel, who calls herself a prophet and is teaching and beguiling my servants to practice fornication and to eat food sacrificed to idols. I gave her time to repent, but she refuses to repent of her fornication. Beware, I am throwing her on a bed, and those who commit adultery with her I am throwing into great distress, unless they repent of her doings; and I will strike her children dead. And all the churches will know that I am the one who searches minds and hearts, and I will give to each of you as your works deserve. But to the rest of you in Thyatira, who do not hold this teaching, who have not learned what some call "the deep things of Satan," to you I say, I do not lay on you any other burden; only hold fast to what you have until I come. (2:19–25)

The Lord examines the minds, hearts, and actions of this church, whose letter begins with the Lord's search results—words of evaluation and commendation that take note of its works, love, faithfulness, service, endurance, and measures of effectiveness. This church will be judged on the merits of its actions and given what its actions deserve—punishment or reward. The church's productivity is compromised by a religion that refuses to admit wrong and excuses sin.

The church in Sardis is the passive church. They need to wake up, come alive, and repent.

> These are the words of him who has the seven spirits of God and the seven stars: I know your works; you have a name of being alive, but you are dead. Wake up, and strengthen what remains

> and is on the point of death, for I have not found your works perfect in the sight of my God. Remember then what you received and heard; obey it, and repent. If you do not wake up, I will come like a thief, and you will not know at what hour I will come to you. (3:1b–3)

The seven Spirits of God (see Isa 11:1–5) can be seen as seven aspects of God's character that bless the church and provide exactly what the church needs in order to wake up and come alive: (1) wisdom—knowing what to do next in all kinds of situations and circumstances; (2) understanding—getting information and comprehending it; (3) counsel—advice for making good decisions ("planning" in the Common English Bible); (4) might—spiritual authority and strength to lead; (5) knowledge—information that is relevant for this life and the next; (6) fear of the Lord—reverence for God based on knowledge of God; (7) justice—what the Lord wears like a belt and gives to the poor.

The church in Philadelphia is the powerless church. They are lacking in prestige, but persistent in piety. They need open doors of opportunity and are exhorted to hold on.

> I know your works. Look, I have set before you an open door, which no one is able to shut. I know that you have but little power, and yet you have kept my word and have not denied my name. I will make those of the synagogue of Satan who say that they are Jews and are not, but are lying—I will make them come and bow down before your feet, and they will learn that I have loved you. Because you have kept my word of patient endurance, I will keep you from the hour of trial that is coming on the whole world to test the inhabitants of the earth. I am coming soon; hold fast to what you have, so that no one may seize your crown. (3:8–11)

The open door that no one can shut is not likely to mean an opportunity for personal advancement; instead it signifies an opportunity for the powerless, impoverished church to multiply the influence of its testimony of the love of Christ.

The church in Laodicea is the prosperous church. They lack self-awareness and need to repent.

> I know your works; you are neither cold nor hot. I wish that you were either cold or hot. So, because you are lukewarm, and neither cold nor hot, I am about to spit you out of my mouth. For you say, "I am rich, I have prospered, and I need nothing." You do not realize that you are wretched, pitiable, poor, blind, and naked. Therefore I counsel you to buy from me gold refined by

> fire so that you may be rich; and white robes to clothe you and to keep the shame of your nakedness from being seen; and salve to anoint your eyes so that you may see. I reprove and discipline those whom I love. Be earnest, therefore, and repent. (3:15–19)

The prosperous church is lukewarm because it has completely acclimated itself to the room temperature of the dominant culture. Because it has adopted and internalized the empire's standards of success and measures of morality, it has deceived itself into thinking it is rich and self-sufficient. Recovery of self-awareness will require a careful recalculation of what wealth enables: to invest in true riches, the gold refined by fire; to address deficiencies by buying white robes as a covering; and to purchase anointing salve to heal blinded eyes.

These seven scenes offer a glimpse of the real or imagined experiences of congregations that are engaged, one way or another, in corporate struggle with the present realities of empire with a view toward the victory and rewards of heaven. The seven letters are direct messages intended to offer guidance and encouragement to congregations whose desired outcomes will result from a willingness to work through their issues, conflicts, and challenges—in other words, to struggle together and not solely as individuals. Their ultimate fate, whether eternal commendation or condemnation, is tied to their collective destiny as communities of faith who are committed to the testimony of truth (or not).

To speak of these congregations in terms of stances is a hermeneutical strategy I have employed to enable listening for how these texts might address modern congregations and denominations that are facing the challenges of meaningful social engagement under extreme economic and political circumstances. This strategy disentangles us from the difficult exegetical question of whether or not these congregations actually existed in particular times and places. In either case, to view the recipients and their circumstances (in terms of stances) can be instructive if we can correlate these stances to the social engagement options facing congregations in our own time.

None of these terms I have denominated "the seven stances" is intended to be pejorative. However, in Revelation 2–3 each stance is subjected to divine scrutiny and serves as a basis for giving instructions for correcting the course for future growth and direction. So in order to overcome the threats and challenges posed by the culture en route to fulfillment of the assignment to be faithful witnesses, the puritanical church needs more love, the persecuted church must resist discouragement, the persevering church must devote more attention to morality, the productive church must resist yielding too readily to compromise, the passive church must wake up and develop strategies for ministry, the powerless church should energize their patient piety with vigilant opportunism, and the prosperous church must cultivate a higher level of self-awareness that can empower them to rebalance their portfolios and reallocate their wealth for the nurture of souls and for the fulfillment of mission and witness.

Songs for an Overcoming Church

The book of Revelation provides the richest source of hymns and songs to be found in the New Testament; there is no other book in the New Testament where music plays a larger role.[4] While there are as many as fourteen or fifteen of these songs in Revelation, there are only two instances in which the words "song" or "singing" are used with the lyrics following:

> They took up a new song, saying, "You are worthy to take the scroll and open its seals, because you were slain, and by your blood you purchased for God persons from every tribe, language, people, and nation. You made them a kingdom and priests to our God, and they will rule on earth." (5:9–10)

> Those who gained victory over the beast, its image, and the number of its name were standing by the glass sea, holding harps from God. They sing the song of Moses, God's servant, and the song of the Lamb, saying, "Great and awe-inspiring are your works, Lord God Almighty. Just and true are your ways, king of the nations. Who won't fear you, Lord, and glorify your name? You alone are holy. All nations will come and fall down in worship before you, for your acts of justice have been revealed." (15:2b–4)

The first of these two songs celebrates the inclusion of every category of humanity in the redemptive work of God. The second remembers the song of Moses and the Exodus narrative of deliverance, proclaiming the accountability of all nations to God's acts of justice. Luke Powery argues that by recalling the Exodus these songs declare that what God did in the past, God also does in the present: "John is attempting to persuade his hearers to oppose the human enslaving powers of imperialism while simultaneously embracing the divine liberating power of God."[5]

Some aspects of the political and cultural context of the book of Revelation should be taken into consideration while seeking to understand these lyrics, their messages, and what they reveal to us about worship in

---

4. Koester, "Distant Triumph Song," 243.
5. Powery, "Painful Praise," 75.

heaven. Powery observes that in John's day the Roman imperial cult was the symbol of the unity of the empire and the most widespread popular religion: "World power was in the hands of the caesars who were worshipped as the embodiment of true divinity. Loyalty of the citizens to the state empire was fostered by religious ceremonies focused on the emperor, linking politics, religion, and economic realities.... Those who refused to participate in the emperor cult awaited death or economic privation."[6]

Powery sees these hymns as functioning as a direct counterpart to the imperial court ceremonial. They not only resist political oppression and pain, but "exalt God and persuade others to do the same, for it is God's power alone that can undo the earthly powers of Roman imperialism."[7] The songs of Revelation are performed in a context of political opposition and struggle. They are "coded musical weapons that struggle against and seek to undermine the ruling empire of its day."[8] I see them as fight songs intended to inspire and to sustain struggle toward the end of achieving victory in God's name against the forces of imperial idolatry and injustice. Robert H. Smith helps us to complete the picture by drawing attention to the fact that "power and wealth" come first on the list of what the Lamb is worthy to receive. He further explains that the songs of Revelation 4 and 5 deliberately picture redemption in economic language and political imagery, "because John rejects not just the cult of the emperor but the entire social world projected and celebrated by that cult. His Revelation will climax with a picture of a new city, and it is not Rome, where a new politics and a new economics are practiced."[9]

Les Hardin's theological study of the hymns of Revelation includes a helpful summary of some key themes. They are directed at the throne (and not at believers); are biblical in content, telling the story of the victory of God and the Lamb (not of the prosperity and well-being of the worshippers); and are inclusive of all who desire to attend the throne (lacking overtones of apocalyptic-style polemic).[10] Hardin insists that worship in heaven is inclusive of all humanity: "John will not permit the worship of heaven to descend into a fallen, class-driven, race-oriented, gender-exclusive imitation. The worship John envisions (and the repentance that precedes it) is open and available to all. The worship of heaven is 'a radical equalizer that

---

6. Powery, "Painful Praise," 71.
7. Powery, "Painful Praise," 73.
8. Powery, "Painful Praise," 71.
9. Smith, "'Worthy,'" 506.
10. Hardin, "Theology," 244.

breaks down all boundaries' and creates an egalitarian *communitas* of those gathered around the throne."[11]

Reading the songs of Revelation through these political, economic, and cultural lenses compels us to consider how our various repertoires of contemporary worship music may influence, and be influenced by, our own political, economic, and cultural predilections. Powery is forthright in bringing a critique to bear upon current worship practices and content based upon his interpretation of the songs of Revelation, arguing that these songs offer a dynamic combination of praise of the God of heaven and resistance to political oppression and pain: "In light of this biblical reflection, it appears that much of contemporary praise and prosperity talk misses the mark when it comes to the embrace of pain as critical to praise, especially a pain that is perpetuated by political oppression. In some way, one might argue that popular praise and prosperity preaching are propped up by the political powers of the economic market and pay allegiance to the empire-state."[12] In Powery's opinion, contemporary praise music and prosperity preaching alike have much to learn from the biblical tradition of the Revelation hymns. Pain does not have to be ignored nor avoided in our music because it will not have the final word in the end. Powery's interpretation of John's lyrical messaging is that "it is God's power alone that can undo the earthly powers of Roman imperialism."[13] If he is correct, then perhaps we can be open to the emergence of new songs that combine praise with resistance, embolden the church to struggle for justice, and assure us that the victory we pursue is ordered and ordained by God.

Symbols: An Open Door, the Throne of Heaven, and White Robes

The book of Revelation is known for its symbolism. Out of the many that appear in the text, I have selected three symbols for discussion on the basis of their potential for inspiring the imagination of an evangelizing church: the open door, the throne of heaven, and the white robes.

My reading of the open door offers an alternative to popular depictions of heaven with St. Peter guarding individual access to the gate with documentation, riddles, and questions. John sees the open door immediately after the reading of the seven letters: "After this I looked, and there in heaven a door stood open! And the first voice, which I had heard speaking

---

11. Hardin, "Theology," 243–44.
12. Powery, "Painful Praise," 75.
13. Powery, "Painful Praise," 73.

to me like a trumpet, said, 'Come up here, and I will show you what must take place after this'" (4:1). If there is one compelling message from Revelation that motivates the ministry of winning converts and nurturing disciples for the kingdom of God, it is simply this: a door stands open in heaven. There are other doors in Revelation. For example, the text where a door is mentioned in the letter to the Laodiceans has often been cited by preachers and evangelists to invite persons to Christian commitment by opening the door to their hearts: "Behold, I stand at the door and knock. If anyone hears My voice and opens the door, I will come in to him and dine with him, and he with Me" (3:20). But the image of an open door to heaven—that is, not the door to one's heart, but a door that leads to God's eternal presence—suggests a different approach to preaching, teaching, and outreach. If heaven has an open door, our responsibility is not to shut the door, or to police the door, but simply to announce that it is open. We can share the invitation to enter the open door unencumbered by inner reluctance or external restrictions. I do not interpret the open door theologically, signifying a doctrine of inclusion, because I discern a clear distinction between having open access to heaven and being called to account and subjected to judgment after arriving there. The heart of evangelism, the good news, is to announce that the door is open. If heaven's door is open, it follows that our churches must find ways to open our doors (both physical and virtual) to welcome all kinds of people to join us in practices of faith, discipleship, and spiritual formation.

The first thing John sees in the Spirit after entering the open door is the throne: "At once I was in the spirit, and there in heaven stood a throne, with one seated on the throne! And the one seated there looks like jasper and carnelian, and around the throne is a rainbow that looks like an emerald" (4:2–3). Powery explains that in the book of Revelation "throne" is a political term, thus meaning that the "throne of God" is a political polemic: "For Roman culture, Rome was the center with worship directed at the emperors, while for John the throne of God is the center. Interestingly, by focusing on and envisioning the throne of God, John implicitly asserts that the ultimate center is outside of the everyday world governed by the Roman imperials."[14] This view of the throne of God at the center of the universe is, in itself, a declaration of political resistance against the imperialist regime of Rome: "John wants his hearers to shower lavish praise on God, and in so doing they will declare political resistance against the imperialist regime of Rome."[15]

Some think the description of the throne is not significant, but I offer an alternative view: the color of the throne, colors around the throne,

14. Powery, "Painful Praise," 74.
15. Powery, "Painful Praise," 74.

and the color of the one seated on the throne should not be overlooked. The throne of heaven is white. It is surrounded by a rainbow, signifying a bright array of the full palette of refracted color combinations ranging from indigo to red and yellow. In the natural order of things, the rainbow appears when the sun breaks through at a certain angle in the aftermath of a storm. The throne conveys a magnificent display of light, sound, and power. Surrounded by a rainbow, with flashes of lightning, and rumblings and peals of thunder (4:5), the throne is the site of a celestial storm. Theologically, the rainbow and the thunderstorm associated with the throne of heaven signify both covenant and judgment.

Color is also specifically attributed to the one seated on the throne, who "looks like jasper and carnelian," two precious stones that bear some combination of shades of brown and red. God is not described here in anthropomorphic terms, but the one seated on the throne clearly is not white. Nor is Jesus white in Revelation, notwithstanding Warner Sallman's iconic 1940 painting *Head of Christ* that renders Jesus as a Nordic blond. The depictions of the risen Lord in Revelation stand in stark contrast to the white Jesus who remains predominant in art, film, sacred architecture, and in the mindset of many Christians, especially in North America:

> I saw one like the Son of Man, clothed with a long robe and with a golden sash across his chest. His head and his hair were white as white wool, white as snow; his eyes were like a flame of fire, his feet were like burnished bronze, refined as in a furnace, and his voice was like the sound of many waters. (1:13b–15)

Granted, his head and hair are described as white in John's encounter of him in Revelation 1, but his feet have the deep brown coloration of burnished bronze. "White as snow" is not an accurate description of the skin color of modern persons who identify as white people, neither do they have woolly hair or dark brown feet. So we can safely assume that Revelation is not intending to depict Jesus as a white man. However, if we want to adhere to the notion that Jesus is white, we must disregard how Revelation colors his feet. On the other hand, if our preferred portrayal of Jesus is black, the texture of his hair suits our imagination better than the color of his head. My resolution of the question of the color of the occupants of the throne of heaven is to acknowledge that together they reflect the full spectrum of coloration represented throughout the human race.

In fact, the color white is referenced throughout the book of Revelation. There is a great white throne, and there are white stones, white horses, and white robes. In the letters to the churches at Sardis and Laodicea, white robes are associated with moral piety, victory, and dignity: "A few persons in Sardis who have not soiled their clothes; they will walk with me, dressed in white, for they are worthy. If you conquer, you will be clothed like them in white robes. . . . I counsel you to buy from me . . . white robes to clothe you and to keep the shame of your nakedness from being seen" (3:4–5b, 18).

One of the most stunning scenarios of all in the book of Revelation is the innumerable global gathering of persons from every nation, ethnicity, and language who stand before the throne of God and the Lamb of God wearing white robes:

> After this I looked, and there was a great multitude that no one could count, from every nation, from all tribes and peoples and languages, standing before the throne and before the Lamb, robed in white, with palm branches in their hands. They cried out in a loud voice, saying, "Salvation belongs to our God who is seated on the throne, and to the Lamb!" . . . Then one of the elders addressed me, saying, "Who are these, robed in white, and where have they come from?" I said to him, "Sir, you are the one that knows." Then he said to me, "These are they who have come out of the great ordeal; they have washed their robes and made them white in the blood of the Lamb." (7:9–10, 13–14)

The white-robed multitude is an unambiguous statement of the universality of the human family, who in heaven are clothed with a white robe of global communion and uniformity that makes the many, one before God. The palm branches in their hands signify victory, but in a jarring contradiction, the whiteness of their robes is the result of their engagement in struggle and bloodshed. Instead of staining their garments red, the blood has served as a cleansing agent to make their robes white. What is inescapable here are the notions of struggle, tribulation, ordeal, and martyrdom that elevate a global community of believers to a posture of solidarity with the Lamb of God who was slain. Their victory as partakers in the same struggle that resulted in the death of Jesus transports them to worship at the throne of God. There they experience the end of the hunger, thirst, and heat that tortured their lives on earth. Their souls are shepherded and refreshed by the water of life. The trauma ends, and there is deep consolation by one who knows the causes, circumstances and consequences of their weeping, and who wipes away every tear (7:15–17).

The white robe is also the chosen garment of the Lamb's bride: "Let us rejoice and celebrate, and give him the glory, for the wedding day of the Lamb has come, and his bride has made herself ready. She was given fine, pure white linen to wear, for the fine linen is the saints' acts of justice" (19:7–8). Clearly, this text correlates the saints' acts of justice with the white garment of the bride, the victorious church, who has enacted justice by struggle and engagement. These depictions of white robes challenge modern churches to consider modifying the focus of our preaching and evangelizing so that our messaging is informed by a vision of the holy intersectionality of heaven.[16] The white robe does not negate racial difference or insinuate white supremacy. Rather, it establishes the equality and inclusion of persons in every human category in the plan of God. The image of the white robe signals a pilgrimage toward unity in allegiance to the testimony of truth, the commitment to struggle, and an abiding thirst for earthly and divine justice, that is, the justice we strive for in our economic and political contexts, even as justice flows from the throne of God.

Conclusion

This overview of some of the scenes, songs, and symbols of the book of Revelation helps us to envision how modern churches can engage in justice-seeking struggle, open-door evangelism energized by enhanced social awareness, and intentional pursuit of an inclusive intersectionality that welcomes all kinds of people to participate together in the practices of Christian faith and formation. It is my hope that these readings of the letters to the seven churches of Revelation can inspire thoughtful reconsideration of the posture so many evangelical churches have assumed in tacit complicity with the prevailing politics of racial and economic injustice. Having considered the place of wonder in the Christian life from the vantage point of social inequality and economic disparities, we acknowledge that the justice imagined in the book of Revelation is issued from the throne of God as vindication and reward for the oppressed of every tribe and nation. John's imagination shapes and empowers our aspiration to achieve social justice for our own tribes and nations by presenting a poignant image of what justice will look (and sound) like in heaven—an unending celebration of equity and equality voiced by a diverse congregation unified in one language of ecstatic praise and proclamation. We need new songs focusing our worship repertoire on the reign of God without idolizing empire or culture. Finally, by re-imagining the open door, the throne, the white robes, and other symbols of Revelation in light of John's vision of eschatological diversity, we can restore and realign the public witness of the overcoming church, under the authority of and in solidarity with the Lamb who has redeemed us to God by his blood out of every tribe and language and people and nation.

---

16. See McCaulley, *Reading While Black*, 115–16.

13

Evangelical Theology and the Christian Church

DAVID LAUBER

Robert McAfee Brown describes the compelling glory of the gospel as he writes, "The gospel is not the mystery of incomprehensible darkness but the mystery of incomprehensible light. It is not that we see so little of what God has done that we are puzzled, but that in the light of God's revelation in Christ we see so much of what God has done that we are dazzled."[1] By gazing on the beauty and glory of God as manifest in Jesus Christ and his gospel, we cannot help but respond in awe, wonder, and gratitude. We do not stare into the abyss of darkness; rather, we turn our eyes to the brilliance of God's light. Dazzled and overwhelmed by God's glorious revelation, we respond in silence and worship. Our worship leads us to take up joyful and patient reflection on the beauty of the gospel as we seek to come to understand God more truly so that we might serve him more faithfully. And we are moved from awed silence to creaturely attempts to speak faithfully about God and his ways. We speak and then must return to silence and worship before we take up our speech once again.[2]

---

1. Brown, "Introduction," 18. This is a description of Karl Barth's approach to the task of dogmatic theology, yet it certainly applies to every theology that is done in jubilant response to the glorious and astonishing light of the gospel of Jesus Christ.

2. In the wise essay, "Silence in the face of mystery," Rowan Williams writes, "[I]f we believe that our humanity is constantly growing, then there have got to be moments

The aim of this essay is to demonstrate that evangelical theology should be marked by wonder in response to the dazzling and incomprehensible glory of God's revelation in Christ. This wonder calls us to humility before God as we acknowledge that God is uncontrollable, unpredictable, and cannot be domesticated. Furthermore, the dazzling wonder of the gospel compels us to be humble, generous, gracious, and loving before others. In making this case, I will reflect on the thirty years of the Wheaton Theology Conference as an example for how evangelical theology can respond faithfully and humbly to the wondrous revelation of God in Christ. In looking back at the significance of the Wheaton Theology Conference—its successes and shortcomings—we will consider a way forward for evangelical theology.

The Wheaton Theology Conference: A Brief History

As their families shared Christmas dinner together, Dennis Okholm and Timothy Phillips developed a plan to host a theology conference at Wheaton College, a Christian liberal arts college outside of Chicago, Illinois.[3] As friends and colleagues, Tim and Dennis had a vision for advancing the discipline of *theology* at Wheaton. People on campus routinely referred to their department as the Bible department, since the majority of professors and classes focused on biblical studies. Trained as theologians, however, Tim and Dennis sought to cultivate the distinctive work of theological studies within the department and at the college. At the same time, Wheaton had a long-standing tradition of hosting an annual Philosophy Conference, and Dennis and Tim thought it was time to host something similar. Beginning in April 1992, and continuing for thirty years, theologians, students, pastors, and church lay leaders gathered for two to three days every April to explore topics significant for the identity and mission of the church, contributing to the development of evangelical theology more broadly in the process.

---

when we are taken beyond the familiar and the controllable. A growing humanity, a maturing humanity, is one that's prepared for silence, because it's prepared at important moments to say, 'I can't domesticate, I can't get on top of this.' God is that environment, that encounter, that we will never get to the bottom of and that we will never control."

3. The content of this essay draws extensively from a conversation that I hosted with three principal organizers of the Wheaton Theology Conference over the years: Dennis Okholm taught at Wheaton from 1989 until 2003, Mark Husbands taught theology at Wheaton from 2001 until 2007, and Jeffrey Greenman served as associate dean of Biblical and Theological Studies at Wheaton from 2005 until 2013. Laubner et al., "Wheaton Theology Conference: A Retrospective" (roundtable, Wheaton Theology Conference, virtual, April 9, 2021).

Okholm and Phillips not only cast the vision for the Wheaton Theology Conference, they also served as its principal organizers for the first decade. The first conference proceedings were self-published; the admission fee was $10; and Tim and Dennis, along with their wives, made the coffee, printed the program and abstract booklets, and oversaw every detail of the event.[4] The conference carried on after Tim's death in the fall of 2000 and Dennis's move to Azusa Pacific University in 2003. Through it all, their original vision remained: to gather theologians to address matters of contemporary significance to the church and the academy. The focus was not primarily Christian doctrine, as important as doctrine is to the life of the church, but rather current realities facing the church and the intersection of theology with other academic disciplines, e.g., the natural sciences, social sciences, and humanities. This was a theology conference squarely within the liberal arts setting of the college.

Okholm identifies the 1995 conference on *postliberalism*[5] as the most significant during his time at Wheaton and the one that persuaded him to rethink his understanding of the task and method of Christian theology. The introduction to the subsequent publication includes a stark depiction of the state of evangelicalism at the time and a call for new direction and a renewed focus on the unique revelation of God in Christ.

> For the last five decades evangelicalism worked through the intellectual and social structures of American life to engage and transform it from within. Across the disciplines evangelical scholars mustered great intellectual vigor in emphasizing the congruence of nature and grace, reason and revelation (since all truth is God's truth), thus presenting Christianity as *the* truth.
>
> Similarly, many evangelicals are now at the center of key occupations. If all truth is God's truth and all vocations can be callings of God, aren't the politicians, the business people and the scientists glorifying God in their professions? . . .
>
> The original evangelical strategy for bringing the gospel to America by emphasizing the commonality between reason and revelation has resulted in the accolades that it currently enjoys.

---

4. Throughout the years the conference benefited from increased institutional support, the efforts of office staff, and the participation of students. The conference also enjoyed a fruitful partnership with InterVarsity Press for over two decades.

5. Okholm and Phillips describe the movement as follows: "At the center of resurgence of confessional Christianity are the postliberals. Postliberalism refers to a theological movement most commonly linked with Yale Divinity School. It seeks to reverse the trend in modern Christianity of accommodation to culture" ("Nature of Confession," 11). George Lindbeck and George Hunsinger, noted postliberal scholars, were plenary speakers at the conference.

> But has this strategy actually worked to subvert the mission? Have evangelicalism's confidence in reason and delight with American culture become its quagmire? So it seems. Fifty years later the question no longer concerns the trivialization of reason but the trivialization of revelation! This concern is crucial.[6]

Here Okholm and Phillips raise a concern about the price paid by evangelicalism in its efforts to gain a hearing and exert influence in various centers of power in the United States—business, politics, and the academy. The cost of this acceptance was the danger of accommodation and minimizing the unique truth and power of God's revelation and saving action in Jesus Christ. In this, the conference aimed to reinvigorate evangelical theology and to encourage evangelical churches to reorient themselves towards God's revelation in the gospel and in Scripture, and from there to embody a theology of the cross in service of the world.

The conference arose out of collegial friendship—Tim and Dennis—and continued to be carried out by an expanded cadre of theologians at Wheaton. This was not a structured plan to develop a "Wheaton school of theology." Rather, it consisted of a group of theologians who brought their own scholarly expertise, denominational commitments, and love for Christ and his church to the task of teaching theology and modeling faithful and serious theological thinking for students.

Audience

The vision for the Wheaton Theology Conference reflected a commitment to both particular and broad audiences. Since the focus of the conference was not primarily Christian doctrine, the envisioned audience was not primarily academic theologians. Academics spoke at and attended the conference, but they directed their lectures to the wider Wheaton College community: students and professors from across the disciplines. A second, but no less important audience was the wider church, including pastors and laypersons. The conference was intentionally scheduled for the end of the week after Easter, in order to accommodate the schedules of pastors. Every year, the college welcomed local pastors as well as pastors and laypeople who traveled long distances to engage in theological conversation around themes essential to the identity, ministry, and mission of the church.

---

6. Phillips and Okholm, "Nature of Confession," 9.

Topics

The earliest years of the conference focused on themes related to the church and culture, including a discussion of religious pluralism and an exploration of a new kind of apologetics. The conference also addressed interdisciplinary questions in theology and science as well as theology and psychology. Finally, it focused on the significant need for racial reconciliation within the church and society—a reality that remains a critical issue for the church and society today.

The second decade of the conference turned to the church and doctrine. Some years focused on Scripture, justification, or the Trinity, while others examined pressing doctrinal issues related to women in ministry and theological aesthetics. During this period, the organizers advanced significant ecumenical engagement, most significantly, a conference on "Evangelicals and Roman Catholics in Dialogue." This was the first conference that consisted exclusively of invited speakers—there was no call for papers, since the complexity of the topic required that the schedule be assembled carefully—and consisted of pairs of Roman Catholic and evangelical scholars treating a range of theological topics and doctrines.[7]

The third decade of the conference continued the trajectory of addressing contemporary issues and doctrines within the church in a multidisciplinary way. These years reflect the changing shape of the theology faculty as well as the state of contemporary evangelical concerns: global Christianity, the political witness of the church, and doctrines such as the Holy Spirit, the image of God, and the humanity of Jesus. One conference commemorated the fifth centenary of the Reformation, while others focused on individual scholars, theologians, and writers—specifically, N. T. Wright, Dietrich Bonhoeffer, and Marilynne Robinson.

The final conference in 2021—"God and Wonder: Theology, Imagination, and the Arts"—invoked themes that were present throughout the conference's thirty years. By attending to the intrinsic and compelling glory and beauty of God, the presentations of the conference highlighted how the corresponding human response is one of awe and wonder.

---

7. One of the highlights of the conference was an evening address in Edman Chapel by Francis Cardinal George, the archbishop of Chicago. Wheaton College's president, Duane Litfin, introduced Cardinal George and prayed for him and for the church at the close of the evening. It was an important and powerful moment of serious ecumenical dialogue *and* prayer for the unity and mission of Christ's church.

Ethos

The vision, audience, and topics of the Wheaton Theology Conference widened the scope of evangelical theology during the conference's three-decade run. The conference highlighted prominent evangelical scholars who worked within evangelical institutions. A few scholars were frequent participants over the years, most notably Alister McGrath in the early years, and then Timothy George and Kevin Vanhoozer later on. The conference also sought to expand the engagement of evangelical theology to include confessional Protestants who do not work within evangelical institutions but frequently taught Wheaton theologians: Bruce McCormack, John Webster, George Lindbeck, George Hunsinger, Geoffrey Wainwright, and Stanley Hauerwas, to name just a few. In describing the conference participants, Mark Husbands and Daniel Treier write,

> Many of the essayists self-identify as "evangelical" or work within evangelical structures and institutions; among these we have sought to represent, within manifest limitations, the variety of ecclesiologies in the movement. Other essayists speak to evangelicalism as friendly outsiders; as confessionally orthodox Protestants, with constructive criticism they invite evangelicals to attach themselves more closely to the church's "great tradition."[8]

As noted, the conference also saw the inclusion of Roman Catholic scholars, including plenary addresses by Richard John Neuhaus, Francis Cardinal George, and others in discussions of the doctrine of justification, the sacraments, and the unity of the church. This practice encouraged a rich theological conversation, pushing evangelicals to engage more deeply from the richness of the church's great tradition.[9]

Okholm sees this broadening engagement with non-evangelical scholars as "pushing the envelope." This was not intended to be provocative in an incendiary kind of way; rather, the intent was to deepen and strengthen evangelical theology and evangelicalism. And, it was not merely a one-way engagement, as if evangelical scholars were only pupils in the conversation. For instance, one remarkable feature of the conference on postliberalism was George Lindbeck's comment during the panel discussion that closed the conference. He said that if there truly is a future of postliberal theology, it will be evangelicals who would lead the way—because of their commitment

---

8. Husbands and Treier, "Introduction," 11.

9. These ecumenical conversations were conducted in the posture displayed in the 1994 document "Evangelicals and Catholics Together: The Christian Mission in the Third Millennium."

to and being steeped in Scripture.[10] In his paper titled "What Can Evangelicals & Postliberals Learn from Each Other?," George Hunsinger similarly suggested that postliberals have much to learn from evangelicals about the centrality of the cross and "an uncompromising insistence on the saving death of Christ as the very heart of the gospel."[11] At the same time, these speakers challenged evangelicals to think more carefully and self-critically about theological method and the need for evangelicalism to develop distinguished theologians to complement esteemed evangelical biblical scholars, philosophers, and historians.[12]

Significance

The Wheaton Theology Conference attests to the growth and maturation of theology at Wheaton College, contributing to the growth and maturation of evangelical theology more broadly. Jeffrey Greenman provides a clear assessment in his comment that "Evangelical theology has matured over the period of thirty years. It has grown. It has become more interested in the rest of the theological landscape—more interested in wide interdisciplinary engagement—more interested in the global church—deeply convinced of the significance of Christian practices." Greenman suggests that historians in the future could look back on the Wheaton Theology Conference and see it as a snapshot for how evangelical theology matured over three decades.

This maturation was not without blind spots, neglected themes, overlooked voices, and missed opportunities. At times the conference reflected the social location of Wheaton College as a historically white institution

10. Lindbeck provided the final comment of the panel discussion, which was the final comment of the conference: "I have not expressed fully enough my enormous gratitude for this conference. I will also say that if the sort of research program represented by postliberalism has a real future as a communal enterprise of the church, it's more likely to be carried on by evangelicals than anyone else" (in Phillips and Okholm, "Panel Discussion," 252–53).

11. Hunsinger, "Evangelicals & Postliberals," 149. Hunsinger continues, "Within the field of Christian doctrine per se, [evangelical theology] has consistently been the standard-bearer of the Reformation in so far as it has stood—often in a lonely and exposed position—for 'Christ alone,' 'grace alone,' and 'faith alone' in all matters pertaining to salvation" (149).

12. Hunsinger writes, "Although evangelicals have consistently produced an impressive number of distinguished biblical scholars over the years, especially in the field of New Testament (and have also produced a distinguished crop of philosophers and of historians of Christianity in North America), they have not done nearly so well in producing truly distinguished theologians, and this shortfall may have something to do with their failure to attend sufficiently to questions of theological method" ("Evangelicals & Postliberals," 150).

in a comfortable suburban setting, and did not engage explicitly and consistently with the pressing societal and ecclesial realities of racism, sexism, and economic disparity. In light of this history, a continued maturation of evangelical theology must include serious and self-critical attention to Willie Jennings's account of an intellectual form of "white masculinist self-sufficiency, a way of being in the world that aspires to exhibit possession, mastery, and control of knowledge first, and of one's self second, and if possible of one's world."[13]

In the current cultural moment, the term *evangelical* is contested and is frequently associated with certain types of politics in the United States—politics that are all too often marked by animus, control, and domination. A way forward for evangelical theology should focus once again on the core meaning of "evangelical": *evangel* or gospel. The three panelists suggested that we need to begin again at the beginning—a claim that is reminiscent of Karl Barth's refrain that theology must always begin again at the beginning, and the beginning is none other than Jesus Christ. We must persist in asking the essential question "What is the gospel?," and this must push us to ask again and again how this gospel is "good news" for those who suspect that at its core evangelicalism is nothing more than a social and political ideology.[14]

In my judgment, this must be done in two specific ways. First, we must identify and reject all forms of a theology of glory—a mode of theology and Christian engagement with the world that grasps after the power, wisdom, influence, and control of the world. We must instead embody a theology of the cross—a way of life that recognizes the power of God in the suffering, humiliation, and the apparent weakness and folly of Christ crucified. Second, as clamors for freedom and liberty pervade our ecclesial and public discourse, we must take up true Christian freedom—a freedom to take up lives of love and obedience to God and self-expending love and service to others.

---

13. Jennings, *After Whiteness*, 29.

14. In a footnote related to what evangelicals might learn from postliberals, Hunsinger makes an incisive observation that continues to be true for some quarters of evangelicalism today: "Perhaps it might also be mentioned here for the sake of future discussion that from a postliberal point of view, American evangelicals have typically been at least as excessive (and with consequences no less unfortunate for the progress of the gospel) in committing themselves to the pathologies of American nationalism and militarism as they have in encumbering themselves with the excesses of modern epistemology. The common thread in both cases, if I may say so, seems to have something to do with a lack of Christian self-confidence, an inordinate, or insufficiently self-critical, desire for external validation, and an aversion (in practice) to the theology of the cross" ("Evangelicals & Postliberals," 149n94). Two current and much discussed books address the point that Hunsinger is making here—one by sociologists and one by a historian (Whitehead and Perry, *Taking America Back for God*; Du Mez, *Jesus and John Wayne*).

A New Future for Evangelical Theology

As we look back over thirty years of the Wheaton Theology Conference and take stock of our current situation, I will provide a brief suggestion for moving forward. My central focus is on the need for humility *and* confidence in a contested and complicated world. Evangelicals are called to serve the world humbly and selflessly. This humility arises out of the confidence that we have in the inherent truth and power of the gospel, and the trustworthiness of God to carry out his intentions for the world and the people he has created and loves. In commenting on Paul's Letter to the Ephesians, Rowan Williams reflects on the utter trustworthiness of God, based on the remarkable claim that "in the events around Jesus Christ, God has at last made his purpose clear; . . . the purposes of God that existed from the world's foundation are now laid bare for us. This and this alone is God's 'agenda': the world he has made is designed to become a reconciled world."[15] Williams links God's act of reconciliation in Christ with the proper human response of praise, "This reconciliation liberates human voices for praise, for celebrating the glory of the God who has made it possible and has held steadily to his purpose from the beginning. This is what God is after, and there is no hidden agenda, nothing is kept back" (8–9).

Secure in Christ, and in the life-giving power of God, we can bear witness in the world without antagonism, without the desperate need for acceptance and validation, and without the aggressive stance of considering any opposition as a mortal and existential threat that must be attacked and defeated. A focus on Christ frees us from the felt need to control our situation and to return opposition with stronger and more aggressive opposition. Our task as members of Christ's church, as witnesses to Christ and his gospel, is not to defeat our enemies. Rather, our task is to commend the truth of the gospel as we proclaim it in word and deed. As disciples of the crucified and risen Christ, we must deny ourselves, take up our cross, and follow our Lord into the world, in order to serve the world.

Christ the Center

We must acknowledge that Jesus Christ is at the center of all that we do and all that we are as Christians. In making this statement, we must be willing to ask the question again and again: *who* is this Jesus who is at the center? Furthermore, if Jesus is genuinely at the center of our lives, then we need to ask *where* he is. We need to be where he is and we need to go where he goes.

---

15. Williams, *Tokens of Trust*, 8.

Who is the Christ who is at the center of evangelical theology? Christ is the exalted one—the one in whom all things hold together (Col 1), the one to whom we are instructed to take every thought captive (2 Cor 10:5), the one in whom all things will be gathered up (Eph 1). Christ who is at the center of evangelical theology is the incarnate Word in whom are hidden all the treasures of wisdom and knowledge (Col 2:3). Christ is intrinsically preeminent and exalted. We need to be aware of the dangerous temptation to craft a picture of Christ in our own image—to make an idol of Christ who serves our own agendas.

We must also recognize that this Christ is also Jesus of Nazareth, from Galilee, the one who ministered to the needy and the outcast. He is the one who healed the sick, fed the hungry, and delivered the possessed from their afflictions. He proclaimed and inaugurated the coming kingdom of God (Luke 4). This Christ is the one true human who lived a life of perfect obedience to the will of the Father in carrying out his vocation. This obedience is manifested in his resistance to temptation—his walking the way that led him to his arrest, trial, suffering, death, and burial. He was vindicated in being raised from the dead and now, ascended and exalted, intercedes at the right hand of the Father even as he is present in the world through the Holy Spirit. It is this Jesus who is at the center of evangelical theology. It is this Jesus who is Lord.

Acknowledging Christ at the center and confessing that Jesus is Lord leads us to ask the risky question of where Christ is. This question is risky because it involves giving up control. It decenters us. In a culture that prizes self-sufficiency, agency, and choice, we are tempted to think that we take Christ where we want to go, as if we fit Jesus into our plans and story. Yet, Jesus might call us to places where we are loathe to go. This question is risky because we must be reminded that we cannot be careless when we confidently declare that we seek to follow Jesus. Jesus' words in response to the request of the mother of James and John for her sons to be with him at his right hand and left hand might also apply to us, "You do not know what you are asking. Are you able to drink the cup that I am to drink?" (Matt 20:22). We desire to enjoy the privilege of reigning with Christ in his kingdom, but his command to us is to be unlike those who exercise domineering power, authority, and control over others. We can never underestimate the call of Jesus that "whoever would be great among you must be your servant, and whoever would be first among you must be your slave; even as the Son of man came not to be served but to serve, and to give his life as a ransom for many" (Matt 20:26–27). We must not be flippant and self-assured in our claim to follow Christ, just as we must not be careless in casually asking the

Spirit to guide us, for as Annie Dillard reminds us, "God may draw us out to where we can never return."[16]

This call to acknowledge Christ at the center and to go where he is present and acting in the world has particular force for me, and for those connected to Wheaton College. The motto "For Christ and His Kingdom" is etched in the stone sign that welcomes people to our campus, it is on our letterhead, and our email signatures. The question always before me, and one I must self-consciously and self-critically ask is, "Do I acknowledge the vast difference between Christ Jesus as Lord and Caesar as Lord, and am I truly committed to advancing the kingdom of Christ in contrast to the worldly, imperial 'kingdoms' of this world?"

Faithful Proclamation

We would be wise to follow Paul's description in 2 Corinthians 4 of his own ministry as we consider a way forward for evangelical theology. It is a word of exhortation that needs to be heard in our churches, colleges, and seminaries. Paul writes: "For we do not proclaim ourselves; we proclaim Jesus Christ as Lord and ourselves as your slaves for Jesus' sake. For God, who said, 'Let light shine out of darkness,' has shone in our hearts to give the light of the knowledge of the glory of God in the face of Jesus Christ. But we have this treasure in clay jars, so that it may be made clear that this extraordinary power belongs to God and does not come from us" (2 Cor 4:5–7). This text directs our attention to the compelling beauty of the glory that shines in the face of Christ. Paul then directs us outward as slaves to the world—slaves to those before whom we bear witness to the truth and power of the gospel—reminding us that in his grace God makes Christ known to us and that through our weakness and frail efforts God bears witness to his own extraordinary power.[17]

---

16. Dillard, *Teaching a Stone to Talk*, 40. The entire quote is instructive: "Why do we people in churches seem like cheerful, brainless tourists on a packaged tour of the Absolute? On the whole, I do not find Christians, outside the catacombs, sufficiently sensible of conditions. Does anyone have the foggiest idea what sort of power we so blithely invoke? Or, as I suspect, does not one believe a word of it? The churches are children playing on the floor with their chemistry sets, mixing up a batch of TNT to kill a Sunday morning. It is madness to wear ladies' straw hats and velvet hats to church; we should be wearing crash helmets. Ushers should issue life preservers and signal flares; they should lash us to our pews. For the sleeping God may wake some day and take offense, or the waking God may draw us out to where we can never return."

17. In commenting on the significance of this text for the function of a pastor and congregation, C. E. B. Cranfield writes, "It is the minister's task to strive to bring himself and his congregation back again and again under the discipline of the gospel, from

Given the dazzling light of the truth of God, we must also take up our theological work in wonder and delight. In other words, evangelical theology must be done responsibly and with self-critical awareness, and it must be done cheerfully and with delight—trusting in the trustworthiness of God and trusting that the truth and mission of God does not depend upon us for the success of our work. A theology focused on the gospel is doxological. Its aim is to point to the truth of Christ and it should not be used as a weapon in a battle against culture or theological opponents. Theology that is doxological is also concerned with being faithful to historical and confessional orthodoxy. This form of orthodoxy arises out of the true and life-giving words of Scripture and points us to the peerless reality of Jesus Christ, who was sent by the Father in the power of the Holy Spirit for the life of the world. As John Webster writes, "The good news of the gospel of Christ is not a weapon with which to attack; it is an invitation to delight in and celebrate the lavish goodness of God." And the function of orthodoxy, therefore, is "to focus the imagination of the people of God in such a way that Jesus Christ is recognized, acknowledged, confessed, worshiped, and served."[18] Theological orthodoxy ought to lead to glorious worship of the true God, faithful and confident witness to the inherent truth of the gospel, and responsible service and participation in the mission of God in the world.[19]

We proclaim Christ, and our proclamation of Christ is dependent upon the prior work of God. Paul compares God's calling light into being at the beginning of creation with God's act of illumination in each of our hearts, so that we might have the knowledge of the glory of God as we gaze into the face of Jesus. God must be active. God must enable us to see his glory in the face of Jesus, in our encounter with the risen Christ who was crucified for our sake. Perhaps the most essential presupposition to theological study and Christian witness and mission is that God is indeed active—God has acted in the past—God is active now—and God will act in the future. The God we study, consider, and behold is living, personal, and other than us—God's ways are not our ways—his thoughts are not our thoughts (Isa 55:8–9). God is "the high and lofty one who inhabits eternity, whose name is Holy," who dwells in the high and holy place, yet God is also

---

which we are all of us ever prone to stray" ("Minister and Congregation," 165).

18. Webster, "Jesus—God for Us," 96.

19. Stanley Hauerwas insists that upholding the beauty of orthodoxy means that "orthodoxy betrays itself if it is used as a hammer to beat into submission those we think heterodox." He continues, "Orthodoxy can tempt us to self-righteousness and a protectiveness that betrays the joy and confidence that should be the heart of the gospel. When orthodoxy becomes defensive rather than a form of love and proclamation it denies its own reality" ("Foreword," x).

the one who dwells "with those who are contrite and humble in spirit" (Isa 57:15). God is the Holy One in our midst—and he announces his holiness and his distinction from mortals by displaying his warm and tender loving compassion (Hos 11:8–9).

The treasure that we have, Paul continues, is stored in clay jars. The jars in which we store the treasure of the gospel—the treasure of the good news of God revealed, embodied, and enacted in the person of Jesus Christ—are fragile. They are weak and easily cracked, chipped, broken, smashed. The fragility of the container, however, does not compromise or jeopardize the precious treasure of the gospel. For the knowledge of the glory of God in the face of Jesus Christ belongs to God and is never to be counted as our possession. This knowledge is not dependent upon our clever minds, earnest hearts, or smooth tongues but relies upon the power and grace of God. The treasure of the gospel that we proclaim does not come from us, it finds its source in God. We are not alone, Paul says, for we are accompanied by Jesus, and in all that we do, especially in times of trial, God is able to work in us to show forth Christ to the world. Paul goes on to say:

> We are afflicted in every way, but not crushed; perplexed, but not driven to despair; persecuted, but not forsaken; struck down but not destroyed; always carrying in the body the death of Jesus, so that the life of Jesus may also be made visible in our bodies. For while we live, we are always being given up to death for Jesus' sake, so that the life of Jesus may be made visible in our mortal flesh. (2 Cor 4:8–11)

Even in the weakness of our human efforts, the power of God is proclaimed through us. We do not proclaim ourselves; we proclaim Jesus as Lord. When we are afflicted but not crushed, we do not demonstrate our own strength alone. When we are perplexed but not driven to despair, we do not prove the sharpness of our minds alone. When we are persecuted but not forsaken, we do not manifest our resolve alone. And when we are struck down but not destroyed, we do not rely upon our own power alone. Rather, in all of these things, we depend upon the strength and power of God to sustain us, and in all of these things we pray that God might make the life of Jesus visible in our bodies, in our mortal flesh. For again, we do not proclaim ourselves; we proclaim Jesus Christ as Lord, and by proclaiming Jesus Christ as Lord we acknowledge, through the illuminating power of the Holy Spirit, the glory and beauty of God that shines in his face.

Admitting that the treasure of the gospel is housed in clay jars does not nullify the task of theology. It does not relieve us of our responsibility to reflect critically on how the gospel is proclaimed in today's world; rather, it reminds us that our work is of relative significance. It reminds us that the goal of our theological work is for God to use our efforts to show forth Christ. It reminds us that in our work as theologians, we are pointing away from ourselves, toward the beauty and glory of God and Christ. We are called to bear witness to God's self-revelation in the face of Christ, to the reconciliation and redemption of the world by God in the life, death, and resurrection of Jesus Christ.

In pride and self-sufficiency, a theology of glory seeks to draw attention to ourselves. It projects an image of Christ that reflects an idealized version of ourselves—a face of Christ that is filled with power, vigor, and strength. In contrast, in humility and dependence on God's grace, a theology of the cross encounters the glorious power and love of God in the disfigured face of Christ crucified. We stand in silence and awe before this wondrous revelation of God, as we bear witness to the glory and beauty of God as displayed in the unsightly face of the crucified. We must hold together both Psalm 45 and Isaiah 53: Christ is "the most handsome of men; grace is poured upon [his] lips; therefore God has blessed [him] forever" (Ps 45:2), while at the same time we must accept the description of the prophet Isaiah that "he had no form or majesty that we should look at him, nothing in his appearance that we should desire him. He was despised and rejected by others; a man of suffering and acquainted with infirmity; and as one from whom others hide their faces he was despised, and we held him of no account" (Isa 53:2–3). As Pope Benedict XVI writes in reflecting on these two passages: "The One who is Beauty itself let himself be slapped in the face, spat upon, crowned with thorns. However, in his Face that is so disfigured, there appears the genuine, extreme beauty: the beauty of love that goes 'to the very end.'"[20]

---

20. Ratzinger, "Feeling of Things, the Contemplation of Beauty."

Postlude

14

Waiting on Wonder

Jeffrey W. Barbeau

I waited patiently for the Lord; he inclined to me and heard my cry. He drew me up from the desolate pit, out of the miry bog, and set my feet upon a rock, making my steps secure. He put a new song in my mouth, a song of praise to our God. Many will see and fear, and put their trust in the Lord.

Blessed is the man who makes the Lord his trust, who does not turn to the proud, to those who go astray after false gods! Thou hast multiplied, O Lord my God, thy wondrous deeds and thy thoughts toward us; none can compare with thee! Were I to proclaim and tell of them, they would be more than can be numbered.

(Ps 40:1–5, RSV)

There's an old story about Thomas Aquinas that emerged about fifty years after his death.[1] It was around the time of his canonization for sainthood, as the individuals commissioned to compile the details about his life and piety looked back over the central events in his career. The story was first

---

1. Originally delivered in undergraduate chapel during the Wheaton Theology Conference on April 9, 2021.

told by Thomas's amanuensis, a close companion for many years of his life. Thomas was nearly fifty years old at the time and had already achieved an astonishingly productive record as a theologian. His writings included not only hundreds of sermons, treatises, and commentaries, but also his greatest achievement, the *Summa Theologiae*. He was so productive as a writer that stories emerged over time that he required multiple amanuenses to take down his thoughts simultaneously, since none could keep up. I personally find that hard to believe, but, whatever the case, there is no doubt that he was writing at a pace that is remarkably unparalleled. And then, on December 6, 1273, Thomas stopped entirely. When questioned why, he stated, "Everything that I have written seems like straw to me compared to those things that I have seen and have been revealed to me."

Thirty years have passed since the beginning of the Wheaton Theology Conference. In that period, the conference has taken up some of the most pressing theological issues of our times. In just its recent history, the conference has worked on major doctrines such as the image of God, topics such as political theology, and influential figures such as Dietrich Bonhoeffer. In this, the final year of the conference, we've decided to close with what might be deemed as something of a nod to Thomas: "God and Wonder."

Wonder, of course, is an inherently difficult word to pin down. And no doubt some who heard the theme this year have had to stop for a moment to consider its meaning.[2] There's a double-sidedness to wonder. As a noun, it indicates a miracle or spectacle; as a verb, wonder suggests surprise, astonishment, or admiration. You might say, "We wonder at God's wonders," but then that might be just as confusing. Perhaps, with Thomas, you might think we'd better just remain silent, for all this is but straw.

I think the psalm today indicates otherwise. In the moving lines of Psalm 40, the psalmist pleads for deliverance from suffering. But the text does not merely describe the feeling of despair, it instructs us in how to respond to life from a position of truth-telling in our weakness. Notice the opening words: "I waited patiently for the Lord; he inclined to me and heard my cry." The psalm immediately signals two themes that we desperately need to hear today: *patient endurance* paired with *eager anticipation*.

Patient endurance surely describes what many of us have felt during the past year. Life in a global pandemic is a life of persistence, requiring fortitude and tenacity over the long haul. This year has also brought to greater public consciousness the injustices that persist in our nation. As we celebrate Asian

---

2. Emily McGowin's excellent essay at the commencement of this volume provides an essential theological exploration of "Wonder and Theology."

Pacific American Heritage Month, we lament the ways that members of our community have been targeted in acts of prejudice and violence.

In the Scriptures, waiting is met with a personal response: "I waited patiently for the LORD . . ." and "he heard my cry." In this, the psalmist speaks of eager anticipation: our present suffering is not the last word. God has not abandoned us. We should wait *and* expect God's deliverance at any moment. Let's be clear: this is not some fanciful response of sentimentality. This is expectation rooted in a history of God's faithfulness in the past and a hope for a future that exceeds the darkness of our present reality.

Some of the most striking lines in the psalm immediately follow—lines that provide an image of instability paired with hope: "He drew me up from the desolate pit, out of the miry bog, and set my feet upon a rock, making my steps secure" (v. 2). When I was a boy, my family frequently spent summers at the ocean. I'm from New York, so it wasn't uncommon for us to travel down to New Jersey or farther south to Florida and spend several days at the beach. Now the sand at a beachfront can certainly be unstable, but mostly the ground beneath the waves at the shore is pretty firm. You could stand at the edge of the water and slowly watch your feet get covered by the rough sand as the waves passed in and out from the shore.

Those experiences at the ocean made all the more memorable my first time swimming in a lake. I'll never forget how startled I felt when, after so many years spent stepping on the gravelly sand of the beachfront, my body recoiled at the feeling as I pressed my feet down on the slimy ground. Seaweed and other plants pressed against my legs as the mud and muck of the algae-covered ground seeped between my toes. In that moment, I searched frantically for something solid to stand on—something firm that would hold my weight and restore my confidence.

The psalmist mentions the mud and mire of a pit, but I can't help but recall another slimy rescue in the Bible. Remember Jonah? God told him to go to Nineveh, but he wanted nothing to do with it. Sometimes I think we've become so accustomed to the story of "Jonah and the whale" that we've forgotten just how scary the divine command was in the first place. The people of Nineveh were terrible—this was Israel's loathsome enemy, a people as wicked and fearsome as any in history. When they vanquished their enemies, they practiced a cruelty that surpasses anything you'll see on Netflix. Can it be any surprise to us what happened next?

Jonah's response to God's call was to get as far away as possible. And when the storms battered the boat in which he traveled, Jonah knew that his disobedience had found him out. The sailors tried in vain to escape but finally relented, casting Jonah overboard. Down he sank to the bottom of the sea, as the texts records: "The waters closed in over me, the deep was round about me; weeds were wrapped about my head at the roots of the mountains" (2:5). Instead of a rock, Jonah's deliverance took a very different turn. A great fish swallowed him up.

In chapter 9 of Herman Melville's *Moby-Dick*, Jonah is the subject of a preacher's sermon. Ishmael visits the church before setting out on the seas, and listens spellbound to Father Mapple, as he begins to speak and calls on the congregation to hear his words:

> "Starboard gangway, there! side away to larboard—larboard gangway to starboard! Midships! Midships!" And then, pausing a little, Father Mapple begins to preach, "Shipmates, this book, containing only four chapters—four yarns—is one of the smallest strands in the mighty cable of the Scriptures. Yet what depths of the soul does Jonah's deep sealine sound! what a pregnant lesson to us is this prophet! What a noble thing is that canticle in the fish's belly! How billow-like and boisterously grand! We feel the floods surging over us; we sound with him to the kelpy bottom of the waters; sea-weed and all the slime of the sea is about us! But *what* is this lesson that the book of Jonah teaches?"

What, indeed? For Melville's Father Mapple, the lesson is one of sin and repentance. The whale that swallows Jonah is a punishment from God no less than any other in the Old or New Testament.

Figure 10. Antonius Wierix, II, *Jonah Cast on the Shore by the Fish.*

But Psalm 40 gives us another perspective on the condition of Jonah or David or even us today—all who wait in a position of grief and lament. *He turned to him.* The problem isn't God's absence, it's just that sometimes we're expecting a rock and we get a fish instead.

The greatest miracle in the story of Jonah is *not* the great fish. The hardest thing to believe, the part of the story that should cause us all to sit back in astonishment and wonder, is the entirely unexpected result of Jonah's witness. For, as the story goes, once he emerged from the fish and finally went to Nineveh, the expression of God's love for a people so profoundly wicked can only be seen as a wonder-working miracle.

And this bring us to a second point: for the psalmist tells us that God's wondrous works lead us to behold in wonder: "Were I to proclaim and tell of them, they would be more than can be numbered" (40:5). And yet, that's just what Jonah does: Jonah's rock—that great fish in the sea—provided space for him to sing of God's faithfulness. Likewise, the psalmist declares, "He put a new song in my mouth, a song of praise to our God." You see, beholding God in wonder is never simple. Patient endurance and eager anticipation don't bring about instant resolution. Our songs come *amidst* the waiting. We sing while we're still in the belly of the whale.

One of the most well-known artistic renditions of this psalm was produced by the band U2. In the song "40," Bono alternately cries out, "I will sing, sing a new song" only to lament, repeatedly afterward, "How long to sing this song?" How long?

Wonder has a double-sidedness to it. We recognize the wondrous works of God and we behold in wonder, and yet the psalmist expresses something that we probably feel far more often: not the resolution of suffering but the position of waiting. Wonder has an inbuilt, eschatological quality. Expectant waiting is a longing for that which we have only begun to see but have not yet realized. As John Wesley explains, our hope rests in the God who will one day wipe every tear from our eyes: "As there will be no more death, and no more pain or sickness preparatory thereto; as there will be no more grieving for or parting with friends; so there will be no more sorrow or crying." Indeed, Wesley explains, the greater deliverance involves "a deep, an intimate, an uninterrupted union with God."[3] In the meantime, we cry out wherever injustice endures and receive comfort from the Spirit who groans within us, knowing that all is not as it should be.

It is this same eschatological quality of wonder that Charles Wesley invokes in his masterpiece hymn, "Love Divine, All Loves Excelling":

---

3. Wesley, "New Creation," 500.

> Finish, then, Thy new creation;
> Pure and spotless let us be....
> Till we cast our crowns before Thee,
> Lost in wonder, love, and praise.

The Wesleys capture the sense that life in Christ involves an expectancy of that which will only find fulfillment in total union with God. In the meantime, we wait in longing.

The poet S. T. Coleridge captures the connection between the longing and wonder in a memorable aphorism: "In Wonder all Philosophy began: in Wonder it ends: and Admiration fills up the interspace."[4] Isn't that true of so much of our lives? We begin and end with wonder, seeking in expectation. Coleridge continues: "the first Wonder is the Offspring of Ignorance: the last is the Parent of Adoration." And isn't that just what Thomas discovered as he searched the mysteries of creation? For we begin in ignorance, but yearn for a time when adoration alone remains.

While we wait, we sing. So, if you are studying the natural sciences, behold the works of God and sing. If you seek to understand the interactions between humans and culture in the social sciences, then do so with an awareness of the gift of wondrous diversity in communities around the world. And if you work in the humanities or the arts, draw on the gift of imagination to speak the truth about this world. Reject the dewy-eyed sentimentality that would gloss over the truth and, in your waiting, be diligent. In your lamentations, be discerning. In the midst of a "desolate pit" and the "miry bog," sing a new song and discover that your feet have been set on solid ground. Perhaps one day we'll look back on these years and find that it has all been but straw. But in the meantime, set your feet upon the rock, and *sing*.

---

4. Coleridge, *Aids to Reflection*, 236.

ON WONDER....
I. The glory of God's beautiful design

MISOOK KIM (2021)
Text by Karen An-hwei Lee

II. The illumination of beloved statutes

III. The field of radiant awe

IV. Eternity under the olives

Bibliography

Albert and Thomas: Selected Writings. Translated by Simon Tugwell. New York: Paulist, 1988.
Anderson, Herbert, and Susan B. W. Johnson. *Regarding Children: A New Respect for Childhood and Families.* Family Living in Pastoral Perspective. Louisville: Westminster John Knox, 1994.
Aquilina, Tyler. "Spike Lee defends Woody Allen against 'this cancel thing': 'Woody's a friend of mine.'" *Entertainment Weekly*, June 13, 2020. www.ew.com/movies/spike-lee-defends-woody-allen-cancel-culture/.
Aquinas, Thomas. *Summa Theologiae.* Cambridge: Blackfriars, 1964.
Aries, Philippe. *Centuries of Childhood: A Social History of Family Life.* Translated by Robert Baldwick. New York: Knopf, 1962.
Aristotle. *Metaphysics.* Translated by C. D. C. Reeve. Indianapolis: Hackett, 2016.
Asbridge, Nigel. "What is a Child?" In *Through the Eyes of a Child: New Insights in Theology from a Child's Perspective*, edited by Anne Richards and Peter Privett, 1–20. London: Church House, 2009.
Augustine. *Confessions.* Translated by Sarah Ruden. New York: Modern Library, 2017.
Bachelard, Gaston. *The Poetics of Space.* Boston: Beacon, 1969.
Baker, Lynne Rudder. *Naturalism and the First-Person Perspective.* Oxford: Oxford University Press, 2013.
Balthasar, Hans Urs von. *Unless You Become Like This Child.* Translated by Erasmo Leiva-Merikakis. San Francisco: Ignatius, 1991.
Barbeau, Jeffrey W. "Introduction." In *Religion in Romantic England: An Anthology of Primary Sources*, edited by Jeffrey W. Barbeau, xvii–xxxvi. Waco, TX: Baylor University Press, 2018.
Barth, Karl. *Evangelical Theology: An Introduction.* London: Weidenfeld & Nicolson, 1963.
Bartholomew, Craig. *Where Mortals Dwell: A Christian View of Place for Today.* Grand Rapids: Baker Academic, 2011.
Barton, Stephen C. "Dislocating and Relocating Holiness." In *Holiness Past and Present*, edited by S. C. Barton, 193–213. London: T. & T. Clark, 2003.
Begbie, Jeremy. "Beauty, Sentimentality, and the Arts." In *The Beauty of God*, edited by Roger Lundin and Daniel Treier, 45–69. Downers Grove, IL: InterVarsity, 2007.
———. *Redeeming Transcendence in the Arts: Bearing Witness to the Triune God.* Grand Rapids: Eerdmans, 2018.
———. "The Sense of an Ending." In *A Place for Truth*, edited by Dallas Willard, 217–39. Downers Grove, IL: InterVarsity, 2010.

———. *Voicing Creation's Praise: Towards a Theology of the Arts.* Edinburgh: T. & T. Clark, 1991.

———. "The Word Refreshed: Music and God-talk." In *Theology, Music, and Modernity: Struggles for Freedom*, edited by Jeremy Begbie, Daniel K. L. Chua, and Markus Rathey, 358–74. Oxford: Oxford University Press, 2020.

Bendroth, Margaret. "Horace Bushnell's Christian Nurture." In *The Child in Christian Thought*, edited by Marcia J. Bunge, 350–64. Grand Rapids: Eerdmans, 2001.

Berry, Wendell. *The Selected Poems of Wendell Berry.* Washington, DC: Counterpoint, 1998.

———. "Two Economies." In *Art of the Commonplace: The Agrarian Essays of Wendell Berry*, edited by Norman Wirzba, 219–35. Berkeley: Shoemaker & Hoard, 2002.

———. *The Way of Ignorance and Other Essays.* Washington, DC: Shoemaker & Hoard, 2005.

Berryman, Jerome M. *Children and the Theologians: Clearing the Way for Grace.* Harrisburg, PA: Morehouse, 2009.

———. *The Spiritual Guidance of Children: Montessori, Godly Play, and the Future.* New York: Morehouse, 2013.

Bhabha, Homi K. "The Commitment to Theory." In *The Norton Anthology of Theory and Criticism*, 2nd ed., edited by Vincent B. Leitch et al., 2353–72. New York: Norton, 2010.

Bitner, Bradley J. "Acclaiming Artemis in Ephesus: Political Theologies in Acts 19." In *The First Urban Churches: Ephesus*, edited by James R. Harrison and L. L. Welborn, 127–70. Atlanta: SBL, 2018.

Blondel, James. *The strength of imagination in pregnant women examin'd: and the opinion that marks and deformities in children arise from thence, demonstrated to be a vulgar error.* London, 1727. https://wellcomecollection.org/works/j56kepdu/items?canvas=28.

Bloom, Harold. *The Anxiety of Influence: A Theory of Poetry.* New York: Oxford University Press, 1997.

Blount, Brian K. "Revelation." In *True to Our Native Land*, edited by Brian K. Blount et al., 523–58. Minneapolis: Fortress, 2007.

Bonhoeffer, Dietrich. *Ethics.* Minneapolis: Fortress, 2015.

Bordwell, David, et al. *Film Art: An Introduction.* New York: McGraw Hill, 2017.

Boring, M. Eugene. *An Introduction to the New Testament.* Louisville: Westminster John Knox, 2012.

Bouma-Prediger, Steven, and Brian J. Walsh. *Beyond Homelessness: Christian Faith in a Culture of Displacement.* Grand Rapids: Eerdmans, 2008.

Brown, Robert McAfee. "Introduction." In *Portrait of Karl Barth*, by Georges Casalis, 1–37. New York: Doubleday, 1963.

Brown, William P. *The Seven Pillars of Creation: The Bible, Science, and the Ecology of Wonder.* Oxford: Oxford University Press, 2010.

Bulgakov, Sergius. *A Bulgakov Anthology.* Translated by James Pain and Nicolas Zernov. London: SPCK, 1976.

Bunge, Marcia J. "The Vocation of the Child: Theological Perspectives on the Particular and Paradoxical Roles and Responsibilities of Children." In *The Vocation of the Child*, edited by Patrick McKinley Brennan, 31–52. Grand Rapids: Eerdmans, 2008.

Bushnell, Horace. *Christian Nurture.* Cleveland: Pilgrim, 1994.

Buxton, Richard. "Metamorphoses of Gods into Animals and Humans." In *Gods of Ancient Greece: Identities and Transformations*, edited by J. N. Bremmer, 81–91. Edinburgh: Edinburgh University Press.

Cairns, Scott. "Shaping What's Given: Sacred Tradition and the Individual Talent." *Image: A Journal of the Arts & Religion* 25 (2000) 73–82.

Carpenter, Humphrey, ed. *The Letters of J. R. R. Tolkien*. Boston: Houghton, Mifflin, 1981.

Casey, Edward. *Getting Back into Place: Toward a Renewed Understanding of the Place-World*. 2nd ed. Indianapolis: Indiana University Press, 2009.

Caulley, T. S. "The Title *Christianos* and Roman Imperial Cult." *Restoration Quarterly* 53 (2011) 193–206.

Champion, Craige B. *The Peace of the Gods: Elite Religious Practices in the Middle Roman Republic*. Princeton: Princeton University Press, 2017.

Chernavin, Georgy, and Anna Yampolskaya. "'Estrangement' in Aesthetics and Beyond: Russian Formalism and Phenomenological Method." *Continental Philosophy Review* 52 (2019) 91–113.

Clements, Jane. "Child, Though I Take Your Hand." In *No One Can Stem the Tide: Selected Poems 1931–1991*. Walden, NY: Plough, 2000.

Coleridge, Samuel Taylor. *Aids to Reflection*. Edited by John Beer. The Collected Works of Samuel Taylor Coleridge 9. London and Princeton: Routledge and Princeton University Press, 1993.

———. *Biographia Literaria*. Edited by James Engell and W. Jackson Bate. The Collected Works of Samuel Taylor Coleridge 7. Bollingen Series 75. Princeton: Princeton University Press, 1983.

———. *Coleridge: Poems and Prose*. New York: Alfred A. Knopf, 1997.

Coles, Robert. *Children of Crisis*. 5 vols. New York: Little, Brown & Co., 1967–1977.

———. *The Spiritual Life of Children*. Boston: Houghton, Mifflin, 1990.

———. "Struggling Toward Childhood." *Second Opinion* 18.4 (1993) 58–71.

Collier, John, ed. *Toddling to the Kingdom: Child Theology at Work in the Church*. London: The Child Theology Movement, 2009.

Cording, Robert. *Finding the World's Fullness: On Poetry, Metaphor, and Mystery*. Eugene, OR: Slant, 2019.

Cosper, Mike. *Recapturing the Wonder: Transcendent Faith in a Disenchanted World*. Downers Grove, IL: InterVarsity, 2017.

Craft, Jennifer Allen. *Placemaking and the Arts: Cultivating the Christian Life*. Downers Grove, IL: IVP Academic, 2018.

Cranfield, C. E. B. "Minister and Congregation in the light of II Corinthians 4:5–7." *Interpretation* 19 (1965) 163–67.

Cronon, William. "The Trouble with Wilderness; or, Getting Back to the Wrong Nature." In *Uncommon Ground: Rethinking the Human Place in Nature*, edited by William Cronon, 69–90. New York: W. W. Norton & Co., 1995. https://www.williamcronon.net/writing/Trouble_with_Wilderness_Main.html.

Crouch, Andy. *Culture Making*. Downers Grove, IL: InterVarsity, 2008.

Cunningham, Hugh. *The Invention of Childhood*. London: BBC, 2006.

Dawkins, Richard. *An Appetite for Wonder: The Making of a Scientist*. New York: Ecco, 2013.

———. "Science, Delusion, and the Appetite for Wonder: A Talk with Richard Dawkins." Richard Dimbleby Lecture, BBC1, November 12, 1996, with an introduction by

John Brockman. https://www.edge.org/conversation/richard_dawkins-science-delusion-and-the-appetite-for-wonder.
Deckard, Michael Funk, and Péter Losonczi. *Philosophy Begins in Wonder: An Introduction to Early Modern Philosophy, Theology, and Science.* Eugene, OR: Pickwick, 2010.
Derrida, Jacques. "Like the Sound of the Sea Deep within a Shell: Paul de Man's War." *Critical Inquiry* 14 (1988) 590–652.
DesRosiers, N. P., and L. C. Vuong, eds. *Religious Competition in the Greco-Roman World.* Atlanta: SBL, 2016.
Dillard, Annie. *Pilgrim at Tinker Creek.* New York: Harper, 1998.
———. *Teaching a Stone to Talk.* New York: Harper & Row, 1982.
Dostoevsky, Fyodor. *The Brothers Karamazov.* Translated by Constance Garnett. New York: Random House, 1943.
Downing, Crystal. *Salvation from Cinema: The Medium Is the Message.* New York: Routledge, 2016.
Driscoll, Jeremy. *What Happens at Mass?* Chicago: Liturgy Training, 2011.
Du Mez, Kristin Kobes. *Jesus and John Wayne: How White Evangelicals Corrupted a Faith and Fractured a Nation.* New York: Liveright, 2020.
Dunn, James D. G. *Theology of Paul the Apostle.* Grand Rapids: Eerdmans, 1998.
Dyrness, William. *Poetic Theology: God and the Poetics of Everyday Life.* Grand Rapids: Eerdmans, 2011.
Egan, Kieran, Annabelle Cant, and Gillian Judson, eds. *Wonder-full Education: The Centrality of Wonder in Teaching and Learning across the Curriculum.* New York: Routledge, 2014.
Eliot, T. S. *Four Quartets.* New York: Harcourt, 1971.
Erickson, Scott. *Honest Advent: Awakening to the Wonder of God-With-Us Then, Here, and Now.* Grand Rapids: Zondervan, 2020.
Evagrius of Pontus. *Évagre le Pontique. Chapitres sur la prière.* Edited by Paul Géhin. Sources Chrétiennes 589. Paris: Cerf, 2017.
Evans, Murray J. *Sublime Coleridge: The Opus Maximum.* New York: Palgrave Macmillan, 2012.
Farley, Edward. *Faith and Beauty: A Theological Aesthetic.* Aldershot: Ashgate, 2001.
The Festal Menaion. Translated by Mother Mary and Archimandrite Kallistos Ware. London: Faber & Faber, 1969.
Fitch, David. *Faithful Presence: Seven Disciplines that Shape the Church for Mission.* Downers Grove, IL: InterVarsity, 2016.
Flint, Anthony. *Wrestling with Moses: How Jane Jacobs Took on New York's Master Builder and Transformed the American City.* New York: Random House, 2009.
Foerger, R. H. "Artists Rescue Us when the Wonder Has Leaked Out." https://moreenigma.com/2020/12/16/artists-rescue-us-when-the-wonder-has-leaked-out/.
Fowden, Elizabeth Key. "Jerusalem and the Work of Discontinuity." In *Uninterrupted Fugue: Art by Kamal Boullata,* edited by Burcu Dogramaci, 109–33. Munich: Hirmer, 2019.
Fujimura, Makoto. *Art and Faith: A Theology of Making.* New Haven: Yale University Press, 2020.
Gates, Henry Louis, Jr. "The Truth Behind '40 Acres and a Mule.'" *100 Amazing Facts About the Negro* (blog). www.pbs.org/wnet/african-americans-many-rivers-to-cross/history/the-truth-behind-40-acres-and-a-mule/.

González-Andrieu, Cecelia. *Bridge to Wonder: Art as a Gospel of Beauty.* Waco, TX: Baylor University Press, 2012.
Gordley, Matthew E. *New Testament Christological Hymns: Exploring Texts, Contexts, and Significance.* Downers Grove, IL: IVP Academic, 2018.
Gorman, Michael J. *Cruciformity: Paul's Narrative Spirituality of the Cross.* 20th anniversary ed. Grand Rapids: Eerdmans, 2021.
Grieb, A. Katherine. "Paul's Theological Preoccupation in Romans 9–11." In *Between Gospel and Election: Explorations in the Interpretation of Romans 9–11*, edited by Florian Wilk, J. Ross Wagner, and Frank Schleritt, 391–400. Tübingen: Mohr Siebeck, 2010.
Gross, Terry. "Mary Karr, Remembering the Years She Spent 'Lit.'" *Fresh Air*, November 3, 2009. https://www.npr.org/templates/story/story.php?storyId=120020266.
Guite, Malcolm. *Parable and Paradox: Sonnets on the Sayings of Jesus and Other Poems.* Norwich: Canterbury, 2016.
Gundry-Volf, Judith M. "The Least and the Greatest: Children in the New Testament." In *The Child in Christian Thought*, edited by Marcia J. Bunge, 29–60. Grand Rapids: Eerdmans, 2001.
Gunn, Daniel P. "Making Art Strange: A Commentary on Defamiliarization." *The Georgia Review* 38 (1984) 25–33.
Gupta, Nijay K. *Colossians.* SHBC. Macon, GA: Helwys, 2013.
———. "'They Are Not Gods!' Jewish and Christian Idol Polemic and Greco-Roman Use of Cult Statues." *Catholic Biblical Quarterly* 76.4 (2014) 704–19.
———. *Reading Philippians.* Eugene, OR: Cascade, 2020.
———. *Worship That Makes Sense to Paul.* BZNW. New York: de Gruyter, 2010.
Guroian, Vigen. "The Office of the Child in Christian Faith." In *The Vocation of the Child*, edited by Patrick McKinley Brennan, 104–24. Grand Rapids: Eerdmans, 2008.
Hadzigeorgiou, Yannis. "Reclaiming the Value of Wonder in Science Education." In *Wonder-full Education: The Centrality of Wonder in Teaching and Learning across the Curriculum*, edited by Kieran Egan, Annabelle Cant, and Gillian Judson, 40–65. New York: Routledge, 2014.
Handelman, Susan. *The Slayers of Moses.* Albany: SUNY Press, 1983.
Hardin, Les. "A Theology of the Hymns in Revelation." *Stone-Campbell Journal* 17.2 (2014) 233–45.
Harding, Anthony John. "Imagination, Patriarchy, and Evil in Coleridge and Heidegger." *Studies in Romanticism* 35 (1996) 3–26.
Hauerwas, Stanley. "Foreword." In *Heresies and How to Avoid Them: Why It Matters What Christians Believe*, edited by Ben Quash and Michael Ward, ix–xi. London: SPCK, 2007.
———. "Go With God: An Open Letter to Young Christians on Their Way to College." *First Things* (2010). https://www.firstthings.com/article/2010/10/go-with-god.
Heaney, Seamus. "The Pitchfork." In *Opened Ground*, 320. London: Faber & Faber, 1998.
Heil, John Paul. *The Letters of Paul as Rituals of Worship.* Eugene, OR: Cascade, 2011.
Hellerman, Joseph. *Reconstructing Honor in Roman Philippi.* Cambridge: Cambridge University Press, 2008.
Hemard, Chuck. *The Pines: Southern Forests.* Hillsborough, NC: Daylight Community Arts Foundation, 2017.

Herman, Bruce. "Wounds and Beauty." In *The Beauty of God: Theology and the Arts*, edited by Daniel J. Treier, Mark Husbands, and Roger Lundin, 110–20. Downers Grove, IL: IVP Academic, 2007.

Heschel, Abraham. *God in Search of Man: A Philosophy of Judaism*. New York: Farrar, Straus, and Giroux, 1983.

Holmes, Arthur F. *The Idea of a Christian College*. Grand Rapids: Eerdmans, 1987.

Holmes, Richard. *Coleridge: Early Visions, 1772–1804*. New York: Pantheon, 1989.

Hooker, Richard. *The Works of that Learned and Judicious Divine, Mr. Richard Hooker*, edited by John Keble. Oxford: Clarendon, 1874.

Hopkins, Gerard Manley. *Selected Poems of Gerard Manley Hopkins*. Garden City, NY: Dover, 2013.

Horrell, David. "The Label *Christianos*: 1 Peter 4:16 and the Formation of Christian Identity." *The Journal of Biblical Literature* 126.2 (2007) 361–81.

Hunsinger, George. "What Can Evangelicals & Postliberals Learn from Each Other? The Carl Henry-Hans Frei Exchange Reconsidered." In *The Nature of Confession: Evangelicals & Postliberals in Conversation*, edited by Timothy R. Phillips and Dennis L. Okholm, 134–50. Downers Grove, IL: InterVarsity, 1996.

Hurley, Amanda Kolson. "The Detested Bradford Pear is Coming to a Forest Near You." Bloomberg. https://www.bloomberg.com/news/articles/2019-07-02/bradford-pears-threaten-forests-native-species.

Hurtado, Larry. *Destroyer of the Gods: Early Christian Distinctiveness in the Roman World*. Waco, TX: Baylor University Press, 2017.

Husbands, Mark, and Daniel J. Treier, eds. *The Community of the Word: Toward an Evangelical Ecclesiology*. Downers Grove, IL: InterVarsity, 2005.

———. "Introduction." In *The Community of the Word: Toward and Evangelical Ecclesiology*, edited by Mark Husbands and Daniel J. Treier, 7–19. Downers Grove, IL: InterVarsity, 2005.

"Ira Glass on Storytelling." *This American Life*, August 18, 2009. https://www.thisamericanlife.org/extras/ira-glass-on-storytelling.

Jacobs, Jane. *The Death and Life of Great American Cities*. New York: Random House, 1961.

Jacobsen, Erik O. *Sidewalks in the Kingdom*. Grand Rapids: Brazos, 2003.

Jellema, Rod. *A Slender Grace of Poems*. Grand Rapids: Eerdmans, 2004.

Jennings, Willie James. *After Whiteness: An Education in Belonging*. Grand Rapids: Eerdmans, 2020.

———. *The Christian Imagination: Theology and the Origins of Race*. New Haven: Yale University Press, 2010.

———. "Overcoming Racial Faith." *DIVINITY Magazine*, Duke Divinity School (Spring 2015) 4–9.

Jensen, David H. *Graced Vulnerability: A Theology of Childhood*. Cleveland, OH: Pilgrim, 2005.

John of Damascus. *St. John of Damascus: On the Divine Images*. Translated by David Anderson. Crestwood, NY: St. Vladimir's Seminary Press, 1980.

Johnson, Elizabeth. *She Who Is*. New York: Crossroad, 1992/2002.

Johnson, Luke Timothy. *Constructing Paul*. Grand Rapids: Eerdmans, 2020.

Julian of Norwich. *Revelations of Divine Love*. Translated by Elizabeth Spearing. New York: Penguin, 1998.

Kandinsky, Nina. *Kandinsky und Ich*. Munich: Kindler, 1976.

Kant, Immanuel. *Critique of the Power of Judgment*. Edited by Paul Guyer. Cambridge: Cambridge University Press, 2000.
Kavanagh, Patrick. "Having Confessed." In *Collected Poems*, 149. New York: W. W. Norton & Co., 1964.
Kearney, Richard, ed. "Dialogue with Jacques Derrida." In *Dialogues with Contemporary Continental Thinkers: The Phenomenological Heritage*, 105–26. Manchester: Manchester University Press, 1984.
Kearns, Laura-Lee. "Subjects of Wonder: Toward an Aesthetics, Ethics, and Pedagogy of Wonder." *The Journal of Aesthetic Education* 49 (2015) 98–119.
Keck, Leander E. *Christ's First Theologian: The Shape of Paul's Thought*. Waco, TX: Baylor University Press, 2015.
Knox, Francesca Bugliani. "Introduction: Why Wonder?" In *Poetry, Philosophy and Theology in Conversation: Thresholds of Wonder: The Power of the Word IV*, edited by Francesca Bugliani Knox and Jennifer Reek, 1–13. London: Routledge, 2019.
Koester, Craig R. "The Distant Triumph Song: Music and the Book of Revelation." *Word & World* 12 (1992) 243–49.
Kristjánsson, Kristján. "Scientific Practice, Wonder, and Awe." In *Virtue and the Practice of Science: Multidisciplinary Perspectives*, edited by Celia Deane-Drummond, Thomas A. Stapleford, and Darcia Narvaez. Notre Dame: Center for Theology, Science, and Human Flourishing, 2019. https://virtueandthepracticeofscience.pressbooks.com/chapter/scientific-practice-wonder-and-awe/.
———. *Virtuous Emotions*. Oxford: Oxford University Press, 2018.
Kuhn, Reinhard. *Corruption in Paradise: The Child in Western Literature*. Hanover, NH: University Press of New England, 1982.
Kunstler, James Howard. *The Geography of Nowhere*. New York: Touchstone, 1993.
Lauber, David, with Jeffrey Greenman, Mark Husbands, and Dennis Okholm. "Wheaton Theology Conference: A Retrospective." Roundtable at the Wheaton Theology Conference, virtual, April 9, 2021.
L'Ecuyer, Catherine. "The Wonder Approach to Learning." *Frontiers in Human Neuroscience* 8.764 (October 2014) 1–8.
L'Engle, Madeleine. *Walking on Water: Reflections on Art and Faith*. New York: Crown, 2016.
LeFebvre, Henri. *The Production of Space*. Translated by Donald Nicholson Smith. Oxford: Blackwell, 1991.
Lewis, C. S. *An Experiment in Criticism*. Cambridge: Cambridge University Press, 1961.
———. "It All Began with a Picture . . ." In *On Stories, and Other Essays on Literature*, edited by Walter Hooper, 53–54. New York: Harvest, 1966.
———. *Letters to Malcom: Chiefly on Prayer*. New York: Harcourt, Brace & World, 1964.
———. *Miracles: A Preliminary Study*. New York: Macmillan, 1947.
Lichtmann, Maria R. "'The Ecstasy of Interest': Contemplation as Parallelism's Praxis." In *The Contemplative Poetry of Gerard Manley Hopkins*, edited by Maria R. Lichtmann, 129–69. Princeton: Princeton University Press, 1989.
Lundin, Roger. *Beginning with the Word: Modern Literature and the Question of Belief*. Grand Rapids: Baker, 2014.
———. "The Life of Culture and the Christian." YouTube video, February 16, 2011. https://www.youtube.com/watch?v=qza_BStlwLQ.

Macarius. *Die 50 Geistlichen Homilien des Makarios.* Edited by Hermann Dörries, Erich Klostermann, and Matthias Kroeger. Patristische Texte und Studien 4. Berlin: De Gruyter, 1964.

———. *Pseudo-Macaire: Oeuvres spirituelles* I. Edited by Vincent Desprez. Paris: Cerf, 1980.

———. *Reden und Briefe. Die Sammlung I des Vaticanus Graecus 694 (B),* edited by Heinz Berthold. 2 vols. Berlin: Akademie-Verlag, 1973.

MacDonald, George. "The Child in the Midst." In *Unspoken Sermons,* 13–23. Whitehorn, CA: Johannesen, 1997.

Malik, Charles H. "The Two Tasks." *Journal of the Evangelical Theological Society* 23 (1980) 289–96.

Maritain, Jacques. *Creative Intuition in Art and Poetry.* Princeton: Princeton University Press, 1977.

Matthews, Gareth. *Dialogues with Children.* Cambridge: Harvard University Press, 1992.

———. "The Philosopher as Teacher: Philosophy and the Young Child." *Metaphilosophy* 10.3/4 (1979) 354–68.

———. *The Philosophy of Childhood.* Cambridge: Harvard University Press, 1996.

———. "Philosophy as Child's Play." *Children's Literature Association Quarterly* (1990) 25–38.

McCaulley, Esau. *Reading While Black.* Downers Grove, IL: InterVarsity, 2020.

McDonald, Alonzo. "Introduction." In *Leaf by Niggle,* by J. R. R. Tolkien, edited by Alonzo McDonald, 7–16. Washington, DC: Trinity Forum, 2003.

McFarland, Thomas. *Coleridge and the Pantheist Tradition.* Oxford: Clarendon, 1969.

McGowin, Emily Hunter. "Children and Childhood in the Full Quiver." In *Quivering Families: The American Quiverfull Movement and Evangelical Theology of the Family,* 125–68. Minneapolis: Fortress, 2018.

———. *Quivering Families: The American Quiverfull Movement and Evangelical Theology of the Family.* Minneapolis: Fortress, 2018.

———. "Response." In *The Wonders of Creation: Learning Stewardship from Narnia and Middle-Earth,* by Kristen Page. Hansen Lectureship Series. Downers Grove, IL: IVP Academic, 2022.

Mercer, Joyce Ann. *Welcoming Children: A Practical Theology of Childhood.* St. Louis: Chalice, 2005.

Merton, Thomas. *Entering the Silence: Becoming a Monk and a Writer.* Edited by Jonathan Montaldo. New York: Harper Collins e-books, 2009.

———. *The Sign of Jonas.* New York: Harcourt, Brace, and Company, 2002.

Michel, Jen Pollock. *Keeping Place: Reflections on the Meaning of Home.* Downers Grove, IL: InterVarsity, 2017.

Miller, Brian J. "Faith in the Suburbs: Evangelical Christian Books about Suburban Life." In *The Routledge Handbook of Religion and Cities,* edited by Katie Day and Elise M. Edwards, 119–35. London: Routledge, 2021.

Miller-McLemore, Bonnie. *In the Midst of Chaos: Caring for Children as Spiritual Practice.* San Francisco: Josey-Bass, 2007.

———. *Let the Children Come: Reimagining Childhood from a Christian Perspective.* San Francisco: Jossey-Bass, 2003.

Milliner, Matthew. "The Enchantment of Lightning: Why Some Bridges to Wonder are Stronger than Others." https://syndicate.network/symposia/theology/bridge-to-wonder/.
Montgomery, Heather, and Martin Woodhead. *Understanding Childhood: An Interdisciplinary Approach*. Hoboken, NJ: Wiley, 200.
Neusner, Jacob. *Introduction to Rabbinic Literature*. New York: Doubleday, 1994.
Newbigin, Lesslie. *Signs amidst the Rubble*. Grand Rapids: Eerdmans, 2003.
Noll, Mark A. *The Civil War as a Theological Crisis*. Chapel Hill: University of North Carolina Press, 2006.
Nussbaum, Martha. *Upheavals of Thought: The Intelligence of Emotions*. New York: Cambridge University Press, 2001.
O'Connor, Flannery. *The Habit of Being: Letters of Flannery O'Connor*. New York: Farrar, Straus, and Giroux, 1988.
Ohaneson, Heather C. "Turning from the Perfection of God to the Wondrousness of God." In *The Question of God's Perfection: Jewish and Christian Essays on the God of the Bible and Talmud*, edited by Yoram Hazony and Dru Johnson, 211–30. Leiden: Brill, 2019.
Oliver, Jessica. "Self-consciousness and Imagination in the *Biographia Literaria*: The Creative Core Connecting the Infinite and Finite 'I Am.'" *The Coleridge Bulletin*, n.s., 53 (2019) 49–56.
Page, Kristen. *The Wonders of Creation: Learning Stewardship from Narnia and Middle-Earth*. Hansen Lectureship Series. Downers Grove, IL: IVP Academic, 2022.
Papamichael, Stella. "Getting Direct with Directors: No. 21: Spike Lee." BBC Home, September 4, 2014. www.bbc.co.uk/films/callingtheshots/spike_lee.shtml.
Parker, David. *Christmas and Charles Dickens*. New York: AMS, 2005.
Parsons, Howard L. "A Philosophy of Wonder." *Philosophy and Phenomenological Research* 30.1 (1969) 84–101.
Peterman, G. W. *Paul's Gift from Philippi*. Cambridge: Cambridge University Press, 1997.
Phillips, Timothy R., and Dennis L. Okholm, eds. *The Nature of Confession: Evangelicals & Postliberals in Conversation*. Downers Grove, IL: InterVarsity, 1996.
———. "The Nature of Confession: Evangelicals & Postliberals." In *The Nature of Confession: Evangelicals & Postliberals in Conversation*, edited by Timothy R. Phillips and Dennis L. Okholm, 7–20. Downers Grove, IL: InterVarsity, 1996.
———. "A Panel Discussion: Lindbeck, Hunsinger, McGrath & Fackre." In *The Nature of Confession: Evangelicals & Postliberals in Conversation*, edited by Timothy R. Phillips and Dennis L. Okholm, 246–53. Downers Grove, IL: InterVarsity, 1996.
Pieper, Josef. *Leisure: The Basis of Culture, including The Philosophical Act*. San Francisco: Ignatius, 2009.
Piersol, Laura. "Our Hearts Leap Up: Awakening Wonder within the Classroom." In *Wonder-full Education: The Centrality of Wonder in Teaching and Learning across the Curriculum*, edited by Kieran Egan, Annabelle Cant, and Gillian Judson, 3–21. New York: Routledge, 2014.
Plato. *Platonis Opera, Vol. 1: Tetralogiae I–II*. Edited by E. A. Duke and John Burnet. Scriptorum Classicorum Bibliotheca Oxoniensis. Oxford: Clarendon, 1995.
———. *Theaetetus*. Translated by M. J. Levett. Revised by Myles Burnyeat. Indianapolis: Hackett, 1992.
Plested, Marcus. "The Spiritual Senses: Monastic and Theological." In *Knowing Bodies, Passionate Souls: Sense Perceptions in Byzantium*, edited by Susan Ashbrook

Harvey and Margaret Mullett, 301–12. Washington, DC: Dumbarton Oaks Byzantine Symposia and Colloquia, 2017.

Polanyi, Michael. *The Tacit Dimension.* New York: Doubleday, 1966.

Powery, Luke A. "Painful Praise: Exploring the Public Proclamation of the Hymns of Revelation." *Theology Today* 70 (2013) 69–78.

Pridmore, John. "Salvation." In *Through the Eyes of a Child: New Insights in Theology from a Child's Perspective*, edited by Anne Richards and Peter Privett, 185–201. London: Church House, 2009.

Quash, Ben. *Found Theology: History, Imagination, and the Holy Spirit.* London: Bloomsbury, 2013.

Quinn, Dennis. *Iris Exiled: A Synoptic History of Wonder.* Lanham, MD: University Press of America, 2002.

Rah, Soong-Chan. "The Sin of Racism: Racialization of the Image of God." In *The Image of God in an Image-Driven Age*, edited by Beth Felker Jones and Jeffrey W. Barbeau, 205–24. Downers Grove, IL: IVP Academic, 2016.

Rahner, Karl. "Ideas for a Theology of Childhood." In *Theological Investigations*, Vol. VIII, 33–50. New York: Herder & Herder, 1971.

Ratzinger, Joseph. "The Feeling of Things, the Contemplation of Beauty." https://www.vatican.va/roman_curia/congregations/cfaith/documents/rc_con_cfaith_doc_2002824_ratzinger-cl-rimini_en.html.

Rawlings, Marjorie Kinnan. *Cross Creek.* New York: Charles Scribner's Sons, 1942.

Reid, Nicholas. "Coleridge and Schelling: The *Missing Transcendental Deduction*." *Studies in Romanticism* 33 (1994) 451–79.

———. "The Satanic Principle in the Later Coleridge's Theory of Imagination." *Studies in Romanticism* 37 (1998) 259–77.

Richards, Anne, and Peter Privett. *Through the Eyes of a Child: New Insights in Theology from a Child's Perspective.* London: Church House, 2009.

Robinson, Marilynne. *Absence of Mind: The Dispelling of Inwardness from the Modern Myth of the Self.* New Haven: Yale University Press, 2010.

Rousseau, Jean-Jacques. *Emile: or, On Education.* Translated by Allan Bloom. New York: Basic, 1979.

Rubenstein, Mary-Jane. *Strange Wonder: The Closure of Metaphysics and the Opening of Awe.* New York: Columbia University Press, 2010.

The Russian Primary Chronicle: Laurentian Text. Translated by Samuel Hazzard Cross and Olgerd P. Sherbowitz-Wetzor. Cambridge, MA: The Medieval Academy of America, 1953.

Sakharov, Sophrony. *Saint Silouan the Athonite.* Tolleshunt Knights: Stavropegic Monastery of St. John the Baptist, 1991.

Santayana, George. *The Essential Santayana: Selected Writings.* Edited by Martin A. Coleman. Bloomington: Indiana University Press, 1980.

Sartwell, Crispin. *The Six Names of Beauty.* New York: Routledge, 2004.

Saward, John. *The Way of the Lamb: The Spirit of Childhood and the End of the Age.* San Francisco: Ignatius, 1999.

Sawicki, Bernard. "Between Rapture and Rupture." In *Poetry, Philosophy and Theology in Conversation: Thresholds of Wonder: The Power of the Word IV*, edited by Francesca Bugliani Knox and Jennifer Reek, 100–113. London: Routledge, 2019.

Sayer, George. *Jack: C. S. Lewis and His Times.* San Francisco: Harper and Row, 1988.

Sayers, Dorothy L. "Is there a Definite Evil Power that attacks People in the Same Way as there is a Good Power that influences People?" In *Asking Them Questions: A Selection*, edited by Ronald Selby Wright, 43–52. Oxford: Oxford University Press, 1953.

———. *The Just Vengeance*. In *Four Sacred Plays*, 275–352. London: Gollancz, 1948.

———. *The Mind of the Maker*. San Francisco: HarperSanFrancisco, 1979.

———. "The Sacrament of Matter." In *The Christ of the Creeds and Other Broadcast Messages to the British People during World War II*, edited by Suzanne Bray, 37–42. West Sussex, England: The Dorothy L. Sayers Society, 2008.

———. "Towards a Christian Aesthetic." In *Our Culture: Its Christian Roots and Present Crisis*, edited by V. A. Demant, 50–69. London: SPCK, 1947.

———. "Why Work?" In *Creed or Chaos?*, 63–84. Manchester, NH: Sophia Institute, 1974.

———. *The Zeal of Thy House*. In *Four Sacred Plays*, 7–103. London: Victor Gollancz, 1948.

Scarry, Elaine. *On Beauty and Being Just*. Princeton: Princeton University Press, 1999.

Schinkel, Anders. "Education as Mediation between Child and World: The Role of Wonder." *Studies in Philosophy and Education* 39 (2020) 479–92.

———. "Wonder, Mystery, and Meaning." *Philosophical Papers* 48.2 (2019) 293–319.

Scorgie, Glen G. "Wonder and the Revitalization of Evangelical Theology." *Crux* 26.4 (1990) 19–25.

Sertillanges, A. G. *The Intellectual Life*. Westminster, MD: Newman, 1959.

Shenk, David W. "Jesus and Muhammad: Two Roads to Peace." In *Where Was God on Sept. 11? Seeds of Faith and Hope*, edited by Donald B. Kraybill and Linda Gehman Peachey, 49–56. Scottsdale, PA: Herald, 2002.

Sherry, Patrick. *Spirit and Beauty: An Introduction to Theological Aesthetics*. Oxford: Clarendon, 1992.

Shklovsky, Victor. "Art, as Device." Translated by Alexandra Berlina. *Poetics Today* 36 (2015) 151–74.

Smith, Robert H. "'Worthy is the Lamb' and Other Songs of Revelation." *Currents in Theology and Mission* 25 (1998) 500–506.

Smith, Robert S. "Songs of the Seer: The Purpose of Revelation's Hymns." *Themelios* 43.2 (2018) 193–204.

Soskice, Janet Martin. *The Kindness of God*. Oxford: Oxford University Press, 2007.

Stapinski, Helene. "Superheroes, trailblazers, and invisible comics men." Review of *Invisible Men: The Trailblazing Black Artists of Comic Books*, by Ken Quattro. *Chicago Tribune*, January 17, 2021. https://www.pressreader.com/usa/the-capital/20210117/282059099650455.

Stevens, Wallace. *Wallace Stevens: The Collected Poems*. New York: Vintage, 1990.

Stortz, Martha Ellen. "'Where or When Was Your Servant Innocent?' Augustine on Childhood." In *The Child in Christian Thought*, edited by Marcia J. Bunge, 78–102. Grand Rapids: Eerdmans, 2001.

Symeon the New Theologian. *St. Symeon the New Theologian, On the Mystical Life: The Ethical Discourses*. Translated by Alexander Golitzin. 3 vols. Crestwood, NY: St. Vladimir's Seminary Press, 1995–97.

The Syriac Fathers on Prayer and the Spiritual Life. Translated by Sebastian Brock. Kalamazoo, MI: Cistercian, 1987.

Taylor, Charles. *The Language Animal: The Full Shape of the Human Linguistic Capacity*. Cambridge: Harvard University Press, 2016.

———. *A Secular Age*. Cambridge: Harvard University Press, 2007.

Tolkien, J. R. R. "On Fairy-Stories." In *Essays Presented to Charles Williams*, edited by C. S. Lewis, 38–89. Grand Rapids: Eerdmans, 1966.

———. *Leaf by Niggle*. Edited by Alonzo McDonald. Washington, DC: Trinity Forum, 2003.

Trapani, John G. *Poetry, Beauty, and Contemplation: The Complete Aesthetics of Jacques Maritain*. Washington, DC: Catholic University of America, 2011.

Tugwell, Simon. "Introduction to Aquinas." In *Albert and Thomas: Selected Writings*, translated by Simon Tugwell, 201–351. New York: Paulist, 1988.

Turner, Denys. *Julian of Norwich, Theologian*. New Haven: Yale University Press, 2011.

Twelftree, Graham. *The Gospel According to Paul*. Eugene, OR: Cascade, 2019.

U.S. Census Bureau, Population Division. "Projected Age Groups and Sex Composition of the Population: Main Projections Series for the United States, 2017–2060." https://www.census.gov/data/tables/2017/demo/popproj/2017-summary-tables.html.

Vasalou, Sophia. *Wonder: A Grammar*. New York: SUNY Press, 2015.

Volf, Miroslav, and Matthew Croasmun. *For the Life of the World: Theology That Makes a Difference*. Grand Rapids: Brazos, 2019.

Vonnegut, Kurt. *Bluebeard*. New York: Random House, 2009.

Walford, E. John. "The Case for a Broken Beauty." In *The Beauty of God: Theology and the Arts*, edited by Daniel J. Treier, Mark Husbands, and Roger Lundin, 87–109. Downers Grove, IL: IVP Academic, 2007.

Ward, Graham. *True Religion*. Oxford: Blackwell, 2003.

Ware, Kallistos. "A Sense of Wonder." In *The Inner Kingdom*, 69–74. Yonkers, NY: St. Vladimir's Seminary Press, 2000.

Warren, Tish Harrison. *Prayer in the Night: For Those Who Work or Watch or Weep*. Downers Grove, IL: InterVarsity, 2021.

Webster, John. "Jesus—God for Us." In *Anglican Essentials: Reclaiming Faith in the Anglican Church of Canada*, edited by George Egerton, 89–97. Toronto: Anglican Book Centre, 1995.

Webster, Suzanne E. *Body and Soul in Coleridge's Notebooks, 1827–1834: What is Life?* Basingstoke: Palgrave Macmillan, 2010.

Weil, Simone. *Waiting for God*. Translated by Emma Craufurd. New York: Harper & Row, 1973.

Werpehowski, William. "In Search of Real Children: Innocence, Absence, and Becoming a Self in Christ." In *The Vocation of the Child*, edited by Patrick McKinley Brennan, 53–74. Grand Rapids: Eerdmans, 2008.

Wesley, John. "The New Creation." In *John Wesley's Sermons: An Anthology*, edited by Albert C. Outler and Richard P. Heitzenrater, 493–500. Nashville: Abingdon, 1991.

———. "The Unity of the Divine Being." In *John Wesley's Sermons: An Anthology*, edited by Albert C. Outler and Richard P. Heitzenrater, 531–40. Nashville: Abingdon, 1991.

Wettstein, Howard. *The Significance of Religious Experience*. Oxford: Oxford University Press, 2012.

White, Keith. "Creation." In *Through the Eyes of a Child: New Insights in Theology from a Child's Perspective*, edited by Anne Richards and Peter Privett, 44–64. London: Church House, 2009.

Whitehead, Andrew L., and Samuel L. Perry. *Taking America Back for God: Christian Nationalism in the United States*. Oxford: Oxford University Press, 2020.

Whitmore, Todd David, with Tobias Winright. "Children: An Undeveloped Theme in Catholic Teaching." In *The Challenge of Global Stewardship*, edited by Maura A. Ryan and Todd David Whitmore, 161–85. Notre Dame: University of Notre Dame Press, 1997.

Williams, Judy Fentress. *Holy Imagination: A Literary and Theological Introduction to the Whole Bible*. Nashville: Abingdon, 2021.

Williams, Rowan. *The Edge of Words: God and the Habits of Language*. London: Bloomsbury, 2014.

———. *Grace and Necessity: Reflections on Art and Love*. Harrisburg, PA: Morehouse, 2005.

———. "Silence in the face of mystery: God is the encounter we can't control." *The Christian Century* (August 21, 2018). https://www.christiancentury.org/article/critical-essay/silence-face-mystery.

———. *Tokens of Trust: An Introduction to Christian Belief*. Louisville: Westminster John Knox, 2007.

Willmer, Haddon, and Keith J. White. *Entry Point: Towards Child Theology with Matthew 18*. London: WTL, 2013.

Winterson, Jeanette. *Why Be Happy When You Could Be Normal?* New York: Grove, 2011.

Wirzba, Norman. *From Nature to Creation: A Christian Vision for Understanding and Loving Our World*. Grand Rapids: Baker Academic, 2015.

Witherington, Ben. *A Week in the Life of Corinth*. Downers Grove, IL: IVP Academic, 2012.

Wolterstorff, Nicholas. *Until Justice and Peace Embrace*. Grand Rapids: Eerdmans, 1983.

World Bank. https://data.worldbank.org/indicator/SP.POP.0014.TO.ZS.

Wright, N. T. *Paul: A Biography*. New York: HarperOne, 2018.

———. *The Resurrection of the Son of God*. Minneapolis: Fortress, 2003.

———. *Simply Christian: Why Christianity Makes Sense*. New York: HarperSanFrancisco, 2006.

———. *Surprised by Hope*. New York: HarperCollins, 2008.

———. "They Sing a New Song." N. T. Wright Page (2005). http://ntwrightpage.com/2016/03/30/they-sing-a-new-song/.

Yarnold, Edward. *Cyril of Jerusalem*. Early Church Fathers. London: Routledge, 2000.

———. *The Awe-inspiring Rites of Initiation: The Origins of the RCIA*. Slough: St. Paul, 1972.

Yelle, Robert A., and Lorenz Trein. *Narratives of Disenchantment and Secularization: Critiquing Max Weber's Idea of Modernity*. London: Bloomsbury, 2020.

Index

Adam and Eve, 73, 134-35, 144
aesthetics, 20, 26-29, 91, 94, 110, 112
    n.27, 134, 136-37, 141, 185
agency
    creative, 20-21, 46-47, 50-56
    divine, 105, 111 n.24
    human, 20-21, 34, 42
anti-Semitism, 141, 145
Aquinas, Thomas. *See* Thomas
    Aquinas.
Arianism, 138, 144
artistry, 91, 97-100
Augustine, 22, 24, 27, 34, 138-39
awe, 6, 28, 60, 89, 91, 102, 126, 128,
    131, 155, 159, 161, 181, 194

Bachelard, Gaston, 85
Balthasar, Hans Urs Von, 35
Barth, Karl, 5, 6, 7, 103, 104, 181 n.1,
    188
Basil the Great, 151, 159-60
Bauckham, Richard, 115
beauty, 25, 27, 52, 60-63, 66-67,
    88-90, 91, 93, 95-99, 105, 112
    n.27, 115, 153-55, 159, 163-
    65, 181, 185, 192 n.19
Begbie, Jeremy, 60, 66
Berry, Wendell, 87-88, 98
Berryman, Jerome, 31, 34 n.15, 41
body or bodies, 13-14, 19, 22-23, 49,
    62, 76 n.9, 115, 131, 139, 157

Bouma-Prediger, Steven, 85
brokenness, 26-32, 68, 90-91, 96-99
Brown, Robert McAfee, 181
building, 55-56, 71, 73, 77
Bulgakov, Sergius, 154-55
Bunge, Marcia, 35, 39
Bushnell, Horace, 35

calling. *See* vocation.
celebration, 68-69, 116, 137, 167-68,
    180
Central Park, 74
Chesterton, G. K., 133-34
children or childhood, xii, 9, 13-14,
    23, 31-43, 105, 164
Child Theology or Child Theology
    Movement, 42-43
Christianity, 124, 162, 183 n.5
church or churches
    Eastern, 153-54
    in the book of Revelation, 9, 167-
        74, 178-80
    local, 9, 23, 28, 31-34, 38, 41-42,
        69, 71, 75, 83, 184-86
    Orthodox, 9, 152, 156-57, 159
cinema (or film or movies), 72, 116,
    133-34, 137-38, 141-46
cities, 71, 74, 78-79, 81
Clement, Jane Tyson, xi, 43
Coles, Robert, 37-38

Coleridge, Samuel Taylor, 9, 15–17, 20, 24, 26, 48, 52
    Aids to Reflection, 17, 47, 202
    Biographia Literaria, 16, 20–21, 28
    Kubla Khan, 44–46, 55–56
Coleridge, Sara, 26
colonialism, 141
color, symbolism of, 177–78
Colossians, Epistle to the, 130–31, 138
communion, 47, 93
    Holy (Eucharist), 68, 156
    of saints, 69, 152, 158, 160, 166, 179
contemplation, 8, 67, 163–64, 166
cosmology (Orthodox), 159–60
Cosper, Mike, 88
creation
    artistic, 72–73, 80, 84, 92, 136, 141, 144
    new, 53, 86, 98–100
    of the world, 9, 16, 21, 47, 83, 91, 113, 133, 135, 138, 159–60
creativity, 16–17, 20–21, 27, 113 n.113, 134–35, 137, 141, 159
cross (or crucifix), 17, 19, 21–23, 96, 130, 150, 157, 188
culture, 27, 48, 71, 73–75, 80, 84, 173, 177, 180

dance, 109, 110, 121
Darsane, Nyoman, 60
death, 60, 63, 66, 68–69, 201
deception, 25
defamiliarization, 108–9
Dillard, Annie, 60, 191
discipline (and wonder), 155–57, 158–59
disenchantment, 86, 95, 104
Divine Liturgy, 151, 156
domestic objects, 109
domestic space and work, 93, 95
doxology, 126, 129, 132, 153, 161, 192
Dunham, Kari, 92–93
Dyrness, William, 15

Easter, 66, 152 n.2, 154
education, 8, 31, 39–41
embodiment, 22–24, 28, 48, 60, 85 n.1, 90, 91, 117

emotion, 39, 66, 91, 146
energy, creative, 107, 135–38, 142
England
    Church of, 136–37
    towns of, 78
Ephesians, Epistle to the, 127, 143, 189
eschatology, 22, 27, 28, 60, 69, 86, 95, 98, 99, 116, 180, 201
Eucharist, 23, 68
Evagrius of Pontus, 165
evangelical or evangelicalism
    churches, 180, 184
    theology, 182–84, 187–88, 189–92
evocation, 51–52
exegesis or exegete, 50, 172–73
expression, 51–52
Ezekiel, Book of, 47

fancy, 16, 19, 24, 25, 28, 46
fantasy (or *phantasia*), 165
fasting, 156
film. *See* cinema.
Foster, John, 14
Fujimura, Makoto, 97, 98

Gadamer, Hans Georg, 48
Genesis, Book of, 48, 60, 133, 134, 140
gentrification, 82
gift, 23, 66, 75, 112–13, 127
Glass, Ira, 64
Godly Play, 31, 41
Gonzalez, Mary, 38
González-Andrieu, Cecelia, 90–91
gospel, 131–32, 147, 181–82, 183–84, 187–89, 191–93
Greenville, SC, 81–82
Gregory of Nyssa, 52
Guite, Malcolm, 113
Guroian, Vigen, 36–37, 39

hallelujah, 68, 126, 128
Handelman, Susan, 48
Heaney, Seamus, 109
Hemard, Chuck, 97–98
Herman, Bruce, 95–96
Holy Spirit, 86, 91, 99, 135, 161, 163
home, 60, 85–89, 92, 93, 95, 97–98, 99–100

homemaking, 89, 93, 94, 97–98, 99–100
Hooker, Richard, 67
hospitality, 88, 93, 96, 98
humility, 6–7, 33 n.13, 40, 132, 182, 189, 194
hymns
  in the book of Revelation, 174–76
  christological, 126, 129–32
  in congregational worship, 84, 118, 156

icon (or icons)
  children as, 36–38
  in worship, 152, 157–59
iconography, 158–59
Idea, 48–49, 135–38
ignorance, 5–6, 87–88, 202
Imago Dei (or Image of God), 133, 134, 135, 136, 140, 141, 148
imagination
  apostatic, 24–26
  artistic, 63, 104, 144
  and children, 37 n.36
  dangers of, 13–14, 24–25, 165
  noetic, 52, 56
  primary, 16–17, 19, 46–47, 53
  sanctified, 27–28, 168, 176
  secondary, 20–21, 23, 46–47, 53
  theology of, 27–29
imperialism, 168, 174–77
incomprehensibility, 106, 163, 181
individualism, 75, 76–80
ineffability, 106, 112 n.27, 116, 163–64
interdependence, 76–80, 135
intersectionality, 180
Isaak the Syrian, 52

Jacobs, Jane, 78, 79–80
Jacobsen, Eric O., 76–77, 81, 83
Jennings, Willie James, 27, 76 n.9, 188
Jensen, David, 35 n.20, 36–37
Jesus
  in art, 94, 178
  and children, 31, 33–34, 36–38, 43
  and crucifixion, 68–69
  as Mother, 22–23
  and new creation, 60, 62, 65, 84, 115
  wonder of, 6, 14–15, 111, 155, 188, 189–93
  worship of, 126–32
John of Damascus, 157
John, Gospel of, 49, 135
Jonah, 199–201
Julian of Norwich, 17–24, 28–29
justice, 62, 96, 147, 167–68, 172, 174, 175–76, 179–80

kairos, 69, 156
Kant, Immanuel, 16, 105 n.7
Karr, Mary, 59, 63
King, Martin Luther, Jr., 143
kingdom of God (or reign of God), 31, 33, 38, 61–63, 65, 71, 83–84, 99, 156, 165, 190–91
Klein, Jordana, 114
Kunstler, James Howard, 73, 75

L'Engle, Madeline, 61
lament, 66–69, 198–99, 201–2
landscape, 72, 75, 76 n.9, 82
Lee, Spike, 141–48
Lewis, C. S., 25, 52, 134, 142, 152, 165
literature, 15, 25, 113 n.31
liturgy, 23, 28, 126–27, 151, 152–53, 156–57
Logos (the Word), 48–49, 155
Lundin, Roger, 25

Macarius of Egypt, 162–66
MacDonald, George, 36, 52
Manichaeism or Manichees, 138–42, 144–46
Matthews, Gareth, 40
Maritain, Jacques, 112–13
Mary, Saint, 3, 13, 19, 23, 36, 114–15
Marty, Martin, 36
Maximus the Confessor, 52
memory, 16, 19, 21, 22, 70
Mercer, Joyce Ann, 36
Merton, Thomas, 67, 161
Michelangelo, 136
Midrash, 50
Miller, Brian, 79
Miller-McLemore, Bonnie, 36, 41
Milliner, Matthew, 111

Miłosz, Czesław, 112
mother or motherhood
　of God, 22, 152, 158
　human, 3, 14, 22–23, 32, 49, 52, 143
　Jesus as mother, 22–23
movies. *See* cinema.
Muir, John, 73
mystic or mysticism, 9, 10, 17, 22, 151, 152, 155, 162, 163, 166

Nashville, TN, 76, 80, 81
naturalism, 106, 107, 110
Nektarios of Aegina, 161
New York City, NY, 74, 79
Neoplatonism, 48–51
Newbigin, Lesslie, 65
Noll, Mark, 139
nostalgia, 83

O'Connor, Flannery, 7
Okholm, Dennis, 182–184
Ohaneson, Heather, 6
orthodoxy, 10, 153, 155, 166, 192
otherness, 79, 90, 91, 93–94, 99, 134–35

painting, 4, 40, 63, 64, 67, 71–72, 82, 83, 93, 95, 109, 110, 136, 159, 178
parenting or parenthood, 23, 24, 31, 33, 34, 202
parks, 73, 74, 81, 84
Parsons, Howard, 32
Paul the Apostle, 9, 13, 103, 104, 112, 116, 118, 119, 120, 121–23, 124–28, 129–32, 138, 143, 162, 163, 164, 189, 191, 192, 193
perception, 5, 14, 16–17, 19, 20–21, 27, 46–47, 52, 87, 96, 104, 109, 162
Philippians, Epistle to the, 126–27, 129–31
Phillips, Timothy, 182–84
philosophy
　children in, 31, 32, 40, 41
　discipline of, 5, 9, 14, 15, 48, 155, 182, 202
photography, 97, 138
Pieper, Josef, 87, 92

Piersol, Laura, 40
place
　artistry of, 70–84
　defining, 60
　making, 85–100
　placelessness, 71
Plato, 5, 48, 95, 155
poetic(s), 15, 20, 21, 28, 109, 115, 128
poetry, 8, 15, 24, 26, 51, 52, 55, 108–10
poet(s), 15, 21, 26, 43, 47, 48, 49, 51, 52, 73, 77, 98, 105, 109, 113, 202
power
　of the arts, 90, 117, 146, 156
　creative (or imaginative), 13, 14–16, 18, 20–21, 46–47, 55, 135–36
　of God, 16, 30, 46, 65, 67, 102, 113–15, 119, 122, 126, 127, 128, 135–38, 155, 162, 174, 175, 176, 178, 184, 188, 189, 191, 192, 193, 194
　political or worldly, 129–30, 134, 175, 176, 184, 188, 190
　of sin and death, 28, 50, 60, 63, 68, 116, 106
　of the word (or literary), 25, 50–51, 64
powerlessness, 33, 172–74
Powery, Luke, 174–77
preachers or preaching, 168, 177, 200
Prescott, Catherine, 135
Psalm(s), 12, 58, 68, 129, 161, 194, 198–89, 201
Puritans, 74, 136, 137

Quash, Ben, 99

racism, 75, 141–46, 188
Rahner, Karl, 35
representation, 16, 19, 60, 98, 105, 108, 116, 117, 156
resurrection, 4, 60, 66–67, 69, 83, 98, 117, 130, 147, 157, 194
revelation(s), 6, 14, 20–22, 28, 162, 181–84, 194
Revelation, Book of, 10, 15, 100, 167–69, 173–80
Romans, Epistle to the, 126, 128

Romantic Movement or Romanticism, 26, 32, 72, 73, 107
Ross, Bob, 71–72, 82

sacrament(s) or sacramentals, 23, 36, 41, 68, 69, 139, 155, 159, 186
saints, 152, 158, 160, 161, 164, 166, 179
Santayana, George, 51–52
Saward, John, 36
Sayers, Dorothy L., 9, 133–48
Schinkel, Anders, 87
Scarry, Elaine, 61, 95–96
secularity or secularization, 104, 106, 111
senses or sensual
    physical, 18, 20, 24, 141, 148, 157
    spiritual, 10, 162–63, 166
sentimentality, 66, 68, 95, 96, 199, 202
Sertillanges, A. G., 64
Shakespeare, William, 61, 136, 141–43
shalom, 62
Sherry, Patrick, 91, 98
Shklovsky, Viktor, 108
silence, 31, 67, 72, 74, 123, 181, 194
Silouan the Athonite, 161
sin, 25, 26, 28, 34, 63, 66, 67, 86, 114, 116, 144, 171, 200
songs or singing, 54–55, 59, 64, 66, 117, 118, 125, 132, 152, 156, 167, 168, 174–76, 180, 197, 201, 202
space
    domestic, 27, 85, 93
    open, 83, 110, 154
    public, 81
    sacred, 83
Spirit. *See* Holy Spirit.
stichic sense, 55
Stomp, 109
suburbs, 71, 73, 74, 79
Symeon the New Theologian, 162–66

Taylor, Charles, 107, 110
theologians, 5–8, 15, 25, 29, 31–35, 39, 41–43, 163, 182–83, 184, 187, 194
theosis, 49, 163
Thomas Aquinas, xvii, 5, 35, 64, 197

Thoreau, Henry David, 73
Timothy, First Epistle to, 127–28, 131
Tolkien, J. R. R.
    Leaf by Niggle, 63
    The Hobbit, 140
Torah, 50–51
Trinity, doctrine of the, 22, 36, 111, 185

vision or visions
    imaginative, 55, 106–7, 138,
    mystical, 19–22, 29, 162, 163, 164, 166
    prophetic or eschatological, 47, 62, 63, 100, 180
virtue, 36, 40, 51, 73, 127
vocation, 8, 9, 32, 38–42, 86, 91, 100, 119, 134, 167, 183, 190
Vonnegut, Kurt, 65

Walford, John, 27
Walsh, Brian, 85
Weil, Simone, 61
Wesley, John, 16, 24–25, 201–2
Wheaton College, 25, 52, 182, 184, 187, 191
Wheaton Theology Conference, 8, 10, 27, 182–84, 186–87, 189, 198
Whitmore, Todd, 32
wilderness, 71–73
Williams, Rowan, 108, 189
Winterson, Jeanette, 25
wisdom, 72, 101, 128, 153–55, 159, 160, 162, 166, 172, 188, 190
Word. *See Logos.*
worship
    contemporary practices of, 9, 27, 31, 78, 83, 176, 180, 181, 192
    historical, 125, 136, 171, 175, 177
    in the New Testament, 167–68, 174–75, 179
    Orthodox, 10, 152–58, 166
    of Paul, 120, 122, 123–26, 128–32
Wright, N. T., 60, 83, 98, 116, 185
writing (the practice of), 52, 59, 64, 67, 76, 82, 95, 134, 135, 137, 142

Volf, Miroslav, 8

www.ingramcontent.com/pod-product-compliance
Lightning Source LLC
Chambersburg PA
CBHW042042240426
43667CB00047B/2943